THE LORD CHANCELLOR

THE LORD CHANCELLOR

by

NICHOLAS UNDERHILL

With a Foreword by
The Right Honourable the Lord Elwyn-Jones, C.H.
Lord High Chancellor of Great Britain

Offices of State
Series Editor: M. M. Reese

TERENCE DALTON LIMITED
LAVENHAM   .   SUFFOLK
1978

Published by
TERENCE DALTON LIMITED
LAVENHAM   SUFFOLK

ISBN 0 900963 81 6

Text photoset in 11/13pt Baskerville

Printed in Great Britain at
THE LAVENHAM PRESS LIMITED
LAVENHAM   .   SUFFOLK

Contents

Index of Illustrations

General Introduction

THE British have great respect for their ancient institutions without perhaps knowing very much about them; and it is a strange fact that, so far, the knowledge has never been easily accessible in a simple and compact form likely to attract readers interested in their origins and historical development.

Thus the publisher, Terence Dalton, has had the excellent idea of projecting a series of short books on the Great Offices of States, or the officers who fill them. The books are as accurate as it has been possible to make them, having regard to the uncertainty and controversy that surround the early origins. English constitutional development has been notoriously haphazard, and in certain areas it is impossible to go beyond conjecture. But where the great offices have suddenly taken long strides or moved in new directions, this has usually been due to statesmen of outstanding calibre or determination. The author's recognition of the quirks and accomplishments of these famous men brings a personal flavour to the narrative and reminds us that constitutional progress has seldom been achieved without passion and struggle.

The Lord Chancellor is one of the first two titles introducing this series. The author, Nicholas Underhill, is a young Oxford scholar whose thorough examination of the evidence has set up some interesting new perspectives. His book should be of value not only to specialists and students but to all readers who wish to understand more about the State that now bulks so large in everyone's life.

M. M. Reese,
Hindhead,
December 1977

Foreword

by the Right Honourable the Lord Elwyn-Jones

THE office of Lord Chancellor is older than Parliament and older than Magna Carta. During the years in which I have held the office I have found that the extraordinary range of responsibilities that belong to the Lord Chancellor as head of the judiciary, Speaker of the House of Lords and member of the Cabinet makes it an object of wonderment and perplexity—particularly to those accustomed to living under different constitutions. I therefore welcome Mr Underhill's absorbing account of its history, to which it owes far more than it does to constitutional principle. It is for this reason that it is unique. No other constitution, not even in Commonwealth countries, has its equivalent.

To understand it involves careful study of its beginnings in the Middle Ages and its subsequent adaptability to changing needs and changing circumstances. Some authorities trace its origins further back to St Swithin or even further. Mr Underhill, however, traces it back into the Anglo-Saxon period and has described its subsequent development attractively and well. It is indeed a remarkable achievement to have covered such a wide span of time in such a short and readable book.

This has required a considerable feat of concentration in which he has successfully resisted a number of temptations. He has not allowed himself to be waylaid either by the legends of Saxon England or by the anecdotes of modern times and he has foregone many fascinating political and legal digressions where these have not been relevant to his central theme. He has successfully surmounted what Lord Campbell, the biographer of Lord Chancellors, has called "the great difficulty in distinguishing between what is authentic and what is fabulous".

He has not attempted to repeat Lord Campbell's biographical study but he does, nevertheless, provide outlines of the more important Chancellors. He has said relatively little about the twentieth century, where as he says, much of the ground is covered by Professor Heuston's excellent *Lives of the Lord Chancellors, 1885-1940*.

Lord Chancellors have always been at the centre of affairs, legal, political and in earlier centuries, religious, so that the history of the office touches on many facets of our national life. Many of those who have held the office have left their imprint on history, men as different as Thomas à Becket and William of Wykeham, Cardinal Wolsey, Thomas More and Francis Bacon, Judge Jeffreys and in more modern times Lord Brougham, Lord Haldane and Lord Birkenhead.

As the author explains, the office reached its pinnacle of power in the career of Cardinal Wolsey, who was Chancellor from 1515-1529. Sir Thomas More, who succeeded him, was a layman trained in the common law, the son of a judge of the King's Bench. The author quotes Sir Thomas More's words on the scaffold, that he died "the king's good servant but God's first" and observes the irony in the contrast between these words from the first of the regular line of lay Chancellors and those of Wolsey, the last of the medieval prelate Chancellors, who died lamenting that he had not served his God as he had his king. Both discovered, as W. S. Gilbert told us, that the Woolsack has sometimes been stuffed with thorns.

Since the days of Cardinal Wolsey the emphasis of the office has varied from reign to reign and from Chancellor to Chancellor and has tended to be of greater legal than political importance although membership of the Cabinet ensures the latter.

Since the contribution made by Lord Brougham in the second half of the last century, Lord Chancellors have been increasingly concerned with the reform of the law and in recent years their responsibility for the administration of justice has grown enormously.

Mr Underhill has not attempted a study in depth of the place of the Lord Chancellor in law and government today but his comments upon it are thoughtful and informative. I have great pleasure, therefore, in commending his study not only to those who are engaged in the administration of justice or in the business of government, but to all who are concerned with the workings of our institutions and who may wonder how they have developed through the centuries, and how they were influenced by the kind of men who have occupied the Woolsack.

Elwyn-Jones, C.,
House of Lords,
April 1978

Preface

THERE are several things this book is not. It is not a history of the Court of Chancery nor of the administrative functions of the Great Seal. It is not a treatise on equity or its place in English law. It is concerned specifically with the Lord Chancellor and I have dealt with these other deep and difficult themes only as they relate to the actual work that the Chancellors at different times have had to do. This is not primarily a work of original research but of synthesis, and where the subject has drawn me into such specialist fields I have gratefully relied on the researches of others. Nor have I attempted a study of the place of the Lord Chancellor in law and government today. This is a history, and as such is concerned with how and when the various functions of this extraordinarily diverse office were acquired and developed. I have thus deliberately touched only lightly on the details of the post-War development of the office and, in particular, the changes following the Courts Act 1971, which cannot usefully be assessed in a work of this scope. The purpose of the book is also in part biographical, if that is not too large a word for what can only be brief outlines even of the more important characters. Here again I have said relatively little about the twentieth century, where much of the ground is covered by Professor Heuston's excellent *Lives of the Lord Chancellors 1885-1940*.

Such definitions and disclaimers are necessary because the history of the office of Lord Chancellor is involved with so many aspects of English history — legal, administrative and political — that any study of the whole can only be made manageable by setting fairly rigorous limits to its scope and refusing to stray outside them beyond what is necessary for an understanding of the development of the office itself. Yet even so restricted a study as this has not been attempted since the

first half of the nineteenth century. For professional historians the
subject has perhaps been too diffuse; and others may have been
deterred by the prospects of having to come to terms with Lord
Campbell's eight-volume *Lives of the Lord Chancellors*, which was
published in the 1840s but is still (deservedly) widely read and
(undeservedly) respected by lawyers and amateurs of history. It is
hoped that this book will be able to give some enlightenment, at rather
less than Campbell's length, to those who wonder how so various a
range of functions has come to be exercised at one time or another by
this venerable office, many of them surviving, if only vestigially, to the
present day. Whether they will draw from it any inspiring lesson of the
profound and ancient wisdom of the British constitution will depend
on their approach to such things. The adaptability of the office of
Lord Chancellor is indeed, if one looks at it that way, remarkable —
but so much so that it is doubtful whether we are really dealing with
one adaptable institution or three or four independent ones each with
a distinct rationale and importance. I do not intend to try to decide
such questions here.

I am grateful to my publishers and editor for their forbearance;
and, for different sorts of help and encouragement, to David Kynaston,
Sylvia Matthews, Thomas Morison, Philip Cayford, Georgina English,
Antony Griffiths, and, above all, my parents, to whom the book is
dedicated.

Note: In the lists of Chancellors and Lord Keepers preceding each chapter I have given
details only of episcopal sees and titles held by them during their periods of office, save
that I have given also subsequently acquired peerage titles in order to avoid confusion,
since they may differ from those by which the Chancellors were known when in office.
From 1770 all Chancellors were either already peers (usually by virtue of having
previously held high judicial office — only Bathurst was heir to a peerage) or were at once
ennobled on accepting the Great Seal: I have not therefore given their dates of creation.
Fuller details can be found in the *Handbook of British Chronology* published by the
Royal Historical Society.

CHAPTER ONE

?1068-?1070	Herfast
?1070-?1078	Osmund
?1078-?1085	Maurice
?1085- ?	Gerard
? -?1093	Robert Bloet
?1093-1101	William Giffard
1101-1102	Roger of Salisbury
1102-1107	Waldric
1107-1123	Ranulf
1123-1133	Geoffrey Rufus
[1133-1135	Robert de Sigillo]
1135-1139	Roger le Poer
1139-1140	Philip de Harcourt
1140-1154	Robert de Gant
1154/5-1162	Thomas Becket
[1162-1173	Geoffrey Ridel]
1173-1182	Ralph de Warneville
1182-1189	Geoffrey
1189-1197	William Longchamp, bishop of Ely
1197-1199	Eustace, bishop of Ely
1199-1205	Hubert Walter, archbishop of Canterbury
1205-1214	Walter de Gray
1214-1226	Richard Marsh, bishop of Durham 1217
1226-1244	Ralph Neville, bishop of Chichester
[1244-1255	see pp. 25-26]
1255-1260	Henry de Wengham, bishop of London 1259
1260-1261	Nicholas of Ely
1261-1263	Walter de Merton
1263	Nicholas of Ely
1263-1264	John Chishull
1264-1265	Thomas Cantilupe
1265-1266	Walter Giffard, bishop of Bath and Wells
1266-1268	Godfrey Giffard
1268-1269	John Chishull
1269-1272	Richard Middleton
1272-1274	Walter de Merton
1274-1292	Robert Burnell, bishop of Bath and Wells 1275
1292-1302	John Langton
1302-1305	William Greenfield, archbishop of York 1304
1305-1307	William Hamilton
1307	Ralph Baldock, bishop of London
1307-1310	John Langton, bishop of Chichester

CHAPTER ONE

The Chancellor in Medieval Government

(I) The Early Middle Ages: The Chancery

Origins

THE title of chancellor is first applied to an English official in a document of 1068, when Herfast, one of the king's chaplains, is described as *cancellarius*. It might seem reasonable therefore to look no further back than the Norman Conquest for the origins of the office of chancellor. But names should not be confused with things. The distinctive duty of the first known chancellors was their responsibility for the work of the king's writing-office (*scriptorium*), in which the secretarial work of royal government was done. In this capacity they had the custody of the king's seal, by which letters emanating from the royal court could be recognised as genuine. These duties were not new, however, for English kings certainly had a *scriptorium* and a seal well before the Conquest; and it would accordingly make little sense not to attempt to trace the origins of the office of chancellor back into the Anglo-Saxon period. What needs if possible to be identified is the point at which the king first acquired a regular staff, however small, whose work it was to produce the letters and documents that he wanted written. Such an office need not have been called the chancery — the Latin term *cancellaria* does not appear until the second half of the twelfth century — nor have been under the authority of a *cancellarius*, but it would nevertheless represent the real origins of the chancellor's job.

Lord Campbell, the Victorian biographer of the Lord Chancellors, believed that the office of chancellor could be traced as far back as the seventh century, and he took his readers on an enjoyable ramble through the quaint legends surrounding such supposed chancellors as

Saint Swithin, "celebrated for his pluvian propensity". But his sources were far from reliable and he admitted to "great difficulty in distinguishing what is authentic from what is fabulous" — a difficulty he was not able wholly to overcome even in the lives of his contemporaries. In fact, an established royal secretariat is unlikely to have emerged much before the tenth century, for the simple reason that there would have been nothing for it to do. The rudimentary government of early Anglo-Saxon England made little use of the written word. Of course, even the most primitive king had occasionally to write letters, but this task could be managed well enough by whatever prelate or chaplain happened to be available. As for royal charters, the formal documents by which, from as early as the seventh century, gifts by the king of land or rights were recorded, these were generally composed and written by their recipients. It is not until the great period of the conquest of England by the kingdom of Wessex, begun by Alfred (871-899) but not complete until the reign of Edgar (959-975), that English kings had either the need or the inclination to make much use of writing in government. Under Alfred's able and energetic successors the foundations were laid of a coherent administrative structure covering the whole of England and based on the units of the shire and the hundred. To convey the king's wishes through his vastly expanded kingdom, the practice developed of sending written instructions and information to local officials to be read aloud, or otherwise given effect to, at the regular assemblies by which the shires governed themselves. Royal letters of this sort on administrative business were known as writs. Writs were to play an immensely important part in English medieval government, and their production was for centuries the chief work of the chancery. Being in origin simply a letter from the king, a writ was not a formal, quasi-ceremonial document like a charter. In form it was short and to the point, with the minimum of fuss and technicality — it is appropriate that the Latin term for a writ is *breve*. Anglo-Saxon writs were in English, unlike charters, which used a self-conscious and highly literary form of Latin. The rare originals that have survived from before the Norman Conquest, all from the reign of Edward the Confessor (1042-1066), are written on small rectangular scraps of parchment, varying from seven to ten inches across and from two to seven inches down, to which a large wax seal was appended; but it is not certain that earlier writs were authenticated by a seal of this sort, or indeed by any at all, for it was not uncommon for messengers simply to be provided with a ring or other small token to show that they were genuine. Here is a typical basic writ of the period:

"King Edward sends friendly greetings to Earl Harold and Abbot Aethelnoth and Godwine the sheriff and all my thegns in Somerset. And I inform you that my will is that Bishop Giso [of Wells] shall discharge the obligations on his land at Chew now at the same rate as his predecessors did before him. And I will not permit that any wrong be done to him."

It would be difficult to devise a terser, more efficient, form of command.

Historians invariably throw up their hands in admiration at the flexibility and functionalism of this all-purpose tool of government. Its potential, given the political will to exploit it, was enormous. Once officials became accustomed to having the king's will thus authoritatively expressed to them by letter, frequent, precise and regular instructions could be sent over the whole country on all the varied business — military, fiscal, judicial, legislative — that a powerful monarch needed to transact. But it is not clear how adventurously the writ was developed by its Anglo-Saxon originators. The surviving texts are almost all of a particular type, notifying the shire authorities of a royal grant or confirmation of lands or rights within the shire, and implicitly or expressly requiring them to ensure that the grantee's interests are respected. These writs have survived because the owners of the land tended to regard them as a more effective form of title deed than the traditional charter; a charter was not addressed to any particular responsible official, and so was easily ignored, and it bore as authentication only a list of purported witnesses, without any royal seal or signature, and so was easily forged. But there was no such special reason why anyone should preserve writs on ephemeral administrative business, and the number and scope of these can therefore only be guessed at. It is probable, however, that, in the eleventh century at least, writs were in extensive use in some areas of government. The elaborate system of assessment for tax, for example, or the military

organisation of the kingdom, suggest an administration too sophisticated not to have relied heavily on the written word, both for
communications and for records.

This has a direct bearing on the origins of the chancery. Writs
needed writers; in any quantity they needed an organised writing-office.
The writs of Edward the Confessor's reign show a consistency of
formula and phraseology that proves that they at any rate were
produced by professional scribes. Whether this was so fifty or a
hundred years earlier is a matter of speculation, since the text survives
of no writ earlier than the reign of Ethelred (978-1016), although it is
clear from other evidence that kings were making some use of writing
in government well before that. In so far as a date can be assigned to
what must in any event have been a gradual development, the most
likely period for the emergence of a royal writing-office is the reign of
Athelstan (924-939), the most successful and respected of Alfred's
descendants. Although no writs of Athelstan are known, the evidence
of his formal charters shows that, in contrast to the usual practice both
earlier and later in the century, these documents were drafted not by
their recipients but at court, for they are distinguished by a style of
bizarre and almost impenetrably idiosyncratic magniloquence, apparently designed to express Athelstan's pretensions as a monarch of
European stature. The clerk or clerks who produced these remarkable
charters, whether or not administrative writs were yet a significant part
of their work, must have formed an elementary secretariat capable of
dealing with the growing business of an increasingly literate
government.

Little can be discovered about the organisation of the Anglo-Saxon
chancery. It is very unlikely to have comprised more than a handful of
clerks, nor will their work have been exclusively secretarial: writing
was only one of the duties of a royal chaplain. Someone must have
been in charge. Under William the Conqueror that someone would
have been the senior chaplain, and he would have been known as the
chancellor. Attempts have thus been made to identify the most
important "king's priests" at various stages of Edward the Confessor's
reign, the earliest for which sufficient evidence survives, and to
conclude that one of these must be the first known English chancellor.
This seems permissible, provided it is recognised that the term

cancellarius itself does not appear in pre-Conquest sources. Certainly in sources of the next generation one or two of Edward's priests are described as his chancellors and were thus presumably regarded as having performed the functions of a chancellor. The first of these is Leofric, the bishop of Crediton (the see that was later moved to Exeter) from 1046 to 1072. It is to his patronage that we owe the compilation of the *Exeter Book*, which contains most of what survives of Anglo-Saxon poetry; it would be pleasing to think of this cultivated man as a predecessor of More and Bacon. A less distinguished candidate is Regenbald, a chaplain of Edward's last years who continued to work for William I and must have been of great assistance to the new regime: two of William's earliest writs are those in which he confirms Regenbald in possession of his extensive estates. In Domesday Book and elsewhere he is referred to as chancellor: this could describe his position under either Edward or William, although if he was William's chancellor he was soon replaced.

It would be possible to make plausible guesses at the identities of "chancellors" of still earlier reigns, but there is a good reason for looking at least no further back than the time of Cnut (1016-1035). The distinguishing mark of the office of chancellor has for centuries been the custody of the king's seal; and Cnut is the first English king who is thought to have had a formal royal seal of what became the conventional pattern. The use of seals began in antiquity, but it was rare in early medieval Europe. Its purpose, when it re-emerged in the tenth century, was primarily that of authentication: in an age of general illiteracy an impression in wax or some soft metal, identifiable as the mark of a particular individual, was far more reliable as a sign that a document was genuine than the crude cross that was all that most laymen could manage with a pen. The use of seals to prevent documents being tampered with was a later development. The only Anglo-Saxon seal of which an impression survives is that of Edward the Confessor; from it all later English "great seals" derive. Edward's seal was circular and about three inches in diameter. It hung from the bottom of the writ on a tongue of parchment, and was thus free to have an impression on both sides, unlike contemporary continental seals, which were simply applied to the face of the document. It has been conjectured that the double-sided seal was devised for Cnut, in order to represent his two kingdoms of England and Denmark, but in the absence of any surviving impressions this cannot be proved. In Edward's case both sides show the king seated, full-length and full-face, though he holds different insignia of royalty on each side. Such a seated portrait has been used consistently on one side of the great seal to the present day; the other has since the Norman Conquest generally borne an equestrian figure.* Around the edge of the seal on both sides runs the legend SIGILLUM EADWARDI ANGLORUM BASILEI, "the Seal of Edward King of the English". The seal was designed to convey as far as possible the majesty of royal authority as if the king were present in person; and its attachment to a document was essential if it was to be recognised as an authentic expression of the king's will. All writs of Edward's reign, and probably also of Cnut's, bore the royal seal. The matrix with which impressions were made (usually itself referred to as "the seal") was thus a good deal more than a mere stamp; and the care of it would almost certainly have been entrusted to the senior royal chaplain, whose clerks constituted the writing-office, and would have been a matter of some dignity. The post of keeper of the seal, if not actually of chancellor, must have existed at the Anglo-Saxon court.

The term *cancellarius* itself was originally the name of the clerk of a late Roman law-court, who sat at the *cancelli*, the screen that separated the court from the public. In the sub-Roman world of Carolingian Gaul the humble *cancellarius* was strangely transformed into the king's secretary and keeper of his seal. As these functions became more widespread with the revival of literacy, so did the functionary: in eleventh-century Europe counts and bishops as well as Popes and Emperors might be expected to have a chancellor. William I clearly felt it necessary to his new dignity as a king to make good his predecessor's omission to have such an official at his court. Herfast, the first English chancellor known to have borne the title, had for many years been one of the Conqueror's chaplains in Normandy, and after only a short term as chancellor he received the standard reward of a royal chaplain when in 1070 he became bishop of East Anglia, with his see first at Elmham and later at Thetford. He was given a poor reputation by the ecclesiastical gossip of his day, perhaps because while a bishop he was incautious enough to fall foul of both Archbishop

---

*The exceptions are seals of Queen Anne and of George V. The one bears a figure of Britannia, the other shows the king standing, with the Grand Fleet in the background.

Lanfranc and Pope Gregory VII, a formidable duo, in the course of a long dispute with the abbot of Bury St Edmunds. He is depicted, through a haze of dubious anecdote, as ignorant, conceited and unchaste. It might have been more seemly had the first English chancellor been the man who was Herfast's successor, Osmund, later bishop of Sarum and the first (if we exclude St Swithin) of four chancellors to be canonised.* But it is not at all certain that either is done justice by his later reputation, especially as the main source for both is the lively but opinionated William of Malmesbury. It is not known that William had any cause to harbour a grudge against Herfast; but he had good Wiltshire reasons for approving of Osmund. In fact it is unlikely that the Conqueror's chaplains were anything more or less than career clerics, of a type hardly yet affected by the Gregorian reform: their loyalty to the king is likely to have been a stronger characteristic than their churchmanship.

The Twelfth-Century Chancery

The Conquest meant little immediate change for the chancery. William I found in England a far more sophisticated system of government than existed in his native Normandy. As duke he had had no chancery, no personal seal, and no instrument equivalent to the writ: his vassals were not accustomed to taking orders in writing—nor, in many cases, to taking orders at all. His local administration was crude and unreliable; the ordered arrangements for taxation and military service available to English monarchs were quite unknown in Normandy. Accordingly the much superior administrative machinery of the Anglo-Saxons was left as it was. For some years the chancery continued to be staffed by English clerks, writing in English; and even when in the 1070s there was a gradual change to Latin the form and appearance of royal writs in other respects hardly altered. The only substantial innovation was the introduction of a brief clause at the end of the writ giving the place at which it was issued (although, curiously, seldom including the date) and generally also the names of one or two witnesses: the more important the document, the greater were the number and standing of the witnesses. The introduction of witnesses somewhat blurred the distinction between writ and charter. As writs came more and more to be preferred to the old-fashioned charter

*The others are St Thomas Becket, St Thomas of Hereford (Thomas Cantilupe), and St Thomas More. A possible fifth candidate is St William of Roskilde, an Englishman with a Danish bishopric who was Cnut's "priest and scribe".

(sometimes called a "diploma") as a record of a royal grant, the Norman chancery evolved what is usually termed a writ-charter, that is to say a document in the form of a letter but employing some of the formality of language and the lengthy witness-lists which had characterised the Anglo-Saxon charter. The writ-charter eventually superseded the charter altogether, and by the thirteenth century the Latin term *carta* means simply the most formal category of royal letter, by which lands and privileges were conveyed.

These changes were gradual and not of great significance in the actual practice of government. The real change brought by the Normans was political. As a conqueror William I was largely free of the conventional restraints that bind established monarchies; and as men of masterful temperament, with an urgent need for money, he and his sons were willing to exploit to its full political potential the machinery of the Anglo-Saxon state which they had acquired. From the very beginning the Norman kings exercised a far tighter control over the activities of their subjects than Edward the Confessor had been able, or indeed probably wished, to do. Their use of the writ both provides the best example of their new approach and records the rise in the activity of government. The scope and variety of Anglo-Norman royal writs, which survive in steadily increasing numbers from 1066 onwards, are remarkable. On the one hand we have writs concerned with matters of great moment, summoning vassals to military service, commanding officials to hold enquiries into disputes, ordering that judicial decisions be enforced, announcing appointments to bishoprics or earldoms. As from before the Conquest, there are many surviving examples of "title-deed" writs, those notifying local officials of grants of land and rights within their shire. But nothing is too trivial to be outside the scope of royal intervention. The bishop of Worcester and the sheriff and men of Worcestershire are ordered to see that the poaching of Walter de Beauchamp's pheasants is stopped. The local magnate in Holderness is required to prevent one of his men from fishing in Hornsea Mere, where the rights are owned by the abbot of St Mary's, York. The abbot of Peterborough is told not to interfere with the collection and transport of stone for the new abbey at Bury St Edmunds. Such writs were not of course all issued on government initiative: many would be sought, and usually bought, from the king by suitors wanting his support in their private troubles. If they were successful they would collect their writs, drafted in the royal chancery and sealed with the king's seal, and publish or use them as they saw fit. But this is only the more striking as evidence of the general recognition of the scope of royal authority. Not an acre was sold or inherited, not a priest was made, not a dispute between neighbours arose, but the king was ready and able to intervene if he thought it to his political or (above all) financial advantage. Such interventions showed little regard for precedent or "the proper channels": writs might go, conventionally, to the sheriff and shire-assembly, but they might equally be addressed to one individual or church or to the kingdom as a whole. And they could be thoroughly peremptory: writs commonly began with a bald *Precipio quod*, "I command", and might often end with such ominous formula as *et vide ne inde amplius clamorem audiam*, "see to it that I hear no further complaints on the matter".

In the long term the new power of central government was bound fundamentally to affect the chancery. As it became busier — not only with the production of writs but with a mass of memoranda and records — it became bigger and better organised; well before the end of the twelfth century it was indispensable to the process of government. But this growth was slow and its early stages are obscure. Hardly more is known of the Anglo-Norman than of the Anglo-Saxon chancery. That it was becoming better defined as an entity distinct from the chapel is indicated by the emergence, apparently around the middle of the reign of Henry I (1100-1135), of a permanent chancery official known as the *magister scriptorii*, master of the writing-office. And the increasing use, apparent in the same reign, of a more rapid and cursive style of handwriting seems to show the effect of increasing business. But fuller evidence of the way the chancery was developing is not available from before the last years of the century, when royal government had been under the stimulus of the Angevin kings, Henry II (1154-1189) and his sons, Richard and John. Their achievement was finally to consolidate the experiments and expedients of the Norman kings into an ordered and durable system of government, so firmly established that it could not be shaken even by the last violent years of John's reign and the minority of Henry III. All over Europe in the mid-twelfth century government was becoming more powerful and more sophisticated, in response as much to the pressures of a more sophisticated and literate society as to the ambitions of monarchs; and England was in the vanguard.

The chancery was both an instrument and a beneficiary of this process. Under the Angevins fixed forms and procedures for the transaction of royal business first begin clearly to emerge. Whole classes of writs were becoming standardised. One example is the writ authorising the payment of money out of a royal treasury, known as a writ of *Liberate*. These were needed in great number, and were thus as brief and businesslike as possible. An example reads simply as follows:

"Henry, by the grace of God king of England, duke of Normandy and Aquitaine, count of Anjou, to R. his treasurer and William Malduit and Warin fitz Gerald his chamberlains, greeting. Pay [*liberate*] from my treasury to the monks of the Chartreuse 25 marks from the 50 which I give them annually under my charter to them. Witness: William of St. Mary's church. At Westminster."

The creation of such basic standard writs was inevitable where routine business had developed in any quantity, as was the case in the field of finance. The pressure for standardisation was equally great in judicial business; its effect can be seen in a work of the late 1180s called *A Treatise on the Laws and Customs of England* but better known as *Glanvill*, after the justiciar of the period who was once thought to have been its author. *Glanvill* contains a detailed commentary on the various types of writ which the king might issue in connection with judicial proceedings — orders requiring the sheriff to bring a case before the king's court, to protect the rights of litigants pending trial, to call a jury, to enforce a judgement, or to perform any other of a multitude of executive duties. The number of ways in which the king might be induced to intervene in disputes between subjects had been greatly increased in the course of Henry II's reign; and for each new extension of royal judicial business he and his servants devised an appropriate standard writ, specifying the procedure that the sheriff was to follow. *Glanvill* gives specimens of all these new writs. Here is one, for the well-known action of "novel disseisin":

"The king to the sheriff, greeting. *N.* has complained to me that *R.* unjustly and without a judgement has disseised [i.e. dispossessed] him of his free tenement in *such-and-such a vill* since *my last voyage to Normandy.* Therefore I command you that, if *N.* gives you security for prosecuting his claim, you are to see that the chattels which were taken from the tenement are restored to it, and that the tenement and chattels remain in peace until the *Sunday after Easter.* And meanwhile you are to see that the tenement is viewed by twelve free and lawful men of the neighbourhood, and their names endorsed on this writ. And summon them by good summoners to be before me or my justices on *the Sunday after Easter*, ready to make the recognition [i.e. declare on the facts of the disseisin]. And summon *R.*, or his bailiff if he himself cannot be found, on the security of gage and reliable sureties, to be there then to hear the recognition. And have there the summoners and this writ and the names of the sureties. Witness, etc."

As the king's courts became more and more popular with litigants, such standard writs, known as "original" or "originating" writs because it was by means of them that litigation was begun, became available as "writs of course", i.e. obtainable *de cursu*, "as a matter of course". To open a case, a would-be plaintiff needed only to come to the chancery, or perhaps to one of its offshoots with the justiciar or at the exchequer, and procure, for the proper fee, a writ appropriate to his grievance. This could then be served on the sheriff, who would begin proceedings accordingly. In a routine case neither the king nor any senior official need be personally involved; indeed the procedure was not essentially very different from that by which actions by writ in the High Court are begun today. Over the course of the next century the issue of original writs was to become a very important, and increasingly distinct, part of the chancery's work, and was itself to develop some judicial features. Under the Angevins it was merely one aspect of the general secretarial business of royal government; but it was already a considerable labour.

Writs on financial and judicial matters were the two most numerous classes of a great mass of largely routine business handled by the Angevin chancery with increasing professionalism. This was probably the heaviest part of the chancery's workload, for writs produced on the direct orders of the king or his ministers cannot have occupied more than a handful of clerks. A new burden was taken on with the systematisation of record-keeping that occurred in the reign of John (1199-1216). Copies began to be kept of the more important outgoing writs — which did not include original writs or other writs of course — on long rolls of parchment compiled year by year for each of several classes of document. In the early stages there were three such classes — charters, letters patent and letters close. The first two were formal letters of the "writ-charter" type, making grants of land or rights: the charter roll recorded grants in perpetuity, and the patent roll the less weighty exercises of royal favour. Letters close were generally not privileges at all but royal commands on administrative business of one sort or another: they form the largest and, for the process of government, most interesting class. The terms "patent" and "close" refer to the different fashions in which these documents were sealed. Letters patent and charters were sealed in the traditional way, with the seal hanging from a strip of parchment or cord that left the face of the document open, or at least openable (for even formal charters were usually folded at this period), for inspection; whereas letters close were folded in such a way that they could not be read without breaking the seal. New rolls soon began to be kept for further different categories of business, but they never covered the whole of the chancery's work, and the distinctions between the categories are sometimes artificial or capricious. Nevertheless the chancery rolls represent a further elaboration of the work of the king's secretariat, and they soon had a keeper and their own staff of clerks. The first known keeper, a distant predecessor of the modern Masters of the Rolls, was William Cucuel, apparently a confidential clerk of King John, who sent him a personal greeting in a postscript to one of his writs — *Saluto vos Willelme Kukku Wel.*

There were other innovations too from around the turn of the twelfth century. A formal dating-clause, based on that used by the Papal chancery, was adopted in royal documents. It gave a full date, and the name of the chancellor or other official responsible for the writ. There were also more new chancery officials. One, the spigurnel, was in charge of the actual process of sealing. It is probable that his office is a specialisation of one of the functions previously performed by the "serjeants of the king's chapel": both terms are found in use in the early years of the thirteenth century, but by the 1230s at the latest chapel and chancery staff were being treated as distinct. Another new office is that of "protonotary", probably a successor of the *magister scriptorii*; this official had not apparently been made redundant by the increasing use of vice-chancellors.* From the first year of John's reign there also survives an ordinance, in the form of a charter addressed generally, fixing a standard scale of fees payable to the chancellor, vice-chancellor and protonotary for royal grants made or confirmed by charter. It does not cover writs "of course", but it is likely that a fixed rate prevailed for these also.

What is particularly remarkable about the professionalism of the Angevin chancery is that it was achieved in very unpromising circumstances. Despite the growth of routine work in which the king could have no personal interest, it was taken for granted that the main body of the royal chancery should travel with him on the ceaseless journeys by means of which the unwieldy Angevin domains were held together: the king's clerks were part of his household, so where he went they went. Henry II and his sons were constantly accompanied by a busy and often disconsolate band of secretaries, living and working out of carts and saddlebags or in makeshift quarters in overcrowded castles. This was the twelfth-century chancery, not a neat office in Westminster or Rouen with permanent files and nine-to-five hours. It is true that some clerks of the royal household appear to have remained in Westminster when the king was overseas, to assist the justiciar, the officer who had charge of the kingdom in his absence, and to take part in the half-yearly meetings of the exchequer, at which the treasury accounts were reviewed: the exchequer held a duplicate of the royal seal, which enabled valid writs to be issued even when the king was out of the country. But these clerks never constituted anything like an independent department, and were absorbed back into the household on the king's return.

In this closeness to the king lay both the chancery's strength and its weakness as an administrative tool. From one point of view, this was the greatest period in the history of the chancery. It was the heart of royal government, pumping out the steady stream of writs on which the health and activity of the organs and limbs of the overgrown Angevin empire depended. Orders came direct from the king himself,

*See pp. 17-18.

were translated into writs, and in that form were despatched to his
subjects and officials from Yorkshire to the Pyrenees. Never again was
the chancery to be so immediately involved in the process of government. But precisely this immediacy prevented the chancery from
developing a strong identity of its own. Its function was purely
secretarial: only the most routine business could be dealt with on its
own initiative. If one were looking for a twentieth-century analogy,
Henry II's chancery was closer to a modern typing-pool than to a great
department of state. Henry did not need a department of state: what
he needed was a reserve of skilled clerks and writers. Indeed the very
term "chancery clerk" is over-precise. The clerks of the king's household
might work on any of a number of assignments that might come their
way. In the early days there was probably little distinction between
treasury and chancery staff, and even after the treasury had, late in
the twelfth century, become a separate department, clerks under the
control of the chancellor continued to assist in the work of the
exchequer. Some clerks might be entrusted with tasks that were not
secretarial at all, as diplomats, for example, or lawyers, for the royal
household attracted many men of ability and ambition who would
have been wasted as full-time scribes.

Under Henry II Hubert Walter, later a distinguished chancellor,
worked not only on the drafting of important royal letters but as a
judge, as a messenger entrusted with money for the payment of troops,
and as a negotiator between the king and the ever-troublesome monks
of Canterbury. In this at least the chancery did differ from the
typing-pool: that the art of drafting letters and formal documents was
learnt only as part of a general legal and literary education, and was a
far rarer and more valued accomplishment than shorthand typing is
today. In spite of the sophistication of much of the work it had to do,
the chancery was a loosely-knit and ill-defined body, containing a
variety of individual talents. Its size is hard to estimate, partly because
chapel and chancery were not yet formally separated, and it is
impossible to know which of the king's *clerici* or *capellani* were
primarily chaplains and which primarily working as scribes. Becket's
friend and biographer, William fitz Stephen, himself a chancery clerk,
claims that the chancellor had fifty-two *clericos* in his service: this
figure is probably a good deal too high for the chancery, for he makes

it clear that not all these were doing what we would regard as chancery work. On the other hand he would probably have considered that distinction meaningless: these were the chancellor's clerks, and they did whatever work they were assigned. Flexibility was essential in the fevered atmosphere of Henry II's court.

The Twelfth-Century Chancellors

Notionally the work of the chancery was the responsibility of the chancellor; but so neat an equation of office and function is unfortunately not possible for any period of the Middle Ages. As the king's senior chaplain, the chancellor was not only the head of the chapel and writing-office but was among the most important and influential figures in the royal entourage. A short document of the first year of Stephen's reign, the *Constitutio Domus Regis*, which outlines the fees and perquisites of the different members of Henry I's household, reveals that the chancellor was in the front rank of household officers, earning the high pay of 5s a day, along with substantial allowances of candles, bread and wine. This was quite apart from the income from the fees charged to suitors who were granted writs from the chancery: these were already considerable, and there are some indications that as early as 1130 the chancellor was expected to pay the king for the privilege of so lucrative an appointment. As a further reward, the chancellors of the Norman and Angevin kings could look forward to promotion to a bishopric within a few years. A man who had risen so far would not be expected to give his whole attention to the purely secretarial work of the chancery. It is not surprising that by the middle of Henry I's reign much of that work seems to have been in the hands of the official described as the *magister scriptorii*, master of the writing-office, or *custos sigilli*, keeper of the seal. If the *magister scriptorii* had charge of the seal, he must have had effective responsibility for at least the day-to-day running of the chancery, for the seal would have had to be in regular use for the authentication of routine writs. Henry I, who had an eye for realities, appears to have decided to take this development to its logical conclusion. When Geoffrey Rufus, his chancellor, was made bishop of Durham in 1133, no successor was appointed, but the wages of the *magister scriptorii* were raised from 10d to 2s a day: presumably he considered that the chancellor as such was performing no useful function that could not be equally well done, and more cheaply, by his subordinate. The chancellorship might indeed have disappeared altogether had not King Stephen decided to revive it for Roger le Poer, a son of the influential Bishop Roger of Salisbury, whose support he badly needed at the beginning of his reign.

Not enough is known of the Anglo-Norman chancellors to make possible any accurate estimate of their places as individuals in the government of the kings they served. They were generally in attendance on the king, and must certainly have been among his intimate counsellors, but none appears to have achieved any special eminence over the other senior members of the household. This may in part be due to the fact that both William II and Henry I relied heavily on a single trusted minister — the notorious Ranulf Flambard in William's reign, and Roger of Salisbury in Henry's. It used to be thought that Flambard had in fact been William's chancellor, but this view has now been abandoned. Roger was indeed chancellor for a short while, from 1101 until he became bishop of Sarum in 1102 and relinquished his office. But his great period of power was in the years that followed, when as Henry's justiciar he was the official who had the responsibility of governing England during the king's absences in Normandy. The authority of the justiciar as viceroy was very extensive, and over the next hundred years it is generally he rather than the chancellor who, if anyone, can be regarded as the chief royal minister, even when the king was in England. For information on the careers of the Anglo-Norman chancellors we are largely dependent on William of Malmesbury, who sheds a fitful and rather lurid light on the Church of his time. He tells us, for example, that Maurice, William I's chancellor from 1082 to 1086, was much given to fornication but excused these lapses by claiming that they were strictly on doctor's orders and were intended to prevent the accumulation of dangerous humours. Whether true or not, this story is unkind to Maurice, who deserves rather to be remembered as the principal builder of Old St Paul's. William resorts to another commonplace of clerical mud-slinging in his account of the death of Gerard, chancellor from 1086 to 1093, who dabbled in the black arts and was found mysteriously dead with a book on astrology beneath his pillow. These stories are probably better evidence of the rancour of monastery gossip than they are of the morals of the royal court; but they are all we have.

Under the Angevin kings the chancellor for the first time comes to the front of the political stage. At least three chancellors, Thomas Becket (1154-1162), William Longchamp (1189-1197) and Hubert Walter (1199-1205), were men second only to the king in the government of the kingdom. But the development of the office is far from straightforward. To some extent the chancellorship continued to be more of an honorific position (though one that brought with it an ever-increasing income from fees) than an office involving specific functions, in the chancery or elsewhere. Certainly the chancery did not need the chancellor. For ten years after Becket had resigned as chancellor on his election as archbishop of Canterbury Henry II omitted to appoint a successor, perhaps to show his disapproval of what he regarded as Becket's disloyal and unnecessarily scrupulous gesture. Over the whole of this busy decade the chancery was efficiently managed by Geoffrey Ridel, a royal clerk who seems to have been given no official title whatever. When Geoffrey duly received a bishopric in 1173 Henry appointed as chancellor Ralph of Warneville, who so much disliked the way of life entailed in constant attendance on the king that he delegated most, if not all, of his duties to a vice-chancellor, Walter of Coutances (despite his name a Cornishman), who is described as *archisigillarius* or *sigillifer*, controller of the seal. When in 1180 Ralph was succeeded as chancellor by the king's bastard son Geoffrey, Walter continued in effective control of the chancery. Geoffrey was the only one of Henry's unpleasant brood of sons to remain consistently loyal to his father — although a cynic might suggest that this was because he was the only one who had no chance of the throne. In any event, he was close in Henry's counsels and one of his best military commanders, despite being in deacon's orders; but he had no interest in administrative work. That the king's son should have become chancellor at all is an indication of how the prestige of the office, along with its income, had risen. Geoffrey was in fact appointed as a form of consolation prize, after the Pope had taken an unexpectedly firm line in refusing to confirm his election as bishop of Lincoln unless he became a priest. Also noticeable is the lapsing of the convention whereby the chancellorship was not combined with a bishopric. Becket had been following this convention when he resigned in 1162, but a generation later Hubert Walter, who had already been archbishop for five years, willingly accepted office as John's chancellor — although this did attract from one contemporary the wry comment that "we have seen a chancellor become an archbishop, but never an archbishop become a chancellor". The chancellorship had become a dignity that none need think beneath him. The more exalted the office, the greater the need for men to do the actual work. Walter of Coutances was the first of many busy vice-chancellors: the chancellor of John's last years and Henry III's minority, Richard Marsh (1214-1226), had so little to do with the chancery that he had to write sternly to the vice-chancellor to remind him to accord him the title of chancellor on official documents.

But if the chancellorship itself could be something of a sinecure, its holders were not thereby allowed to relax comfortably on the profits of office. If Henry II did not choose to use his chancellors as secretaries it was because he had more demanding work for them to do. At the centre of the Angevin system of government was a small group of royal friends and advisers, the king's *familiares* as contemporaries called them. To be a royal *familiaris* was to be not an official with a defined sphere of duties but an extension of the king himself, ready to take his place in the field, at the exchequer, on the judicial bench. Henry was not interested in the social status of his *familiares*. Some were from baronial families, but many were from more humble backgrounds. Most had made careers in the Church, since only clerics were educated for the sort of administrative and legal skills that royal government required. The case of Thomas Becket is typical. The son of a prosperous London merchant, Becket seemed set for a moderately successful career in the Church when, after studying canon law on the Continent, he entered the household of Archbishop Theobald of Canterbury. But within a few months of Henry II's coming to the throne, he was chosen as the royal chancellor, apparently on Theobald's recommendation. He was soon established as the king's intimate friend and one of his two or three most trusted servants. Over the next eight years he is to be found assisting Henry in not only the mass of judicial and financial business that absorbed so much of the king's time, but

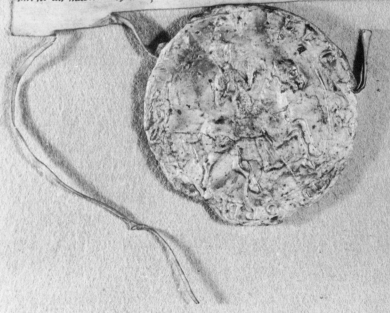

This is one of the earliest surviving English writs, dating probably from 1095. It is addressed by William II to the Archbishop of York and to his subjects generally and announces the confirmation in favour of the see of Durham of its title to a group of northern estates. In size (5" × 3") and general appearance it is a fairly typical royal writ of its period, though it is unusual in that its scribe was a Durham scribe rather than a chancery clerk: a chancery "duplicate" was in fact also written, but this version is illustrated because of the exceptionally fine state of preservation of the seal. Note how one strip of parchment has the seal impressed over it; the other is for wrapping round the folded writ. *Durham Dean and Chapter Muniments, Misc. Ch. 973;*
by permission of the Dean and Chapter of Durham Cathedral

The fine contemporary effigy of William of Wykeham in his chantry in Winchester Cathedral.   *Photograph by A. W. Kerr*

An idea can still be had of the power and profits enjoyed by a medieval chancellor by looking at the buildings they left behind them.

Winchester College, only one of several lavish pieces of conspicuous expenditure by William of Wykeham.

Thomas Wolsey's palace at Hampton Court. The first two courtyards are in essence his, though altered by Henry VIII.

Photograph by A. W. Kerr

Crown Copyright

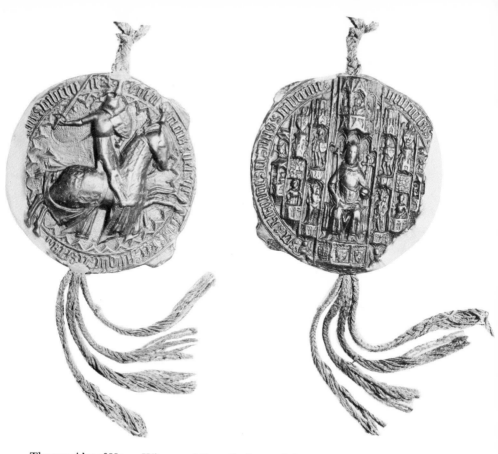

The two sides of Henry IV's second Great Seal, one of the most elaborate of the Middle Ages.

Public Record Office

By courtesy of Christies

No early matrix of the Great Seal survives. This reverse of one of Queen Victoria's Great Seals is, however, not very different from those of the Middle Ages. The projecting "lugs" enable obverse and reverse to be kept in register.

The Court of Chancery in about 1460, from the Whaddon Folio. The Chancellor sits in the centre, addressed by advocates from the bar of the court. On the table are several writs already folded and ready for issue. The clerk on the right is using a type of rolling-pin to press the wax into the matrix of the Great Seal.

By permission of the Masters of the Bench of the Inner Temple

Thomas Wolsey. An anonymous portrait.   *National Portrait Gallery*

Sir Thomas More, by Holbein. The SS chain was worn by senior royal officials and councillors. *Copyright, The Frick Collection, New York*

Sir Christopher Hatton, a miniature by Nicholas Hilliard. On the table are the Lord Chancellor's Mace (a symbol of authority) and Purse (containing the Great Seal).

Crown Copyright, Victoria and Albert Museum

undertaking such duties as taking charge of the income of vacant sees and abbeys (one of the most lucrative sources of royal revenue), leading a notoriously ostentatious embassy to King Louis VII of France, overseeing the rebuilding of the Tower of London, and raising and commanding a force of knights in the Toulouse campaign of 1161. Indeed, had Henry had his way Becket would also, as archbishop of Canterbury, have been responsible for ensuring that the English Church was as fully subject to royal authority as the rest of the kingdom. None of these tasks had anything to do with Becket's responsibility for the chancery: they were the sort of work that any *familiaris* might be called upon to do. Thus when his biographer, William fitz Stephen, claims proudly that the chancellor is to be considered as second only to the king, and cites indiscriminately both Becket's care of the seal and the chancery and the multitude of other work that Henry piled on him, he is over-simplifying. No doubt the dignity of the office was great and custody of the seal a valued honour, but these did not make the chancellor, in Becket's time at least, automatically "prime minister". Even he was not as pre-eminent as his biographers liked to believe: it has always been tempting to see Becket the chancellor only in the light of Becket the martyr and to play up the worldly success of his early career, and especially his friendship with Henry, in order to point the dramatic quality of his conversion and the tragedy of his quarrel with the king. Nevertheless, Becket does stand out among the royal servants of his time for the public show of success that he insisted on making and which must have made the office of chancellor appear briefly to contemporaries as something more splendid than in fact it was. He adopted what has aptly been described as "the manner of a grand vizier", built on lavish hospitality and stylish overspending, rather out of place in Henry II's businesslike court. The puzzle of Becket's career has always been to interpret his conversion to the cause of the Church after he became archbishop. Does it represent a genuine sanctification of the qualities of confidence and self-advertisement that he had shown as chancellor? Many of his fellow-churchmen, who were in a position to know, preferred to believe that the see of Canterbury simply provided a yet more exalted stage for the ex-chancellor's vanity. Neither view need exclude the other.

Despite the flexibility of the Angevin royal household, the ties between the chancellor and the chancery never became merely nominal. Someone had to be in charge of the seal and the secretariat, and, other things being equal, the most convenient person was still the chancellor. Of course other things were often not equal. But in the informal *mêlée* of an itinerant court even those chancellors who were most involved in other business could not, if they were at court at all, avoid regular contact with their clerks. This need not have involved a very detailed supervision of the work of the chancery, but it is difficult to believe that when the chancellor appears among the witnesses to an important royal document he did not play some part in its drafting, and the sources do occasionally reveal the king and the chancellor discussing together the wording of an important charter. The more informative dating-clause that was introduced on writs in the reign of Richard I makes the chancellor's activity easier to trace. Hubert Walter, John's first chancellor, appears in these clauses at the beginning of his period of office with a frequency that suggests a close involvement with the workings of the chancery. It seems likely that he was also personally responsible for the important reforms in the scale of official fees and the keeping of records that were made at this time. Hubert was the quintessential royal servant. He was from a minor baronial family and in Henry II's last years he entered the royal service through the household of his uncle, Ranulf Glanvill, the justiciar. In the next reign he acquired a bishopric, followed in a few years by the see of Canterbury itself; travelled with Richard I on the Third Crusade, where he distinguished himself as both a soldier and a counsellor; helped to negotiate the king's release from imprisonment in Germany; and, as justiciar, governed England during Richard's long absence in France. His six years as chancellor from 1199 were less eventful, but his administrative experience and value as an elder statesman made him indispensable to John's government. Hubert's interest in chancery procedures was exceptional, but even chancellors without his background could not altogether ignore the staff they supposedly controlled. For one thing, chancery business provided the bulk of their official income, an income for which they had already in most cases made a substantial payment. Longchamp in 1189 paid Richard I over £3,000 on his appointment as chancellor, a very large sum which, never-the less, probably represented no more than about two years' income from fees. This was a solid incentive to take some interest in the running of the chancery.

The royal seal was for the most part simply a tool of administration, and its custody and use a matter of routine. But it did give the office a potential political significance of its own. In the absence or incapacity of the king, the seal was the only incontrovertible guarantee of royal authority. The power this might give to the office of chancellor was demonstrated during Richard I's absence on the Third Crusade. As his predecessors had generally done while in France, Richard took his seal with him, for it was still thought of as the personal seal of the king and not the seal of the kingdom. But his chancellor, William Longchamp, a man of humble origin but a trusted friend who had been in Richard's service while he was duke of Aquitaine, remained in England and was given the use of a smaller seal by which the necessary work of government could be authenticated while the king was away; this was perhaps the duplicate seal already kept by the exchequer for its own business. The chancellor was originally intended to share power, as co-justiciar, with Hugh de Puiset, the bishop of Durham, but it soon became clear that Longchamp's position as chancellor put effective control of the government solely into his hands. For over a year he exercised an increasingly autocratic and unpopular rule. Hugh de Puiset was disgraced; Geoffrey, Longchamp's own predecessor as chancellor and now archbishop of York, was seized and imprisoned; and royal offices and patronage were lavishly distributed to the chancellor's family and friends. It was not long before Longchamp was hated even by his own clerks: the Pipe Roll for 1190-91 includes a mocking caricature of his brother Osbert, drawn in the O of his initial, as well as a derisive comment aimed at Longchamp himself. Only the intervention of the old vice-chancellor, Walter of Coutances, hurriedly sent home by Richard to restore the situation, prevented civil war. Longchamp fled the country in October 1191, dressed, it is said, as a tinker woman or, according to another source, as a prostitute — disguises which caused him much embarrassment when passers-by tried to buy his wares, for he could speak no English. These malicious stories are typical of Longchamp's almost uniquely bad reputation in contemporary sources. Nevertheless he was a man of character and ability, and to some extent earned his unpopularity by being too zealous in the king's service. Certainly Richard continued to trust him, for Longchamp remained his chancellor until his death in 1197, although wisely he stayed with his master in France and left most of his chancery work to a vice-chancellor.

This episode shows that, although under an active monarch the office of chancellor was no more than the king allowed it to be, in a political vacuum the chancellor's control of the seal gave him tremendous power, for with the control of the seal went control of the administration. King John showed that he recognised this when, after what he chose to interpret as a show of independence by Hubert Walter, he confiscated the seal from him and for a few days acted as his own chancellor: the gesture emphasised that government was the king's government. In the troubled years of Henry III's minority the custody of the seal was a critical matter. For the first two years of the reign it was resolved to make do with the personal seal of the regent, William Marshal. When, in 1218, a seal was made for the young king, its use was hedged about with restrictions. Even so, when William Marshal died the next year, the first thought of his would-be successor, the papal legate Pandulf, was to send a barrage of letters to the vice-chancellor, claiming his support and enjoining the utmost caution in the use and safekeeping of the seal. However little some chancellors might themselves employ the seal, its central place in the administrative process meant that its custody could never be an empty dignity.

The Chancery and the Household

By the middle of the fourteenth century the chancery had lost the central place in government that it had occupied under the Angevins. As it was to do for the rest of the Middle Ages, it continued to handle the bulk of the routine secretarial work of the administration, formally issuing and recording the mass of day-to-day communications that were necessary for effective government. But it no longer did so as the immediate royal secretariat, directly dependent on the king. It had become an independent and largely autonomous department. The chancery had once been the office through which the whole administrative machine was co-ordinated; but by the reign of Edward III it was itself only one of the parts of that machine, and its co-ordinating role had been assumed by a smaller private secretariat that had developed to serve the king and his council. The fundamental reason for this change was the pressure of business on the chancery organisation. The expansion of royal government in the twelfth century showed no signs of slackening in the thirteenth. Because of the increasing size of its staff and the elaboration of procedure that was required in order to cope with the new work, the chancery became a less and less apt instrument for a busy monarch. Much of the chancery was too preoccupied with routine work, above all with the rising tide of business connected with the issue of original writs, to be of use to the king when it came to the urgent and intimate work of government and the instant execution of decisions as soon as they were made. What was essential in the king's personal secretariat was availability and flexibility; the chancery had become too muscle-bound to provide either.

The new secretariat was initially formed by the department known as the wardrobe. The officials of the wardrobe had originally had the purely domestic task of looking after the care and transport of the king's valuables, which included cash and important documents as well as clothes. In the thirteenth century they began to acquire governmental functions. The clerks of the domestic offices, notably the wardrobe and the bedchamber, were always liable to become involved in duties beyond their nominal responsibilities, for they necessarily remained close to the person of the king and were men whom he would know and trust. It was to them that he naturally turned when other departments proved too cumbersome for his immediate needs: the chamber had already in the twelfth century become the centre of royal financial administration, for stationary treasuries and exchequer were unable to supply the needs of the king in war-time (which was most of the time). Reliance on these domestic departments is often referred to as "household government", but the phrase is misleading if it obscures the fact that all successful medieval monarchs relied on the small staffs available in their immediate entourage as the first and most valuable tool of government. Personal monarchy could not work through distant, impersonal departments. When, in the twelfth and thirteenth centuries, the chancery was at the peak of its importance, it was an integral part of the royal household. Conversely, when, later in the fourteenth century, the "household" office of the wardrobe itself became too burdened with inessential business the king resorted to still more intimate clerks, such as the chamber or the "signet office" under an official known simply as "the king's secretary". However elaborate the process of government might become, the king's household was necessarily the centre from which it was directed. It was when the chancery became detached from the household that its governmental importance decisively declined.

The change in the standing of the chancery was very gradual, and it was often modified or disguised by short-term political circumstances. The first experiments in the greater use of the wardrobe occurred not so much in response to the pressure of business on the chancery as to the problems caused by Henry III's long minority. When, in the mid-1220s, the royal household again became the centre of power, the administration had been for a decade without firm royal control, and its loyalties had been shared among a variety of regents, officials and ambitious magnates. It was staffed by men whom Henry did not know and who had not hitherto been dependent on his favour. The chief officers and their clerks were naturally re-absorbed into the household, but it was not from among them that the king chose his *familiares*. In the aftermath of the fall in 1232 of his overbearing justiciar, Hubert de Burgh, it was not a new justiciar or the chancellor who took charge of the government or was closest in the king's counsels, but a clique of domestic officials of the royal household, Henry's personal associates and dependants. The chancellor was Ralph Nevill, who had held office since 1226 and had been vice-chancellor for the absent Richard Marsh since 1218. He was bishop of Chichester and came from a prominent baronial family. As an associate of Hubert de Burgh he had already twice been confirmed in office for life. But after 1232 the main influence in Henry's government was that of Peter des Rivaux, a Poitevin of obscure family who held the offices of custodian of the king's wardrobe and chamber and treasurer of the household; and although he was temporarily driven from power in 1234 he was succeeded in the king's confidence by others like him. Peter was also the first formally appointed keeper of the king's privy seal, a post of some significance in the later history of wardrobe and chancery. From, at the latest, the reign of John, the king had, as well as the long-established "great seal" kept by the chancellor, a smaller private seal of which he had personal control, for use in authenticating private documents and also in the financial business handled by the chamber. There are indications that under Peter des Rivaux the privy seal was for the first time being more widely used where Peter wished, for reasons of speed or secrecy, to by-pass the normal machinery of the chancery. One of the charges made against him in 1234 was that only "Peter's seal" — presumably the privy seal — was effective to command any matter of moment, while the king's seal counted for nothing. Although this may not have had much significance at the time, there are clearly the seeds in this period of the later development of the wardrobe as an alternative chancery, with the privy seal taking the place of the chancellor's seal as the necessary authentication.

Such a development was rendered for the time being unnecessary when in 1238 Henry III, after a quarrel with the chancellor, confiscated the great seal and entrusted it to officials of his wardrobe, leaving Nevill the mere title of chancellor. There was a reconciliation in 1242, but after Nevill's death in 1244 Henry reverted to the practice of giving the care of the seal to a series of keepers chosen from among his household clerks. This was good sense. Once the chancery organisation and the great seal were under the control of the inner ring of Henry's trusted officials, to which Nevill had never belonged, there was no call to experiment with alternatives — which the wardrobe was in any case not yet equipped to provide. Henry was reducing the office of chancellor to its functional origins. The new keepers of the seal* had none of the status or independence that the chancellors had been acquiring since at least the time of Longchamp. They were not accorded the title of chancellor, and they were not entitled, as previous chancellors had been, to keep for themselves the fees charged on their behalf for the issue of writs under the seal: a new department, known as the hanaper, was set up to account for these fees to the wardrobe. It was only in the period of baronial rule after the rising of 1258 that the title of chancellor definitely re-appeared, and even then the chancellors were insignificant creatures compared with their Angevin predecessors. Their dependent status was emphasised by the institution by the barons in 1260 of a fixed annual salary of 400 marks‡ for the

---

*At this stage in his *Lives* Lord Campbell gleefully devotes a whole chapter to Henry III's wife, Queen Eleanor, as the only "Lady Keeper of the Seal". The pedestrian truth, however, is that, although the seal was indeed formally entrusted to her and the king's brother as regents during Henry's absence in France in 1253, it was never used, and the keeper of the seal, a wardrobe clerk called William of Kilkenny, was ordered to employ the duplicate seal kept by the exchequer.

‡A mark was a unit of account worth 13s 4d.

chancellor, an innovation which the king chose to retain: no more than the keepers of the seal were the restored chancellors to be allowed to keep the profits of office. This is not to say that they were necessarily impoverished. Walter de Merton, chancellor from 1261 to 1263 and again under Edward I, was rich enough to endow the college at Oxford that bears his name.* Official fees formed only a small part of the income of a royal clerk from the thirteenth century onwards. Ecclesiastical benefices were systematically exploited to subsidise an expanding civil service. John Mansel, who as Henry III's most confidential clerk held many of the reins of the administration in the 1250s and was several times keeper of the seal, was alleged to have accumulated over 300 benefices.

The chancery was not greatly affected by the down-grading of the office of chancellor. It is true that the more influential royal servants already tended to be those associated with the wardrobe rather than the chancery; but the clerks of the chancery had certainly not yet lost their place at the king's side. Indeed it is unlikely that distinctions between wardrobe and chancery were rigidly adhered to among the clerks who jogged around England in the king's immense baggage train. The chancery was an integral part of the royal household, directly available to the king and not yet seriously hampered in its duties as the king's private secretariat by its more extensive routine business. This is well illustrated by an entry noted by Professor Galbraith in one of the chancery rolls for 1242. A long list of bizarre debts supposedly owed to the king by one of his courtiers — such things as "24 hogsheads of wine which he bought for the king at Mussac, where he dreamt he saw the Emperor Otto" — is solemnly entered on the roll under this explanatory note from the clerk:

> "The lord king, when playing dice with Peter of Poitou on the ship when he crossed from Gascony to England, ordered all these items to be enrolled, and then, when Peter was not looking, they were to be immediately cancelled."

*Merton was the first of several chancellors to found an Oxford college. He was followed by Wykeham (New College), Waynflete (Magdalen) and Wolsey (Christ Church — originally called Cardinal's College). Stapledon Hall was re-founded as Exeter College by Edmund Stafford, chancellor and bishop of Exeter. At Cambridge Jesus was founded by Alcock, and Magdalene was re-founded by Henry VIII's chancellor, Thomas Audley.

The clerk must have been close at hand to be a party to the king's practical joke. The rolls give other evidence of Henry's sense of humour. In 1254 they record an order for a new suit of clothes for the court jester, to replace those torn up by the king; three years later his successor needs another special issue after having been thrown into the water by his master.

It is in the reign of Edward I (1272-1307) that the chancery began decisively to be replaced by the wardrobe. The trend was for a while concealed by the influence of Robert Burnell, Edward's chancellor from 1274 to 1292 and his closest friend and adviser. Not since Becket had there been such a partnership of king and chancellor. Edward was not exaggerating when in a letter to Burnell and his other trusted friend, Otto of Granson, he told them that they understood his will as well as he himself and that their decisions had all the authority of his own. Many historians have seen Burnell as the chief originator of the great period of legislation that marks the first half of Edward's reign — though in the sources he is most in evidence as a diplomat. Nothing was too good for Burnell in the king's eyes. He twice tried to have him elected archbishop of Canterbury, but this plan foundered on the Pope's doubts about the suitability of a man whose career had been so exclusively devoted to the royal service, and Burnell had to settle for Bath and Wells. For him Edward revived the practice of allowing the chancellor to take for himself the profits from the chancery fees, and Burnell's wealth and self-esteem were displayed in the magnificent palaces he built for himself at Wells and at his family home of Acton Burnell in Shropshire. Under such a man the chancery, being the chancellor's peculiar staff, was naturally very closely involved with the other household offices in the important royal business for which its master was responsible. But after Burnell's death Edward reverted to the appointment of less eminent servants as chancellor. He restored the fixed annual salary (though at the higher rate of £500 a year) and showed no inclination to distribute bishoprics to go with the office; and it became clear that the place of the chancery at the centre of power had largely depended on the importance of Burnell himself. During his chancellorship the chancery had been leading a double life. One section, consisting no doubt of the more valued clerks, had formed Burnell's personal staff of assistants, but it was another

detachment, larger and with more specialised skills, that had handled
the routine judicial and administrative writs and records. This
separation can be seen quite clearly during Edward's absence in
Gascony from 1286 to 1289: Burnell and his clerks accompanied the
king to France, as did the wardrobe, but a large part of the chancery
remained in England to be at the service of the regent. Some such
division of labour must have been in force for many years, but never
before had it been so evident. As a way of organising the government it
was difficult to justify. It made better sense for the chancery to confine
itself to the single role of a national administrative secretariat. The
flexible and intimate wardrobe office was, by the 1290s, quite well
enough equipped to take over as the private secretariat of the king. It
had formed Edward's personal staff while he was abroad from 1270 to
1274, and in the subsequent twenty years it developed fast in size and
sophistication in response to the heavy governmental demands of
Edward's wars. It now had a large number of clerks, its own
permanent records, and the regular use of the king's privy seal, which
made recourse to the chancery to have documents authenticated
unnecessary. Nor was any of Burnell's rather mediocre successors as
chancellor in Edward's confidence to the same extent as such
"household" officials as John Benstead, the keeper of the privy seal. In
these circumstances, and under the continuing pressure of work
generated by wars in France and Scotland, the king began habitually
to deal only with the clerks of the wardrobe when he wanted anything
done. His orders might have to be passed on to the chancery if they
needed to be embodied in a document under the great seal; but only
exceptionally would chancery clerks receive royal commands directly.

It thus became less necessary for the chancery to dog the king's
footsteps as faithfully as it had done in the past. In Edward I's later
years it might move temporarily to Rhuddlan or to York or wherever
might be convenient for the king's summer campaigns, but once
settled for the season it followed him no further. In subsequent reigns
even this degree of movement became unusual. Edward III set up a
"branch" of the chancery in the tents around Calais during the long
siege of 1346-7, and in 1392 Richard II ordered the chancery and the
other administrative offices and courts to be transferred to York,
where they remained for a few inconvenient months; but these moves

were quite exceptional. From the 1320s at the latest the chancery had permanent headquarters in Westminster Hall. This brought great benefits for both officials and clients of the chancery. Clerks were freed from the appalling task of trying to organise a peripatetic national administration, while litigants and others with business at the chancery at last had a fixed place where they knew they could find the officials they wanted — the elusiveness of the royal offices had been a matter of complaint from at least as early as Magna Carta. That the detachment of the chancery from the royal household was officially recognised is shown by the grant in 1293 to John Langton, Burnell's successor as chancellor, of an annual allowance of £500 a year, which was to cover both his personal salary and the maintenance of a *hospicium extra curiam regis*, a household outside the court. This no doubt represented an administrative rather than a decisive physical separation; "going out of court" was a gradual process. It was not until the middle of the reign of Edward II that the hanaper, the financial department of the chancery, ceased to account to the wardrobe for its income, thereby breaking the last institutional link between chancery and household.

Independence from the royal household relegated the chancery to secondary role in the process of government. In a system where all important decisions were taken by the monarch or his immediate advisers, governmental and political influence depended on regular and direct contact with the king and his entourage. This the chancery had lost. Of course medieval government was never so formalised that the king could not deal directly with his chancery when it was convenient to do so, and individual chancery clerks were on occasion used in duties far outside the normal scope of their office — many had skills too valuable to be devoted solely to bureaucratic drudgery. But as an institution the function of the chancery in the later Middle Ages was to give formal effect to decisions taken at higher levels of government.

The chancellor never became as detached from the king as did the chancery. It was not unusual for the chancellor and a few clerks, with or without the great seal, to accompany the king while the bulk of the chancery remained behind at Westminster. Even when, as was the case with Edward I's later chancellors, they were not in the king's inner circle of confidants, their administrative experience often meant that they were required at court; and the king needed sometimes to have the great seal by him. In 1306, for example, when Edward I went north on his last campaign against the Scots he ordered the chancery to remain behind, but by January of 1307 he had the chancellor, the seal, and five chancery clerks with him at Carlisle for a meeting of parliament. But it is not in his responsibility for the chancery that the continuing importance of the chancellor in later medieval England principally lies, but in the development of new powers and functions in connection with the king's council.

(II) The Later Middle Ages

Chancery and Council

THE principal theme of the history of the office of chancellor in the earlier Middle Ages is the history of the chancery, and thus of the development of royal government in England. But while the significance of the chancery in government had declined by the middle of the fourteenth century, the chancellor nevertheless remained a central figure in politics and administration. This survival of the office was largely due to its association with the royal council, which from the late thirteenth century had become the most important organ of government in the kingdom. The term "council" is here meant—for the Latin word *consilium* used by contemporaries is ambiguous—neither in the sense of the king's informal advisers, or counsellors, nor of that form of "great council" that came to be known as parliament, but to connote a permanent and defined institution to which the king regularly delegated a part of his governmental functions. The council in this sense is generally described as the "administrative" or "executive" council. It was quite unlike the chancery and other secretarial departments such as the wardrobe: it existed to take decisions itself on behalf of the king, not to implement the decisions of others. But its development became necessary as a result of the same increasing pressure of work that had overloaded the chancery as a secretariat. The king could no longer rely, as had been possible under the Angevins, on *ad hoc*, unsystematic delegation.

The formation of the administrative council was a gradual process. It was in effect a formalisation of some of the functions of the loose group of *familiares* who had always assisted, and would continue to assist, the king: "counsel" and "council" were concepts that in reality necessarily overlapped. The decisive period for the emergence of the council as an institution seems to have been the reign of Edward I (1272-1307), whose successive wars added greatly to the burden of government while leaving the king himself less time and energy with

31

which to attend to it. Under Edward III (1327-1377), an equally belligerent monarch who spent long periods campaigning in Scotland and France, the council finally settled into regular habits and constitution. By the end of the 1330s it had acquired permanent headquarters in Westminster and had the privy seal and its secretariat at its disposal. Except at times of political crisis when the leading magnates were able to force their way on to the council, it consisted principally of the king's more important officials, the chancellor, treasurer and keeper of the privy seal. In the long absences of the king, and still more during a royal minority, such as occurred from 1377 to 1383, the council came to direct the whole government of the realm, taking major decisions on such matters as foreign policy, the raising of revenue, and rudimentary social and economic legislation. Even the more circumscribed role of the council under an active and capable monarch left it very important functions both of advising on policy and of deciding on its own responsibility a range of routine or detailed business with which the king could not be concerned. It was at the centre of the late medieval system of government.

From the beginning the chancellor seems to have been the most important official member of the council, and by the middle of the fourteenth century he was certainly established as its *de facto* president. Quite why this should have been so is not entirely clear. The office does not seem in the reign of Edward I to have carried with it any greater status, and certainly not necessarily any greater power, than that of the treasurer or the keeper of the privy seal. The answer probably lies in the uniquely wide influence in the administration generally which the chancellor derived from his personal portfolio, the chancery. Though now subordinate to the privy seal and to the various household secretariats, and increasingly redundant in many of its functions, the chancery still formally processed a very wide cross-section of government business. This was due to its continued monopoly of the use of the great seal. For all personal business the king now used the privy seal or one of a number of still more private seals that were brought into use when the privy seal itself began to become too cumbersome and "public". But throughout the Middle Ages and beyond many decisions had conventionally to be embodied in documents under the great seal. Probably the largest number were original and judicial writs,* but every branch of the administration had to use the great seal on occasion.

Some idea of the scope of chancery work in the later Middle Ages, outside the specialist areas of finance and justice, can be had from looking at the entries on the chancery rolls for 1377-8, the opening months of the reign of Richard II. The writs and letters recorded there cover matters from the highest state policy to the most trivial administrative detail. Of great importance, for example, was a series of writs to the sheriffs, mayors, and assorted castellans of the South Coast, commanding them to put their defences in readiness against the threat of a French invasion; these arrangements involved also such minute instructions as that to the keeper of the Kingswood Forest near Bristol to deliver twenty oaks for the defence of the town. Similarly, appointments and re-appointments at the beginning of the new reign recorded in the patent roll range from judges and officials of the exchequer down to a coroner to enquire into the death of one of the archbishop of Canterbury's men, drowned in the Thames, who was lying unburied for want of an inquest. Appointments also included the grant to Geoffrey Chaucer of the office of controller of the custom and subsidy of wools, hides and wool-fells in the port of London. There is frequent reference in the rolls to the forthcoming coronation of the new king, which involved much activity. The chancery was ordered to issue writs authorising the collection of teams of plumbers, tentmakers, carpenters and other workmen. Matters of ceremonial and procedure had to be decided and disputes about precedence settled; the decisions made were recorded in full on the close rolls. And the king's ancestors were remembered among the preparations for the new reign: an order was sent under the great seal for the renewing of the wax preserving the body of Edward I.

Meanwhile, the usual miscellaneous business of government had to be carried on. The chancery sent a series of writs to local officials consequent on the deaths of the earl of Devon and the earl of Pembroke so that their estates should pass into the proper hands. Successful petitions for favours had to be given effect. A licence was issued to one Robert de Hokenale of Hull to buy in Grimsby and transport to Hull for sale 1000 barrels of ale, despite any proclamations

---

*"Judicial" writs were those issued in the course of legal proceedings, embodying judgements or orders of the court, as opposed to original writs, which initiated an action. From early in the reign of Edward III, when the courts of King's Bench and Common Pleas acquired their own seals, judicial writs were removed from the scope of the chancery.

and orders to the contrary. The abbot of Bury St Edmunds was to be permitted to stay in his comfortable manor at Elmswell and not move to Worlingworth where he would be closer at hand to repel the French but which was in "strait miry and difficult" country. A pardon was given under the great seal to a Nottingham man who was guilty of homicide in self-defence. The escheator of Newcastle, the principal royal agent, was commissioned to investigate whether the son of a deceased creditor of the king should be paid the £90 owed to his father.

This is but a small selection of some of the types of document that the chancery had to produce — licences, pardons, commissions, appointments, records. It is evident that, though indeed the duties of the chancery were purely secretarial, the custody of the great seal assured that the chancellor had a finger in most administrative pies. This was potentially a matter of the greatest political importance: few contacts between a subject and his king could not be intercepted, impeded or promoted by the chancellor.

Something should be said of chancery procedure and organisation at their later period. In most cases the chancery would issue a writ or charter in obedience to written instructions sent by the king under his privy seal. This procedure was formally endorsed by the Ordinances of Walton made by Edward III's government in 1338. Edward was shortly to leave England on campaign and was anxious to ensure that he kept a strict control of the administration: chancery and great seal in England would be at the command of the king and his privy seal in France. It is unlikely, however, that the Ordinances did much more than formalise existing procedure. By the end of the fourteenth century these "privy seal warrants" would themselves probably have been at second-hand. The privy seal office acted on orders sent by the king under his "secret seal" or signet, kept by his secretary, who actually received the original verbal order of king or council. Despite the absurdly cumbersome nature of this system it was rarely by-passed. Richard II liked to send commands directly under his signet to his friend and chancellor, Michael de la Pole (1383-6), and his clerks; but Pole's successor, Archbishop Arundel, refused to allow this practice, presumably believing that administrative elaboration, especially if hallowed by an irrational tradition, was a safeguard against autocracy:

the Merciless Parliament of 1388 described signet warrants as "to the disturbance of the law and danger of the realm".

It was natural, with so many governmental decisions being processed through the chancery, that its responsibilities in respect of some of them were not purely secretarial. Officials of the chancery, usually the chancellor himself, were in some limited areas of government allowed to take decisions for themselves; this was recognised in the Ordinances of Walton. One such area already mentioned was the issue of original writs. Other duties which were to have a long history included the disposal of some of the lesser ecclesiastical patronage of the king, benefices whose value was under twenty marks a year, and appointments to a variety of middling and lesser royal offices; perhaps the most important being that of the justices of the peace when that office was created in the mid-fourteenth century. The chancery had, besides, a variety of miscellaneous duties, arising in large part from the fact that, with the exchequer, it was the main permanent settled office of the administration. Royal officials came to it to take their oaths. The results of national enquiries could be reported back to the chancery and filed there. It provided the clerks who attended and administered meetings of parliament. Most important of all, it acquired a role as a court.*

Providing the *raison d'être* for such a busy office, the great seal was far from being a mere ceremonial object. It was an important piece of working apparatus. The seal itself consisted of two round pieces of silver (though the Lancastrian kings also had a golden seal) about 4½ inches across, with the design of the seal cut in negative. Designs were a good deal more sophisticated than in the time of Edward the Confessor and were often of great beauty. The seated portrait on one side from the reign of Edward III showed the king on an elaborate canopied throne. The equestrian portrait became increasingly intricate and decorative. Changes of title or other accidents often required a new seal in the course of a reign, and monarchs who were often abroad had a "seal of absence" and a "seal of presence". The chancellor's responsibility for the seal generally meant actual custody. In normal circumstances he would preside in person when batches of documents were sealed, and if he were away documents would have to be forwarded to him for sealing. But for one reason or another he might

*See Chapter Three.

delegate care of the seal, for periods sometimes of months, to senior clerks of the chancery.

The chancery of the later Middle Ages was an elaborately organised department. At the bottom were the cursitors, who wrote ("engrossed") the routine "writs of course". At the end of the fourteenth century these numbered twenty-four. Above them were twelve "clerks of the second grade". Most of the more important writs and charters were written by them—or at least drafted, since each was allowed one subordinate clerk who may have done the actual writing. It was generally one of these who had charge of the hanaper, the department which kept account of the fees and fines paid in. Fees were standard sums, charged on the issue of a document, whereas fines were extra charges, at first unauthorised, demanded by the chancery staff: even when fines were themselves standardised it was impossible to exclude the exaction of additional gratuities for preferential treatment. The chancery was dominated by twelve "clerks of the first grade". They might draft documents of first importance, but their main duties were managerial and supervisory: all other than routine writs had to be checked by them in their capacity as "examiners". As suited their superior status, they were entitled to three subordinate clerks each. These twelve senior clerks came to be known as the "Masters in Chancery". Traditionally, the senior master was the master of the rolls, the "keeper of the rolls" of an earlier period, whose original responsibility for the records had widened into a general pre-eminence in the chancery. In the mid-fourteenth century he acquired a permanent headquarters at the *Domus Conversorum*, an old hospital in what is now Chancery Lane. He was entitled to six subordinates, the "Six Clerks" who later gained an important status in the chancery as the masters concentrated more and more on judicial work. Outside this hierarchical structure the chancery employed also such special officials as the spigurnel and his assistant, the chafewax, who dealt with the actual process of sealing, and the portejoie, who looked after the chancery rolls.

This amounted to a staff of over a hundred, but it is likely that it was supplemented by a fair number of unofficial assistants, ushers and hangers-on. No chancery official was given a salary as such, though the bulk of the chancellor's salary of £500 was intended to be used to provide at least the senior clerks with food and clothing. Their basic income would come from the ecclesiastical patronage that they received as a matter of course; and besides this they were well placed to benefit from tips, retainers and other perquisites. They certainly prospered. The commons in 1381 described the clerks of the chancery as "too fat in body and in purse, and too well furred, and their benefices badly managed, through their grievous oppressions of the people . . .". They asked for a "wise, discreet chancellor, a layman or a cleric, the best who can be found in the kingdom", to examine and reform the state of the chancery. The commons always resented the expense involved in almost any contact with the chancery and periodically protested against one aspect or another of its procedures. But only rarely, when their protest coincided with the political aims of the aristocracy, was any attempt made to reform the chancery or the administration generally. Archbishop Arundel in his first chancellor-ship, from 1386 to 1389, produced a set of chancery ordinances regulating procedure and organisation, but there is no evidence that they made the chancery fundamentally more efficient or less venal. It was not the administrative triumph that it had been two centuries earlier; but it was adequate for its purpose.

It is not possible neatly to differentiate the powers exercised by the chancellor by virtue of his control of the chancery from those he enjoyed as a principal councillor of the king. The two overlapped and complemented one another. But it is from this dual position that the multifarious duties and functions of the chancellor, which determine so much of the later history of the office, derive. The extraordinary congeries of responsibilities that belong to the Lord Chancellor even at the present day can rarely be understood or explained without reference back to the fourteenth and fifteenth centuries when the chancellor had the entire government of the kingdom under his control and was the figure to whom authority was naturally delegated. It was as chief councillor of the king that the chancellor acquired his role in parliament, the most elaborate manifestation of the royal council. It was through both chancery and council that he exercised the right of appointment of judges and justices of the peace and a range of other government patronage; also much of the ecclesiastical patronage of the Crown and such duties as that of visitor to all royal foundations. It was by reason of his control of the great seal of the kingdom that he played a role of special importance at times of constitutional crisis. And both chancery and council contributed to his development as a judicial officer. All these features of the office were to persist with continued or growing importance after the pre-eminence of the chancellor in government had waned.

CHAPTER TWO

1310-1314	Walter Reynolds, bishop of Worcester, archbishop of Canterbury 1313
1314-1318	John Sandale, bishop of Winchester 1316
1318-1320	John Hotham, bishop of Ely
1320-1323	John Salmon, bishop of Norwich
1323-1326	Robert Baldock
1327-1328	John Hotham (see above)
1328-1330	Henry Burghersh, bishop of Lincoln
1330-1334	John Stratford, bishop of Winchester, archbishop of Canterbury 1333
1334-1335	Richard de Bury, bishop of Durham
1335-1337	John Stratford (see above)
1337-1338	Robert Stratford, bishop of Chichester
1338-1340	Richard Bintworth, bishop of London
1340	John Stratford (see above)
1340	Robert Stratford (see above)
1340-1341	Robert Bourchier
1341-1343	Robert Parving
1343-1345	Robert Sadington
1345-1349	John Offord
1349-1356	John Thoresby, bishop of Worcester, archbishop of York 1352
1356-1363	William of Edington, bishop of Winchester
1363-1367	Simon Langham, bishop of Ely, archbishop of Canterbury 1366
1367-1371	William of Wykeham, bishop of Winchester
1371-1372	Robert Thorp
1372-1377	John Knyvet
1377-1378	Adam Houghton, bishop of St David's
1378-1380	Richard Scrope
1380-1381	Simon Sudbury, archbishop of Canterbury
1381	William Courtenay, bishop of London
1381-1382	Richard Scrope
1382-1383	Robert Braybrooke, bishop of London
1383-1386	Michael de la Pole, Earl of Suffolk 1385
1386-1389	Thomas Arundel, bishop of Ely, archbishop of York 1388
1389-1391	William of Wykeham (see above)
1391-1396	Thomas Arundel (see above), archbishop of Canterbury 1396

1396-1399*	Edmund Stafford, bishop of Exeter
1399-1401	John Scarle
1401-1403	Edmund Stafford (see above)
1403-1405	Henry Beaufort, bishop of Lincoln, bishop of Winchester 1404
1405-1407	Thomas Langley, bishop of Durham 1406
1407-1409	Thomas Arundel (see above)
1410-1411	Thomas Beaufort, Earl of Dorset 1412, Duke of Exeter 1416
1412-1413	Thomas Arundel (see above)
1413-1417	Henry Beaufort (see above)
1417-1424	Thomas Langley (see above)
1424-1426	Henry Beaufort (see above)
1426-1432	John Kemp, archbishop of York
1432-1450	John Stafford, bishop of Bath and Wells, archbishop of Canterbury 1443
1450-1454	John Kemp (see above), archbishop of Canterbury 1452
1454-1455	Richard Neville, Earl of Salisbury
1455-1456	Thomas Bourchier, archbishop of Canterbury
1456-1460	William Waynflete, bishop of Winchester
1460-1467	George Neville, bishop of Exeter, archbishop of York 1465
1467-1470	Robert Stillington, bishop of Bath and Wells
1470-1471	George Neville (see above)
1471-1473	Robert Stillington (see above)
1473-1474	Laurence Booth, bishop of Durham
1474-1475	Thomas Rotherham, bishop of Lincoln
[1475	John Alcock, bishop of Rochester]
1475-1483	Thomas Rotherham (see above), archbishop of York 1480
1483-1485	John Russell, bishop of Lincoln
1485-1486	John Alcock (see above), bishop of Worcester 1476
1486-1500	John Morton, archbishop of Canterbury
1500-1502	Henry Deane, archbishop of Canterbury [keeper of the seal]
1502-1515	William Warham, bishop of London, archbishop of Canterbury 1503 [keeper of the seal 1502-4]
1515-1529	Thomas Wolsey, archbishop of York—also bishop of Bath and Wells (1518-24), Lincoln (1524), Durham (1524-9) and Winchester (1529-30)

*P. 57n.

The Chancellor in Medieval Politics

The Growth of Opposition

THE history of the office of chancellor in the later Middle Ages cannot be written, as it can for the earlier period, mainly in terms of the chancellor's administrative work. Essential though its administrative functions remained, in the council and, to a decreasing extent, in the chancery, the office came more and more to be affected by political pressures. This development reflected an important change in the attitudes of the governed towards royal government in the late twelfth and thirteenth centuries. In a society that was rapidly becoming richer and more sophisticated even the greatest magnates increasingly accepted the growing powers of central government, in a way that had been unimaginable in the feudal kingdom of the Normans. But the corollary was this: the more deeply the king's authority soaked into the political structure of the country—above all by means of the distribution of royal offices and other patronage—the less acceptable it became that that authority should remain purely under the direction of the king himself. It had always been recognised as a duty of the king's greater subjects that they should give him their *consilium* on matters of importance. This duty to give counsel now came to be regarded as a right, and a right not merely to advise but to take a real share in the making of political and administrative decisions. These aims could in part be attained through the institution of parliament; but for an effective control of the machinery of government it was essential that the magnates should acquire a hold of the permanent "administrative council" which handled the day-to-day affairs of the kingdom, and of the officials of whom the council was primarily composed.

The council, and with it the office of chancellor, was thus in the front line of political conflict in the later Middle Ages. Appointments to the council and to the chancellorship were for much of the period liable to be influenced, or indeed dictated, by shifts in the balance of power between the king and his greater subjects. It is to this development that the emergence of the concept of the chancellor as an "officer of state" must principally be traced. For the changing political pattern was reflected by a changing constitutional theory. Council and officials were no longer seen as owing responsibility simply to the king: their duty was a wider one, owed to the kingdom as a whole. Thus demands were sporadically voiced for the appointment of the chancellor and other officials in parliament; attempts were made to establish a formal "continual council" through which the king could be compelled to govern — and in which the chancellor was generally the dominant figure; and it became possible for the chancellor on occasion to refuse to obey the commands of his king in the supposed interests of the kingdom. There were indications of a new status when in 1351 the chancellor (with the treasurer and judges) was included by statute with the king and his heir among those whose killing constituted the crime of treason. At the same time it was made a treason to counter-feit the great seal. These provisions remain on the statute book.

Changing attitudes are well illustrated by an episode in 1376 when the ex-chancellor, William of Wykeham, was summoned before the council to answer for alleged misdeeds during his period of office. Wykeham refused to answer "for at that time he was chancellor, the secondary in England next to the king, which office is of such authority that he that is chancellor is not bound to account for his office". The judge, William Skipwith, replied "Sir bishop, the law is that every of the king's officers, in whatsoever office he be, is bound to account for his office, as well the chancellor and treasurer as any other". Nor was this merely a matter of words. Ten years later, in the parliament of 1386, when the baronial leaders demanded that Richard II dismiss his chancellor, Michael de la Pole, the king refused, declaring that he would not at their request dismiss even a scullion from his kitchen. Richard's reply was the conventional view of medieval monarchs; but it was out of date. Under the Angevins the chancellor was indeed simply a servant of the royal household, as much so as the king's falconer or his physician. But by 1386, though still in form appointed and dismissed by the king, the chancellor might be made answerable to the kingdom: Pole was impeached,* found guilty, fined and imprisoned. He fled into exile, and in 1388 was in his absence declared guilty of treason and sentenced to death. Such proceedings would have been inconceivable a century earlier.

The origins of the new attitudes can be found in the years leading up to the baronial revolt of 1258. In preferring, as he did, to govern through a small group of friends and household officials, Henry III was doing nothing that his predecessors had not done. But his magnates were no longer content with the methods of the past. They chose to regard themselves as being deliberately excluded from the king's counsels by a band of upstarts and foreigners. They believed that the restoration of the great offices of chancellor, justiciar and treasurer (which had, as we have seen, been allowed to lapse) would serve as a check on Henry's "kitchen cabinet" of wardrobe officials. Thus the middle years of the reign are punctuated by demands for an independent chancellor and by ambitious schemes of political reform. One such plan, probably dating from 1244, proposes that there should be "a chancellor and justiciar to be chosen by all", who are to be members of a permanent council of "conservators" watching over royal government — "and if for any reason the king takes the seal away from the chancellor, whatever is sealed in the interval shall be null and void". It was perhaps under the influence of such ideas as these that, in an incident which historians have always found obscure, the keeper of the great seal, Simon the Norman, refused in 1240 to seal a document concerning the taxing of wool which he considered to be *contra coronam* — "unconstitutional". He was promptly dismissed.

Exasperated by the futility of their efforts, the baronial leaders in 1258 staged a *coup d'état* and took full command of the government. The pattern of events that followed is a warning against attaching too much importance to the changes in theoretical attitudes outlined above. In the first place, it is important to note that it was not constitutional tinkering which won power for the barons, but armed force. By no other means could an obstinate or insensitive king be induced to part with full control of his council and administration.

*Impeachment was a process whereby the commons as a body brought a charge against, usually, a royal minister before the lords, who heard and adjudicated on the charge. In the developed procedure it was generally the chancellor who presided at an impeachment, either in his own capacity or (where the accused was a peer) as "Lord High Steward", an office to which he would be specially appointed for the purpose.

Whatever the constitutional theory, the medieval administrative system centred naturally on the person of the king, and it was rarely possible to suborn his officials from the side of a king who wished to rule: an "independent" chancellor, appointed in opposition to royal wishes, would be effectively powerless unless the king himself were subject to *force majeure*. This lesson had to be painfully re-learnt by the enemies of Edward II and Richard II.

Secondly, it is evident that once direct power had been assumed by the opposition, the demand for accountable "officers of state" became an irrelevance. The barons in 1258 simply re-appointed Henry's keeper of the seal, Henry de Wengham, with the title of chancellor, and required him to swear an oath limiting the circumstances in which he might use the seal: writs "of course" could continue to be issued automatically but grants of royal patronage, such as wardships, could not be sealed without the consent of the new governing council, and in no event was the chancellor to seal anything contrary to the Provisions of Oxford or other ordinances of "the Twenty-Four". It was also resolved that his tenure of office should be reviewed after a year, and in 1260 the salary of the office was fixed at 400 marks a year. None of these measures was calculated to restore the supposedly independent status of the chancellors of Henry III's minority—rather the reverse.. This too is characteristic of the late medieval pattern. Only in times of crisis did the opposition seek a division of power, with the chancellor standing against the king: once a faction were firmly established, in the king's favour or in his despite, no more than he did they want to be saddled with officials whom they could not control. Thus for the rest of Henry's reign the chancellorship was held not by "great officers" but by a succession of insignificant nominees of the dominant party.*

The third point of importance is that under Henry's able and forceful successor, Edward I, the issue apparently disappeared. Edward was a strong and subtle enough ruler to be able to resist all pressures on his council and administration and to maintain an entourage of advisers and officials entirely of his own choice. The truth was that under monarchs of even average ability, who were able to bully, coax or bribe their aristocracy into acquiescence, the council

---

*One of these who deserves at least footnote mention is St Thomas Cantilupe, who was briefly Simon de Montfort's chancellor in 1265. Cantilupe was an aristocratic episcopal magnate, and, though he was learned and conscientious according to his lights, his claim to sanctity is puzzling. He engaged in a bitter dispute with the genuinely saintly Archbishop Pecham, whose reforming enthusiasms he considered vulgar and ill-advised, and he had the rare distinction, for a saint, of dying excommunicate.

could operate as a hard-working apolitical body under royal control, consisting chiefly of a few professional civil servants. When it came to it, magnates were as little attracted to the mundane business of government as they were equipped to perform it. Only when the intransigence or incompetence of the king provoked serious political opposition were genuine attempts made to establish councillors, chancellor and officials as a source of authority independent of the monarch.

The later medieval chancellors can thus be divided broadly into two types. One consists of the professional administrators, men often of influence and ability but lacking any political power independent of that of the king whom they served. This is the old tradition of a Becket or a Burnell. The other comprises the men who were imposed on the king as the instruments or, more rarely, the leaders of political faction. It would be unreal to attempt to give a general estimate of the political or constitutional role of the chancellor in the later Middle Ages when the functions and importance of the chancellors could differ so widely. In a system that depended on men, above all the king, and not on institutions, no office could acquire an authority greater than that of its current holder. Only with the development of responsible government could the concept of an officer of state have a real political meaning.

The Fourteenth Century
1307-1330

In the troubled reign of Edward II (1307-1327) and its untidy aftermath the office of chancellor became the target of political faction as it had not been for over forty years. It would only be possible to explain the history of the office during this reign with a complex political narrative: the career of Walter Reynolds, chancellor from 1310 to 1314, is in its essentials typical. Reynolds had been one of Edward's household officials before his accession. We are told that he was a humble clerk of no great learning, but highly valued by the prince for his skill as a producer of court theatricals. With such qualifications he was clearly bound for high office in the Church: Edward procured him the bishopric of Worcester in 1308 and the see of Canterbury in 1313 — Papal scruples had become dulled since the rejection of Burnell. In 1310 the then chancellor, John Langton, allowed himself to be chosen as one of the "Ordainers" appointed in parliament to make ordinances for the reform of the government. Edward's consent to their appointment had never been genuine, and as soon as the magnates had safely dispersed he dismissed Langton and replaced him with Reynolds. That his purpose in this move was purely to thwart the Ordainers is clear from instructions he sent to Reynolds early the next year, ordering him to scrutinise all the Ordainers' decisions and to allow none of them to be put into effect until they had been referred to the king. In any situation short of open rebellion the king held all the aces: any number of proposals and schemes could be made by the reformers but without the control of the administrative machine, in which the office of chancellor was the essential cog, they could not be implemented; and the chancellor looked to the king. The barons were perfectly well aware of what Edward was about. Reynolds' appointment was unpopular from the start; indeed there were hints that it was unlawful because the consent of a parliament had not been sought. For several months in 1313-14 he lay very low, delegating the care of the seal to chancery subordinates, presumably as a conciliatory gesture to an angry opposition. But it was only in the aftermath of Edward's defeat at Bannockburn in 1314 that the barons were able to obtain Reynolds' dismissal. His successor was John Sandale, a royal clerk who had been an associate of Henry, earl of Lincoln, the original leader of the Ordainers. As archbishop, Reynolds continued to exercise a rather inconstant influence on affairs, but he never regained the chancellorship.

Reynolds' career was the model for those of his immediate successors. Edward II's chancellors were not politicians in their own right. They were politicised civil servants, promoted in order to channel the rewards of power to the faction that appointed them, and to deny them to opponents. John Hotham, a tough Yorkshireman who was chancellor from 1318 to 1320, received orders, like Reynolds, to thwart the programme imposed on the king by the Treaty of Leake and the York parliament of 1318. Robert of Baldock, chancellor from 1323 to 1326, was the highly efficient, and correspondingly unpopular, agent of the Despenser faction who dominated the king in his last years. On their fall he was lynched and died in the Tower.

The only exception to this pattern was Henry Burghersh, bishop of Lincoln, who became chancellor in 1328 and is an early and isolated example of the type of magnate chancellors of the later Middle Ages. Burghersh was no mere clerk. He came from a prominent baronial family and emerged in the 1320s as the political heir of his uncle, Bartholomew Badlesmere, the baronial leader executed after the victory of the Despensers in 1322. He rebuilt Badlesmere's following in support of Edward's queen, Isabella, and her lover Roger Mortimer who overthrew the king in 1326. From his position as chancellor he was able conveniently to exploit the political power he had thus acquired. The record happens to survive of one piece of chicanery which must have been typical of the opportunities available to the chancellor or those who controlled him. A certain Geoffrey Cotes, a political opponent of Burghersh and of Isabella's government, had been presented by Edward II to the living of Fishlake in Yorkshire; the Pope meanwhile granted it to an Italian, Peter Vaurelli. In support of Vaurelli's claim Burghersh, according to Cotes, repealed a judgment which he had obtained in his favour in the king's court; blocked all further proceedings by Cotes both in the chancery and in the other royal courts, while promoting Vaurelli's litigation; emasculated a petition presented by Cotes to parliament when it passed through the council; and finished by simply ordering him in the king's name to resign the living. Cotes had no choice but to submit, though he had his revenge after Isabella's fall. It is a trivial enough case, but it was on this sort of petty favour and victimisation, multiplied many times over, that the political strength of a faction depended; and the possibilities it offered for financial exploitation were unlimited.

In such a context the constitutional demands of Edward's opponents must be viewed with caution. The Ordinances of 1310 and 1311, the manifesto of the baronial opposition, contained some high-sounding provisions. Clause 14 required that the chancellor and the other principal governmental officials should be appointed "by the counsel and assent of the baronage, and that in parliament". The chancellor, with the council, was to nominate the sheriffs, the key officials in local administration, and he and his colleagues were to swear an oath to maintain the Ordinances. This did indeed reflect the desire of the barons in opposition to have a say in the government, but it was quite unrealistic as a programme. The fact was that as long as Edward was in power such provisions would not be implemented; and once he was overthrown the victors could appoint whom they liked. Parliamentary consent was useful as a stick with which to beat the king, but no-one in the fourteenth century valued it for its own sake.

1330-1371

The reign of Edward III, after the overthrow of Isabella and Mortimer in 1330, was for the most part politically untroubled. Edward rapidly and naturally established a *modus vivendi* with his aristocracy, based on a common interest in warfare and an even-handed distribution of its rewards. In his reign the art of kingship looks unexpectedly easy. The role of the chancellor was consequently very different. Edward's chancellors were generally career adminis-trators, either lawyers or clerics, with no opportunity or inclination to develop an independent political position. Few came from families of any importance: perhaps the most distinguished fourteenth-century chancellor, William of Wykeham, was the son of a Hampshire peasant — though a "gentry" background of some sort was more usual. Entry into the royal service generally followed some years in the household of a prelate or lay magnate, and often a period at the university in Oxford. Within the administration there was no particular pattern of promotion leading to the chancellorship. Richard de Bury (1334-5) had been the tutor of the young Edward III. He was a noted patron of literature and in his *Philobiblon* he admits to having used his high office to increase his collection of books: suitors were told that the gift of a rare volume was a sure way to the chancellor's favour. More conventionally, John Thoresby (1349-56) had been a clerk in the chancery and master of the rolls. William of Edington (1356-63) had been a notably efficient royal treasurer, while Wykeham had first gained the king's favour as clerk of works at his new palace of Windsor. Of all these varieties of a career in the king's service the chancellorship was the summit.

The bulk of the chancellor's work, like that of any senior official, was performed in the small professional council which managed the internal affairs of the kingdom and was supreme during the king's long absences on campaign. It directed every aspect of royal government, money being generally its most urgent problem. The chancellor might also be expected to be sent or to accompany the king on diplomatic missions: for example, John Stratford, who was chancellor for much of the 1330s, was Edward's principal adviser in the negotiations that preceded the Hundred Years War. An increasingly important task, as the king's military commitments became heavier, was that of setting his financial needs and any other matters to be discussed before parliament in an opening address: this was occasionally done by the chief justice but soon became established as a duty attached to the office of chancellor. In all this work Edward III's chancellors acted as professional royal servants, no more and no less, unswayed by faction or by personal political ambition.

This is not to say that individual chancellors might not be figures of considerable political influence by virtue of their closeness to the king. Two at least enjoyed Edward III's confidence to an exceptional degree. John Stratford, a clever and ambitious man, who was archbishop of Canterbury from 1333, was the dominant influence at court during the king's youth and young manhood. "So close were we," recalled Edward "that I would call him 'father' and he was recognised by the whole kingdom as second only to the king". And when Edward, in the 1360s, began to sink into a premature old age, William of Wykeham, at first as keeper of the privy seal and from 1367 to 1371 as chancellor, "stood so high in the king's favour" in the words of the contemporary writer Froissart, "that everything was done with his consent, and without him nothing". Wykeham fell from power in 1371, but he continued to have an active career in government and politics in the changed circumstances of the 1370s and 1380s.

Some historians have believed that the remarkable influence of John Stratford rested on more than his relationship with the young king, and that he represented an independent "constitutionalist" tradition in the administration, a tradition which finally came into violent conflict with the king and a small group of his most intimate advisers in a dramatic crisis in 1340-1. The crisis began in this way. In late 1339 Stratford, who had been with the king in Flanders, was sent back to England, as Edward's most reliable minister, to cajole the country into more generous supplies of money for the war. Early in 1340 he resumed the chancellorship (which he had resigned in 1337 in favour of his brother Robert) the better to supervise the raising of the taxes which by now the king urgently needed. Despite his efforts and eloquent appeals to parliament, the money produced was in no way adequate, and in desperation the king returned unannounced in November 1340. He was eager for a scapegoat. Robert Stratford, briefly chancellor once more, was dismissed, and the ministers who had accompanied Edward from France prepared a violent denunciation of Archbishop Stratford's misdeeds, the so-called *Libellus Famosus*. This was a mistake. Stratford, sharp-witted and Oxford-trained, was more than a match for them in pamphlet warfare: the king suddenly and disconcertingly found himself enveloped in a noisome cloud of unsuspected political and constitutional controversy. Could the archbishop, as a peer of the realm, be condemned otherwise than in a parliament? Was the king entitled to impose the heavy taxes on the Church that he was now demanding? (Stratford ignored the point that it was he himself who had promoted these taxes the previous year.) Was Edward not in the grip of a clique of avaricious "evil counsellors"? Were the principles of Magna Carta in danger? Stratford combined extravagant protestations of loyalty with dark hints of the fate of Rehoboam. The real issue—the government's failure to keep the king in funds—was wholly obscured as Church, nobles and commons rallied to their supposedly threatened liberties. Shaken, Edward backed off hurriedly, promising concessions on all sides, and Stratford was restored to favour.

It is difficult to resist the belief that Stratford thoroughly enjoyed this battle of words. He clearly admired himself in the mantle of his predecessor (as archbishop and as ex-chancellor) Thomas Becket—though he failed to impress the king's friend Sir John Darcy, who, when Stratford declared that he was willing to face martyrdom, replied sourly: "No such thing—you are not so worthy, nor we so foolish". The issues which Stratford publicised were undoubtedly of genuine importance, but they were invoked in his aid only by a masterly piece of political sleight of hand. Any appearance of independent power on the part of a royal official to resist the king was plainly spurious. In normal circumstances the chancellor, like any royal minister—like Stratford himself before the crisis—depended for what influence he might have not on any political resources of the chancery or any other part of the administration but on his closeness to the king. It was indeed the very fact of Stratford's separation from his master in 1339-41 that enabled the rivalries and misunderstandings to arise by which his position was threatened.

The crisis did have one result of interest. The Stratfords' immediate successors — Robert Bourchier (1340-1), Robert Parving (1341-3) and Robert Sadington (1343-5) — were all laymen and lawyers. Part of the reason for this departure from convention may have been, as Edward is reported to have said, that he wanted no minister whom he could not hang if he chose. A more likely reason is that it was thought that a clerical chancellor could not give wholehearted support to the heavy taxation of the clergy that Edward proposed. This was a sensitive matter in the heated atmosphere of 1340-1, although divided loyalties do not seem unduly to have worried later clerical chancellors. In any event, by the middle of the fourteenth century educated laymen were no longer a rarity. The law had provided an alternative *cursus honorum* for the public service, and since the amount of legal work coming before the chancellor was rapidly increasing the appointment of a lawyer was not inappropriate.

However, the majority of royal servants with administrative experience were still churchmen, and the chancellorship reverted quite naturally to a cleric in 1345. One advantage of clerical chancellors was that they could be rewarded suitably at little cost to the king. Chancellors Stratford, Offord (1345-8) and Langham (1363-7) were all appointed archbishop of Canterbury (though Offord died in the Black Death before he could be consecrated). Thoresby was archbishop of York. Edington was offered and declined the primacy, but his see of Winchester left him rich enough to build a magnificent church at his birthplace in Wiltshire and to begin the rebuilding of Winchester Cathedral that was completed by his successor in the see, William of Wykeham. Langham and Thoresby too were lavish benefactors of their sees. The lawyer chancellors, by contrast, depended entirely on their official salaries (some £500, along with what could be had by way of unauthorised fees and gratuities) which consequently had to be supplemented by the king; and the London palaces of helpful bishops had to be borrowed in order to house the senior chancery clerks, accustomed to archiepiscopal comfort at Lambeth.

It was under Edward III that the chancellor finally consolidated his place as the senior in honour and dignity of the king's officers, "the secondary in authority next to the king", in Wykeham's words. The enormous responsibilities entrusted to his chancellors by the king, and the reflected glory and prodigious wealth accruing to them from their positions in the Church, gave them what was to be an enduring status, however low the real influence of individual chancellors might sink in later years.

1371-1413

In his last years Edward III took little part in government, and his death in 1377 was followed by the minority of his grandson, Richard II. The consequent vacuum at the centre of power created a vortex of political faction. Richard's majority did little to improve matters, for his autocratic dealings with his nobles kept alive the tensions of the previous decade and culminated in his deposition in 1399. His successor, Henry IV (1399-1413), a sick man surrounded by an ambitious family, was unable to restore lasting stability. The chancellorship was inevitably drawn into the conflicts of the period: only by means of the chancellors' management of council and chancery could contested policies be implemented and political rewards be distributed. This aspect of the chancellor's functions was clearly illustrated in 1382, when the young Richard was first beginning to assert himself. On the death of the wealthy earl of March, leaving his hands in the custody of the Crown, Richard proposed to distribute this windfall among a small group of his associates, to the exclusion of the magnates who would normally have expected a share. The chancellor, Richard Scrope, was ordered to have the necessary charter drawn up and sealed. But Scrope was a client of John of Gaunt, duke of Lancaster and the king's uncle, who was reluctant to abandon the domination of the government that he had built up during Edward's last years and Richard's minority. The chancellor therefore refused to co-operate in the grant, and was promptly replaced by the king's private secretary, Robert Braybrooke.

But of course there was more to politics than patronage. The fall of Wykeham in 1371 shows two persistent themes in the history of the office of chancellor in these years — the strength of anticlerical feeling, and the growing importance of the commons in parliament. This was a time of war and high taxation. The clergy were a favoured target for taxation and certainly believed that they were its chief victims; they were thus involved in a running battle with the advocates of an aggressive and expensive foreign policy, whose leader was John of Gaunt. But the Church could not usually count on the alliance of the other sufferers from over-taxation, represented in the commons, for laymen tended to believe that the clergy escaped their full share of the fiscal burden. Clerical chancellors were suspected by the one side of sabotaging military enterprises by failing to keep them properly financed, and by the other of favouring their fellow-clergy in the distribution of taxes. Both sides united in parliament in 1371 to demand the resignation of Wykeham, the very embodiment of clerical vested interests. He was succeeded by an unexceptionable lawyer, Robert Thorp, who died the next year and was in turn succeeded by John Knyvet, a man of like stamp; neither was primarily a politician. But the clergy, especially on the rare occasions when they dropped their feud with the commons, were a formidable enemy for the precarious governments of the 1370s and early 1380s, and Gaunt twice attempted appeasement by appointing as chancellor a compliant bishop who might persuade his brethren to generosity. These experiments were not successful. Adam Houghton, the bishop of St David's, resigned in 1378 in mid-parliament when confronted with the awe-inspiring sight of the primate and a full bench of bishops descending on him howling accusations of sacrilege. He was hurriedly replaced by Richard Scrope, a layman of stronger nerve, who proved an astute manipulator of commons opinion and was able at least partly to retrieve the situation by dividing the opposition. Gaunt's other clerical chancellor, Simon Sudbury, the archbishop of Canterbury, proposed the lucrative poll-tax of 1380 and managed to bully both his clergy and a reluctant parliament into accepting it. It proved a Pyrrhic victory, for the tax provoked the Peasants' Revolt the next year, of which Sudbury himself was the most eminent victim: he was brutally killed on Tower Hill and his head carried in procession through the City to be displayed on London Bridge. After the stop-gap appointment of William Courtenay, the bishop of London, Richard Scrope resumed office.

Parliament was increasingly an important arena for political action, and the chancellor was the main spokesman there for the government and promoter of its policies. His opening address would set the tone for the meeting—as Bishop Stafford signalled the royalist revival of 1397 with his text from Ezekiel "There shall be one king for all". Many days of debate and negotiation might follow, in which adroit management was needed; incompetence could spell disaster, as in the "Good Parliament" of 1376, where Knyvet failed to prevent the impeachment of several of John of Gaunt's associates. Richard II's favourite and chancellor, Michael de la Pole, personally conducted the parliamentary impeachment of the renegade Bishop Despenser of Norwich in 1383, though this was not a precedent which was followed, probably because of difficulties if clerical chancellors had to demand the death sentence.

Under Henry IV parliament entered a phase of precocious development when for a brief while the commons attempted to secure a degree of control over the administration. Their motives were not so much political as fiscal: it was hoped that a close supervision of royal government would restrict the king's inordinate demands for taxation. The principal aim of the commons was to require Henry to act always through a fixed "continual council" whose composition had been approved in parliament. They had one clear success in March 1401, when, apparently as a direct result of representations made in parliament, the then chancellor, John Scarle, was dismissed and replaced by Edmund Stafford, the bishop of Exeter. Scarle had been a humble clerk of the chancery, who, in Lord Campbell's words, "may enjoy the celebrity of being the most inconsiderable man who ever held the office of chancellor in England"; while Stafford was an opportunist aristocratic cleric who had been Richard II's chancellor from 1396 to 1399. No more than Henry III's barons did the commons like to see the administration in the hands of men of low status who owed their position solely to the king. They preferred lords. More generally, the commons sought to ensure that the chancellor be fully subordinate to their approved council, and they clearly did not intend that the council should be dominated, as it usually had been in the past, by the chancellor and his official colleagues. In 1406 they forced Henry to agree, among many other restrictions, that the chancellor should act only on instructions passed to him through the council—a limitation which, if it meant what it said, deprived the king of all direct contact with his own administration.

The bark was loud enough, but in fact parliament's bite was feeble. Though his vulnerability as a usurper and his urgent need for money induced Henry to consent to the commons' demands in 1406 and on other occasions, there was no way in which they could be enforced once parliament had been dispersed and the supplies granted. Besides, a king who was in a position to take a strong line could generally over-awe the commons, who tended only to be troublesome when they thought they could be sure of covert support from a faction within the court. In 1407, when the commons complained that the concessions of the previous year had not been carried out, the chancellor, the forceful Archbishop Arundel, refused to accept the complaint: not only had the chancellor and his colleagues on the council "well and loyally performed their labours" but they had not received proper gratitude for their effort and expenditure in the common interest; they no longer considered themselves bound by their earlier undertakings. This brusque treatment called the commons' bluff and the usual subsidies were granted.

Wykeham and Arundel

Most of the chancellors of this period were civil servants of little significance in politics or were the instruments of powerful patrons. They gained office because of their allegiance, or acceptability, to the dominant faction. But the rule is overshadowed by the exceptions. The most remarkable was William of Wykeham. Wykeham might have been expected to disappear from the political scene after 1371, with the decline of his royal master. But he showed astonishing resilience. Throughout the next decade he was the leading figure in the opposition to John of Gaunt, procuring the impeachment of the duke's associates in 1376, and surviving Gaunt's attempt later in the same year to ruin him by raking up charges of misgovernment in the 1360s — charges which, if anything, praise him with the faintness of their damns. In the series of councils and committees that governed England during Richard's minority and much of the troubled 1380s, his experience made his participation indispensable to proper govern-

ment, and he eventually attained that reputation for elder statesmanship that attaches to all politicians who survive long enough for their
mistakes to be forgotten. After eighteen years out of office, he was
re-appointed chancellor by Richard II in 1389, in the cautious
aftermath of the crisis of 1386-8. He performed his duties capably for
two and a half years before retiring peacefully, to die full of years and
honour in 1404. Wykeham's enduring influence was not the result
simply of ability and tenacity. His rise had been due wholly to his
career in the administrative service of Edward III, and his outlook was
always that of a professional royal servant. Government was a job, to
be taken seriously. It was this attitude, together with his strong
clericalism, that brought him into so violent a collision with the
extravagant and irresponsible John of Gaunt. It was also the attitude
that inspired his twin foundations—unprecedented in scale and in
thoroughness of planning and execution—of Winchester College and
New College, Oxford, designed to produce men of learning who could
be of equal use to Church and state. Wykeham was a serious-minded
man—the self-made can rarely afford not to be.

Of a quite different background was Thomas Arundel, arguably the
greatest of the aristocratic chancellors of the later Middle Ages.
Arundel, a younger son of one of the wealthiest and most powerful
families in the kingdom, four (perhaps five) times chancellor, and
successively bishop of Ely (to which see he was appointed at the age of
twenty), archbishop of York and archbishop of Canterbury, emerged
into politics at the parliament of 1386, as a spokesman and leading
figure of the magnate opposition to Richard II. He became chancellor
in the government of the "Appellants" and for three years controlled
the administration on their behalf. He apparently began to implement
the governmental reforms called for by the Appellants, including the
issue of new regulations for the chancery. Dismissed in the counter-
coup of 1389, he was chancellor again from 1391 to 1396, when
Richard was attempting a policy of conciliation; but he suffered the
king's belated revenge in 1397 and was sent into exile. He returned in
1399 as the chief adviser of the usurper Henry Bolingbroke (the eldest
son of John of Gaunt) and handled the negotiations with Richard at
Conway and in the Tower of London which secured his abdication.
Arundel had given up the chancellorship in 1396 on his appointment

to Canterbury, and it was probably because of his duties as archbishop
that he did not at once resume it under the new king.* Throughout the
early part of the reign Arundel was a counsellor of enormous
influence, whose advice Henry could rarely disregard on matters of
importance. He attended the council more frequently than any other
non-office-holder, and it was he, rather than Scarle, who had
addressed the two parliaments of 1399 which compassed Richard II's
deposition.

The last phase of the archbishop's political career was dominated by
the bitter rivalry which developed between Arundel and the older
generation of Henry's councillors on the one hand and the young Prince
of Wales (later Henry V) and his ambitious Beaufort kinsmen (the sons
of John of Gaunt by his mistress Katharine Swynford) on the other. It is
not clear whether Arundel's resumption of the chancellorship in
January 1407 was connected with this developing hostility, but he
certainly did much to foster it by insisting that words specifically
excluding the Beauforts from the line of succession be introduced into
the act of parliament by which their legitimacy was confirmed. The
insertion of the proviso may have been prudent, but it was regarded by
contemporaries as a deliberate insult. The Beauforts managed to
secure Arundel's resignation in December 1409 and Sir Thomas
Beaufort succeeded him in the following month. The choice was
surprising, since Thomas's elder brother Henry, bishop of Winchester,
had already been chancellor from 1403 to 1405 and was the most
prominent member of the family: Thomas, being a layman, was
probably preferred as a concession to the strength of anticlericalism in
parliament. But the prince and his uncles overplayed their hand.
Henry Beaufort's alleged suggestion to Henry IV that he abdicate in
favour of his son typified the arrogance with which they sought and
exercised power. Arundel was restored to office in January 1412 and
remained chancellor until Henry IV's death in March 1413. He died
the next year.

Arundel's initial rise was no doubt principally due to the eminence
of his family, and his basic political attitudes were those of an
aristocratic conservative. Like most of Richard II's magnates he found
himself in opposition to a king who cultivated a small group of

*He may have been briefly chancellor in August 1399, at the very start of Henry's
invasion.

parvenus at the expense of his "natural counsellors", men of influence and experience — among whom as a prelate and the son and brother of an earl he would certainly have numbered himself. But what in many of the Appellants and their supporters was a mere prejudice, and usually half-baked in its political expression, was transformed by Arundel's thoroughness and determination into forceful action. At the very start of his political career, in 1386, he was willing to threaten Richard II with deposition, and he justified Henry IV's usurpation in 1399 on the pragmatic ground that the kingdom needed to be governed by a man of maturity and experience. Like Wykeham, Arundel was a realist, but a man who took power and its responsibilities seriously. It is not surprising to learn that while in exile he met, and later corresponded with, the humanist Florentine chancellor Salutati, the arch-exponent of the Ciceronian ideal of civic virtue. Arundel's sense of purpose is most notoriously illustrated in his relentless and effective persecution of the Lollard heretics, against whom he was ideally placed to invoke both spiritual and temporal penalties. It was he who was responsible for the introduction of the auto-da-fé to England. He was a firm defender of the rights of the Church against repeated anticlerical attacks in parliament. He rode day and night to forestall the execution, in 1405, of the rebel Archbishop Scrope, which would have been in flagrant breach of clerical immunity; but Henry, not daring to contest the matter with his old counsellor, had Scrope beheaded while Arundel was still sleeping after his journey. On a humbler level, when a group of the king's knights proposed commandeering the horses of the archbishop and his fellows, Arundel is reported to have replied that the first to try any such thing would receive "as good a knock as ever Englishman had".

The most sympathetic picture of Arundel comes from the eccentric Norfolk housewife and mystic Margery Kempe, who visited the archbishop in his palace at Lambeth and rebuked him for the worldliness of his household: "full benignly and meekly he suffered her to speak her intent and gave her a fair answer, she supposing it would then be better. And so their dalliance continued until the stars appeared in the firmament". Evidently the chancellor with all his worldly qualities was a man of spiritual discernment — or at least of patience.

The Fifteenth Century

1413-1454: The Age of Cardinal Beaufort

Henry Beaufort, who succeeded Arundel as chancellor in 1413, was born with a spoon of even purer silver in his mouth than his predecessor. The brother of Henry IV and uncle of Henry V, he had already held the office of chancellor for two years, and in 1404 he had succeeded William of Wykeham as bishop of Winchester, the richest see in England. In material terms he made the most of his enormous advantages. He was three times chancellor, became a cardinal of the Church, amassed a huge fortune, and was for more than twenty years after the death of Henry V in 1422 the most powerful figure in English government and politics. His period of supremacy coincided with the long minority of Henry VI (who was aged only six months when his father died) and with the feckless first decade of his personal rule, and Beaufort must take much of the credit for the at least superficial stability of these years. A competent and businesslike council dominated by himself and his protégés maintained a long and costly war in France without final insolvency, aristocratic rivalries were repressed and the machinery of royal government kept in working order — no mean achievement for a royal minority in the Middle Ages. This was indeed the heyday of the later medieval council, and the officials who comprised it enjoyed a corresponding importance and prestige: it was at this period that the chancellor acquired the honorary "lord" before his title. There was once much talk of the "Lancastrian constitutionalism" said to characterise this long lull before the Wars of the Roses; but it is difficult to know whether Beaufort was in fact as statesmanlike as this picture suggests. The most consistently recurrent themes in his career are threefold — his pursuit of money, his ambitions in the Church, and his bitter feud with his nephew, Humphrey, duke of Gloucester.

Beaufort's financial prowess was remarkable, and was arguably as much to the advantage of the kingdom as of himself. Over forty years he made loans to the government totalling some £200,000 (three times the average annual income of the Crown) which alone enabled the war in France to be carried on. Quite where his wealth originated is not clear, but the terms which, as chancellor and councillor, he was able

to negotiate for himself were never less than generous — to the lender —
and while his capital earned him such returns as the entire customs
revenue of the port of Southampton for an indefinite period he had no
difficulty in finding cash or credit. Professor McFarlane has unravelled
some of Beaufort's more discreditable dealings, in particular his
foreclosure on a selection of the Crown jewels which when chancellor
he had offered himself as a wildly disproportionate security for an
urgent loan which he well knew could not be repaid; he has also traced
the reluctant awakening of the old man's conscience in his last years.

Many of Beaufort's energies were expended in the ecclesiastical
politics of Europe, and he was willing to run considerable domestic
risks for the sake of advantage at Rome — not surprisingly if, as is
likely, his eventual aim was the Papacy itself. It was in order to attend
the great reforming council at Constance that he resigned the
chancellorship in 1417, and in the years that followed he played a
leading part in conciliar politics and in organising the crusade against
the Hussite heretics. These efforts earned him his cardinal's hat and
the position of Papal legate in England, honours he refused to
renounce despite the resentment they caused in the English Church.

Beaufort's only real rival in England was Humphrey, duke of
Gloucester, Henry V's brother and thus an uncle of the young king.
Gloucester was undeniably a more attractive character than the
avaricious and calculating Beaufort, but he was incompetent and
unreliable: it was as well for the country that he seldom got the upper
hand. From 1417 to 1424 the chancellor had been Thomas Langley,
the bishop of Durham, an able royal servant who had already held the
office from 1405 to 1407. During Henry V's almost permanent absence
on campaign in France, the government of England was effectively in
Langley's hands, a responsibility he undertook with impressive success:
nominally he shared power with another of Henry's brothers, John,
duke of Bedford, and had the assistance of a council, but more often
than not meetings of the council comprised only a handful of
subordinate officials and on occasion only the chancellor himself. But
a professional like Langley was out of place in the struggle for power
that followed Henry V's death. Beaufort replaced him and was
sole ruler of the kingdom for two years, during most of which time
Gloucester was away on a characteristically hare-brained private

expedition to Flanders. Equally characteristically, Beaufort took the opportunity to grant himself £2,000 a year on top of his official salary on account of additional expenses. On Gloucester's return in late 1425 strife broke out almost at once, with a nasty fracas between supporters of duke and chancellor at the gates of London. Civil war was only prevented by the efforts of the duke of Bedford at the so-called "Parliament of Bats". As a result of Bedford's mediation Beaufort had to give up the chancellorship, but the concession was an empty one, since his successor, John Kemp, was one of his own protégés. Kemp was a skilled civil servant and diplomat who had been, as keeper of the privy seal and chancellor of the duchy of Normandy, Henry V's right-hand man in the government of his new French conquests. An ambitious and unyielding man, he climbed the ladder of ecclesiastical preferment with unattractive single-mindedness: he had already become successively bishop of Rochester, Chichester and London, and archbishop of York, and before his death he was to add a cardinalate, the position of Papal legate and eventually the archbishopric of Canterbury. These sees saw little of their distinguished occupant. In 1432, in a reshuffle of offices, Kemp was replaced, without losing any of his influence, by John Stafford, a man of similar background to himself. Like Kemp, Stafford had trained as a lawyer and worked his way to the chancellorship by service as keeper of the privy seal and treasurer. A cautious and conscientious man (*a tempore infancie non ymaginativus eram* he said of himself — "I have always kept my feet on the ground"), he was never as active a politician as his predecessor; but he held the office for eighteen years, and kept Kemp out of the see of Canterbury from 1443 until his death in 1452.

The government dominated by Beaufort and Kemp, and latterly also by the young Beaufort duke of Somerset and his associate, the duke of Suffolk, was unashamedly the government of a faction. With the docile compliance of Chancellor Stafford, Beaufort and his friends grew fat on lavish royal patronage and kept a tight control over the council. Gloucester mounted an occasional futile protest. In 1440 he denounced Kemp and Beaufort to the young Henry as having cheated him of his lands, wealth and regal honour and having arrogated to themselves the government of the realm. Their reply was ruthless: the next year Gloucester's wife, Eleanor, was accused and tried for witchcraft, publicly humiliated and forcibly divorced from her husband.

Beaufort died in 1447. Three years later, Suffolk, who had taken over the leadership of the faction, was overthrown, and Stafford resigned the chancellorship. His successor was Kemp, who had fallen out with Suffolk but remained on good terms with the up-and-coming duke of Somerset. Their association continued profitably to both parties until Kemp's death in 1454. Henry VI later mourned him as "one of the wisest lords in the kingdom". Kemp, like his mentor Henry Beaufort, was certainly worldly-wise, but whether the kingdom had been as well served as they had themselves by their rule over three decades is more questionable. Though as the overbearing ministers of a feeble king such chancellors as Beaufort and Kemp had immense power, in the changed circumstances of civil war and a revived monarchy the role of the chancellor was necessarily more subdued.

1454-1471

With the return of open conflict in the 1450s and 1460s the office of chancellor again became a disputed political prize. In a period when the power of the rival factions at court depended to a great extent on their ability to procure favours and patronage for their local followings, the chancellor's position in government, and increasingly also his role in the handling of petitions and litigation, made control of the office essential. The famous Paston letters show how important the favour and support of successive chancellors were to the local ambitions of one prominent group of Norfolk gentry. One letter, for example, from the rich Sir John Fastolf to his lawyer cousin, John Paston, asks Paston to intercede with Bishop William Waynflete (chancellor from 1456 to 1460) to obtain him a licence for the building of a college at his home at Caister, and asks him to secure the services of one of the bishop's chaplains to keep up the pressure when Paston himself was away. A letter of 1465 shows the Pastons themselves benefiting from the "singular good lordship" of the chancellor, Bishop George Neville, when at their request he removed an important part of the family's unending series of law-suits out of the exchequer into his own court of chancery. This was the essential small change with which party loyalties were secured during the Wars of the Roses.

The chancellorship was controlled for much of this period by the powerful Neville family, the chief supporters of the duke of York and, for a time, of his son Edward IV (1461-83). Richard Neville, the earl of Salisbury, did not intend to be hampered by acting through agents who might prove unreliable, especially in the fevered uncertainties of court politics. When Kemp died in 1454, with the king in his first period of madness, Salisbury had York, who was Protector, appoint him chancellor. His administrative experience was negligible, but that was not the point: his real aims were shown in such acts as the extension to all prominent Neville clients of the special privileges of the chancellor's servants to conduct litigation in his court. It was also very convenient to be able to tour his northern estates and impose fines and penalties on his local enemies with the instant authority of the great seal.

Salisbury was forced out of office in early 1455 by the revival of the anti-Yorkist faction around a king now restored to sanity. He was replaced by Thomas Bourchier, the archbishop of Canterbury, a half-brother of the loyal but pacific duke of Buckingham. He in turn proved insufficiently partisan for the king's forceful wife, Margaret of Anjou, who in 1456 installed her own nominee, William Waynflete. Waynflete had been the first warden of Henry's new college at Eton and had since been made bishop of Winchester. In 1460 York defeated Margaret in battle and the next year Edward IV took the throne. The new chancellor was George Neville, aged only twenty-eight in 1460, but the son of the earl of Salisbury and brother of the notorious Richard Neville, "Warwick the Kingmaker". For most of the next decade the Nevilles were the effective masters of the kingdom, and the chancellor was able to see that they received their proper reward: the flood of patronage towards the Nevilles revealed in the patent rolls is of awe-inspiring proportions. George Neville was a politician as flamboyant as he was able, and he saw no point in success if its fruits could not be displayed: at the feast celebrating his installation as archbishop of York in 1465 the fare included some 104 oxen, 1,000 sheep, 500 deer, 400 swans, 2,000 geese, 2,000 chickens and 13,000 jellies, tarts and custards. More sympathetically, a part of his wealth went in an intelligent patronage of scholarship: he was chancellor of the University of Oxford, and a lavish benefactor of his own college, Balliol.

Edward IV grew increasingly restive under Neville domination. On 8th June, 1467 he and a small group of companions appeared without warning at the London palace of the chancellor, where he was lying sick, and summarily relieved him of the seal. There was no immediate retaliation, but in 1469 a rebellion broke out in the Neville lands of the north, and the next year Warwick landed from Calais, expelled the king, and proclaimed the restoration of Henry VI. The so-called "Re-adeption" was short-lived. Edward returned in 1471 and defeated Warwick at Barnet: George Neville, again chancellor, attempted to rally London behind the decrepit king, but without success, and he and Henry were captured and imprisoned in the Tower. Though Neville, luckier than the old king, managed to buy a pardon, Edward, no doubt rightly, did not trust him; and in 1472, while awaiting the king for a hunting party at his sumptuous palace in Hertfordshire, he was instead summarily arrested and his enormous treasure appropriated. He was released from captivity two years later, but died, still aged only forty-four, in 1476, the last of the aristocratic political chancellors of the Middle Ages.

1471-1515

The chancellors of the Yorkist period did not carry the same political weight as their immediate predecessors. Edward IV (1461-83) and Richard III (1483-5) were able and active rulers who required as their officials not political allies but professional servants and advisers. Bishops Stillington (1467-73), Booth (1473-4), Alcock (chancellor briefly in 1475 and again under Henry VII) and Russell (1483-5) were all trained in the civil and canon law and had risen to prominence by means of the normal mixture of ecclesiastical preferment and royal office. Bishop Rotherham (1474-83) was not a lawyer, but he had served an administrative apprenticeship as a diplomat and as keeper of the privy seal, an office also held by Stillington, Booth and Russell before their final elevation. They were men of intelligence and education. Russell in particular was a distinguished writer whom Sir Thomas More later described as "a wise man and a good . . . one of the best learned men, undoubtedly, that England had in his time". His address to Richard III's first parliament is of more than conventional interest as an expression of contemporary constitutional ideas, and he is now thought to have been the anonymous continuator of the *Croyland Chronicle*, whose work provides one of the best and most sophisticated sources for the history of this period. The Yorkist chancellors showed a proper respect for the education which had earned them their success. Among the tale of benefactions are Alcock's foundation of Jesus College at Cambridge, and Rotherham's gifts to both universities, especially to Lincoln College, Oxford, of which he is regarded as a second founder. The universities were, throughout the century, playing an increasing part in the training of future royal servants, particularly through the study of law. Wykeham's foundations provided three chancellors of this period — Waynflete, Russell and Warham — and even the aristocratic George Neville was a Balliol man. In a more and more secular society, devotion to learning was tending to replace devotion to the Church: Bishop Stillington visited his see of Bath and Wells only once in twenty-six years.

To stress the essentially ministerial nature of the chancellors of Edward IV and Richard III is not to deny them all political influence. Rotherham and Russell especially were among the most prominent royal advisers, much relied on in council and in diplomatic business. Rotherham ably coaxed parliament into granting handsome supplies for Edward IV's expedition to France in 1475, and he was at the king's side in the negotiations at Picquigny in which Edward allowed himself to be bought off by King Louis XI. Louis was sufficiently impressed with the chancellor to include him on his list of pensioners at the English court. Nor could the chancellors keep aloof from the intrigue of the Yorkist court. The highest rewards in the king's service could only be obtained with the help of powerful friends: only a careerist could hope to make a really successful career. The best friends to have at Edward IV's court were his wife's family, the Woodvilles. Rotherham came to Edward's notice through their patronage, while Stillington, who was not a Woodville client, spent some uncomfortable months in the Tower in 1478 for expressing too indiscreetly his resentment against them. The usurpation of Richard III broke the Woodvilles' power: Rotherham fell with them and Stillington came back to favour. Stillington, alas, had lost the knack of spotting winners. He was imprisoned when Richard was overthrown by Henry VII and, though he was soon released, in 1487 he gave his support to the pretender

Lambert Simnel and promptly found himself back in prison, where he remained till his death. As ambitious and experienced courtiers, such men were bound to figure in the politics of their time; but they had little power to do more than follow where others led.

John Morton, archbishop of Canterbury, cardinal and Henry VII's chancellor from 1486 to 1500, though he has a higher reputation than his Yorkist predecesors, was essentially a man of the same sort as they. Trained in the civil law, he had entered the chancery of Henry VI under the patronage of Archbishop Bourchier and become master of the rolls in 1473. He was thus a highly experienced lawyer and administrator. He was an equally experienced politician. Exiled with Henry VI, he abandoned the Lancastrian cause after 1471 and became a trusted counsellor of Edward IV. He chose the wrong side in 1483 and went again into exile having organised and perhaps instigated the duke of Buckingham's abortive rebellion against Richard III. While in Flanders he was able to warn the future Henry VII, then also in exile, of a plot against his life, organised on Richard's behalf by Bishop Stillington. The diplomat Mancini described him at this date as "a man of great resource and daring, skilled in party intrigue since King Henry's time". After Bosworth Field he returned to England to be offered the great seal.

Morton's enormous political and administrative experience rendered him invaluable among Henry VII's counsellors. He attended almost invariably at council and was rarely absent from court when matters of importance were at issue. Thomas More, who was a page in Morton's household, testifies that "the king put much trust in his counsel, and the weal public also in a manner leaned unto him". More had a strong regard for the old chancellor and his "deep insight in politic worldly drifts . . . got by great experience, the very mother and mistress of wisdom", his wit, legal acumen and learning—for Morton was chancellor, and a generous patron, of the University of Oxford. It is now impossible to assess Morton's particular contribution to the government of Henry VII, extensive as it must have been. The one policy popularly associated with him, "Morton's Fork"— the argument that justified benevolences on the grounds that those who spent little must have savings to spare and those that spent much must be able to afford to pay—should probably be attributed, if to anyone, to Bishop

Foxe. But such anonymity should be no surprise: the closer a chancellor worked with his king the greater his power.

Henry Deane (1500-2) and William Warham (1502-15) are unfortunately placed between the two great cardinals, Morton and Wolsey. Henry VII seems to have been unwilling to put them on a level with his old adviser: Deane was described not as chancellor but simply as keeper of the seal, and Warham was only given the full title after over a year in office. But neither was a non-entity. Both were made archbishop of Canterbury, a dignity now given almost as of right to the chancellor. Deane was a royal servant who had played a valuable part as right-hand man of Sir Edward Poynings, and later his deputy, on one of the least unsuccessful attempts of the Middle Ages to strengthen English control in Ireland. Warham was a civil lawyer practising in the ecclesiastical courts who in 1494 had been made master of the rolls, as Alcock and Morton had been before. He was also an exceptionally experienced and active diplomat who conducted important commercial negotiations with the Hanse and in Flanders and served on embassies to the courts of Rome, Burgundy and Spain, including the mission that arranged the fateful marriage of Prince Arthur to Catherine of Aragon. In the complex diplomatic web of early Renaissance Europe skill in foreign policy was a vital qualification for chancellors as for all royal servants. Warham and Morton might leave the actual travelling to younger men after they became chancellor, but their experience was essential in advising the king and in dealing with envoys to England. But no chancellor was more preoccupied with foreign policy than Warham's successor, Thomas Wolsey.

Wolsey

Thomas Wolsey was chancellor for almost fourteen years, from December 1515 to October 1529, and during that period he had solitary control of English government. For the sheer extent of his power he is unique among English chancellors and it is natural to enquire whether his career represents an important stage in the history of the office. The simple answer is that it does not. Wolsey's extraordinary power depended essentially on the peculiar relationship between himself and King Henry VIII (1509-47) and was thus personal to himself. He was impatient of institutions, ignoring where possible those already existing and creating none. His only influence on the chancellorship is perhaps the indirect one that his notoriety made monarchs and their advisers wary of bestowing it on men of real authority. Nevertheless Wolsey is interesting specifically as a chancellor as well as as a statesman. His tenure of the office illustrates most of the range of powers available to medieval chancellors and, to some extent, to their later successors.

Wolsey was born in 1472 or 1473 in Ipswich, the son of a moderately prosperous townsman, by tradition a butcher. From Oxford (where he was a fellow and bursar of Magdalen) he passed as a chaplain through the households of Archbishop Deane and the deputy of Calais into that of Henry VII. Under the patronage of Bishop Foxe, one of the old king's chief ministers, he became in 1509 the almoner of the young Henry VIII. It was in this position, whose duties kept him permanently at court, that Wolsey began to acquire the confidence of the king, a trust confirmed by his management of the commissariat and organisation of Henry's French campaign of 1513: wartime, when more formal methods of government were suspended, gave an excellent opportunity for those close to the person of the king to make themselves indispensable. Henry rewarded his campaign-companion with the sees of Tournai (then newly conquered) and Lincoln, and in 1514 Wolsey was appointed archbishop of York. In 1515 he replaced Warham, who was eager to retire, as chancellor. Unfortunately retirement suited the old archbishop: he lived another seventeen years, thus denying Wolsey promotion to Canterbury. The chancellor, however, was able by means of judicious diplomatic pressure on the Pope to have himself made a cardinal and, in 1518, legate *a latere*, a title which gave him effective power over the English Church.

Wolsey's rise thus depended on his personal influence at court and in the king's service. It is noteworthy that he had no formal administrative or legal training—like Wykeham, whom he in many ways resembles, but unlike most of his recent predecessors. This is a lack which is very evident in his later career. Wolsey continued as he began. He did not have, nor did the chancellorship offer, any political or governmental base on which his authority might rest. He relied wholly on the young king's willingness, indeed his wish, to resign all his authority into the hands of one minister. Henry knew exactly what he wanted. He was not interested in government. Limited delegation to such a group of responsible advisers as his father had left him, men who would work to royal orders and make frequent reference back to him for the confirmation and co-ordination of policy, suited him not at all. Wolsey on the other hand was a single strong-minded minister who showed no desire to trouble the king for instructions and decisions with which both of them knew Henry could not be bothered. Contemporary speculation that Wolsey had the king bewitched under-estimate the degree of residual independence that Henry always retained: in the few public matters that did interest him — mostly war and competitive diplomacy — he took an active part. But in general it was highly satisfactory to both parties for the king to leave to his *consiliarius intimus et primarius*, "first and closest counsellor", undivided control of government. Wolsey never tried to establish his power on any other basis but this. He did not seek friends or allies at court, where he was consequently little liked, nor did he attempt to build up a caucus of support in the institutions of government. Thus when the king's loyalty failed him his fall was precipitate. Appropriately, Wolsey forfeited Henry's support not for any governmental or diplomatic failure — such things would not have concerned the king unduly — but for his failure in a far more personal matter, the obtaining of his divorce from Catherine of Aragon. Wolsey for two years made increasingly desperate efforts to extract the desired consent from a reluctant Pope and an unfavourable diplomatic situation; as it turned out, the only real solution was to cut away from the Pope entirely, and that Wolsey was too committed to the *status quo*, out of which he had done so well, to contemplate. Wolsey's failure became finally plain in the summer of 1529; though he lost his office, Henry did not allow at once his old servant to be wholly disgraced. But it was on his way from York to fresh humiliation at Westminster that Wolsey died in November 1530.

How did Wolsey use his supreme power? It is notorious that he enjoyed his position enormously and went to extraordinary lengths to display not only the reality but the semblance of vice-regal authority. He amassed a huge income, principally from his ecclesiastical benefices, which he accumulated quite systematically and without any regard for the rules against pluralism: poorer sees and abbeys were exchanged for richer as they became available (when, that is, he did not simply keep both) and vacancies were ruthlessly exploited for income by virtue of the cardinal's legatine powers. It is estimated that in 1529 his annual income was not less than £50,000 a year, about the same as that of Henry VII in the early years of his reign. The money was spent with due ostentation. Wolsey's house at Hampton Court was finer than any palace in the kingdom. The poet Skelton wrote sourly:

> "*Why come ye not to court?*
> To which court?
> To the king's court,
> Or to Hampton Court?
> *Nay, to the king's court,*
> The king's court
> Should have the excellence,
> But Hampton Court
> Hath the pre-eminence."

Skelton reflected a general resentment and envy of the cardinal's pomp and arrogance. *Why Come Ye Not to Court?* ends with an enumeration of Wolsey's "lewd conditions":

> "Presumption and vainglory
> Envy, wrath and lechery,
> Covetise and gluttony,
> Slothful to do good,
> Now frantic, now stark wood."*

Something like this probably still represents the popular view of Wolsey, but he is in fact one of the (few) great figures in English history who improve on closer acquaintance. His undoubted faults appear great only because they were exercised on a grand scale; there was little in them that was truly vicious. More importantly, Wolsey was considerably more than a mere power politician, in the mould of Beaufort or Morton. It seems clear that Wolsey was genuinely motivated by a sincere and over-riding belief that he alone was capable of bringing justice, peace and good order to the kingdom and, for that matter, to the world. This is the key to Wolsey's quality. What is characteristic of his chancellorship is not so much the pursuit of

Wood = mad.

personal aggrandisement as the pursuit of good intentions. This had much to do with his success. As is often the case with such people, his certainty of himself created the same belief in others and from this came his remarkable power of attraction even over those who disliked and distrusted him. It also explains his astonishing energy. For Wolsey was indefatigable. "Alone," wrote the Venetian ambassador Giustiniani, "he transacts the same business which occupies all the magistracies, offices and councils of Venice". Though Wolsey had, naturally, to make use of a number of able subordinates, whom he had an excellent eye for choosing, he had a rooted resistance to substantial delegation. The old medieval executive council ceased to function under Wolsey's chancellorship, meeting only on formal occasions or, increasingly, as a judicial body; otherwise Wolsey, in effect, *was* the council, taking on his own as chancellor the decisions that would normally have been taken only with conciliar assistance. The dominant position of the chancellor on the council was only important to him in that it entitled him to ignore the council altogether. The same may be said of Wolsey's use of the great seal. It was necessary to his untrammelled authority that he be able to issue properly authenticated royal commands at will; but Wolsey was never bothered with the technicalities of chancery procedure and kept the seal constantly by him for use as was convenient — even when diplomacy took him out of the country, to the serious disruption of both the law and the administration. In the history of both council and chancery Wolsey's chancellorship was no more than an erratic episode.

The good intentions on which Wolsey expended his energy were various. One example is his foreign policy, which probably occupied more of his attention than any other matter. Wolsey was once thought to have been no more than a slavish follower of the interests of Rome aiming primarily at securing the Papacy for himself. Recently, however, his policy has been convincingly re-interpreted as a serious attempt to secure a stable peace between the war-happy European nations. If the policy was doomed to fail it at least had one spectacular temporary success in the treaty of universal peace launched in London in 1518. Wolsey knew that war was wasteful and that its high cost made for discontent. He was also an educated man who was well aware of the trend of contemporary humanist opinion summed up in the title of Erasmus' tract *Sweet is War to Those Who Do Not Know It*. Both Erasmus and his friend, Thomas More, who worked under Wolsey's regime for many years, had high hopes of him as a patron of learning — and his foundation of Christ Church at Oxford shows that they were not wholly misguided. In domestic affairs Wolsey made one of the few determined efforts to investigate and solve the great social problem of enclosures: in 1517 a commission was set up which in due course presented a massive report to the chancery, though its practical effects were disappointing.

Of greater effect were Wolsey's political and judicial policies. Wolsey was convinced that the greatest threat to the king's authority in the kingdom was the power of the great territorial lords and their lesser hangers-on and imitators, whose dominance of their "countries" allowed them to avoid or ignore the king's laws. Much valuable research has been done in recent years into the interaction of local and national politics at this period, and a provisional view is now possible of Wolsey's considerable importance in the long process of the collapse of local autonomy in England. He acted on both the large and the small scale. The two greatest magnates of the time, the duke of Buckingham and the earl of Northumberland, were systematically humiliated and oppressed. They were kept at court, denied the right to return to the estates from which their power was derived, and their followers were harassed and cut off from royal patronage. Buckingham was executed on a trumped-up charge of treason in 1523, and though Northumberland, luckier, was eventually allowed to return to the north when it became clear that his influence there was indispensable, he was by then perforce a tamed and loyal servant of the Tudors. Meanwhile local autonomy was being sapped from below. A survey of Yorkshire in the 1520s shows how Wolsey was active in the acquisition of land and the exploitation of patronage in the county, buying the king into a position of rivalry with the local lords. In 1513 there were twenty-nine local men on the commissions of the peace for the West Riding and only five outsiders; twelve years later the proportions were almost equal and among the outsiders were six lawyer-clerics promoted by Wolsey. In this sort of minute work the office of chancellor was central. The great majority of royal appointments, including, crucially, those of the justices of the peace, were made under the great seal and were thus directly in the chancellor's control. These were the bricks that were being pulled away from the foundations of aristocratic territorial power and slowly being constructed into a centralised royal structure of government.

Wolsey's policies in the field of justice also had a large political element. The common law* courts he regarded — correctly — as favouring the rich and powerful, those who could afford to wait for, buy, or ignore justice. To strike at the power of the lords he must promote more effective tribunals for the enforcement of the law or, to put it another way, of the king's authority. The appropriate instrument was the royal council, in which judicial and executive functions were simply two aspects of a single political responsibility. Wolsey made deliberate and extensive use of the council's jurisdiction to repress the independence and lawlessness of the king's great subjects. In May 1516, in what was evidently intended as a notable display of royal authority, the earl of Northumberland, lately imprisoned in the Fleet after a trifling incursion on the king's rights, was allowed to make a humiliating submission before the council in its normal meeting-place in the Star Chamber; and this show of strength was followed by a formidable oration from Wolsey declaring the king's desire to halt "the enormities usually exercised in this his realm to the derogation of indifferent justice". Justice and government went hand in hand. Yet even where there was no political motive Wolsey was very active in the cause of justice. He offered indiscriminate encouragement to litigants, especially the poor who could not afford to go to law, to bring their grievances to the council and (it seems, though there is very little research on the point) to the chancery, where they would be heard on an equal footing with the privileged; among the numerous committees of councillors established to deal with the resulting flood of petitions was the original "Court of Poor Men's Requests".

Despite the generous spirit that Wolsey put into his projects the conventional judgment tends to be along the lines of that of Professor Elton — "Wolsey turned out to be the most disappointing man who ever held great power in England and used it for so long with skill and high intelligence". Wolsey, it is true, failed in much of what he attempted, and he never even attempted many of the things which today excite the approval of historians. He put his mind to no revolution in government,

*See p. 80n.

or at least in administration; and current research seems to show that his judicial initiatives only served to swamp the tribunals that he so freely made available, and that he did little to assist the development of the Courts of Chancery and Star Chamber other than to bring them work. Energetic as he was, Wolsey never appreciated the care and application required if abuses are to be reformed and new institutions replace old; he allowed himself time for neither of those qualities. Nor can it be denied that his personal failings of arrogance, acquisitiveness and impatience often obstructed his better nature. Nevertheless Wolsey has an important place in English history. It is becoming increasingly clear that the process whereby the feudal independence of territorial power came to yield to royal authority—the taming of the aristocracy who had fought the Wars of the Roses—effectively began not in the reign of the cautious Henry VII but with Wolsey's campaign against the "lords". His methods were later to be refined and altered by more sophisticated operators, but it was Wolsey who took the initiative for a united kingdom.

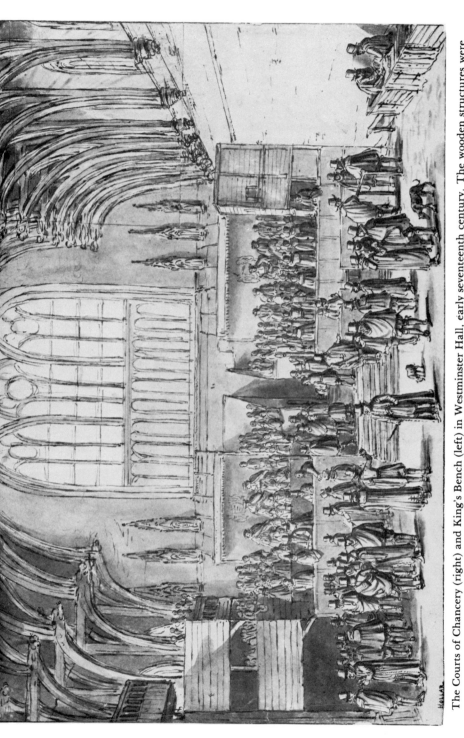

The Courts of Chancery (right) and King's Bench (left) in Westminster Hall, early seventeenth century. The wooden structures were replaced by permanent court-rooms in 1740. The draughtsman is anonymous, possibly Dutch.

Sir Francis Bacon, by Vanderbank (1731) — epitomising the later image of the philosopher Chancellor.

National Portrait Gallery

Clarendon, after A. Hanneman—a portrait well conveying the satisfied melancholy of
the Lord Chancellor's character.   *National Portrait Gallery*

By courtesy of the Guildhall. Photograph by the Cooper-Bridgeman Library

By courtesy of the Guildhall. Photograph by the Cooper-Bridgeman Library

Lord Somers, by Kneller. *National Portrait Gallery*

Two plates from Ackermann's *Microcosm of London* (1812).

A debate in progress in the House of Lords, with the Lord Chancellor presiding on the Woolsack.

A sitting of the Court of Chancery in the Old Hall of Lincoln's Inn, which was used for vacation sittings from the mid-eighteenth century.

The bland Lord Hardwicke, a mezzotint from a portrait by Thomas Hudson.

By courtesy of the Trustees of the British Museum

This mezzotint is from Reynolds' portrait of Camden as Chief Justice of Common Pleas, commissioned by the City of London after his famous judgements in favour of John Wilkes.   *By courtesy of the Trustees of the British Museum*

"Blood and Thunder Fording the Red Sea", by Gillray (1788). Thurlow is carrying
Warren Hastings: the reference is to the Lord Chancellor's unconcealed support for
Hastings during his trial.   *By courtesy of the Trustees of the British Museum*

"Sin, Death and the Devil", one of Gillray's best-known satirical prints, adapted from
an illustration to Milton by Fuseli. Thurlow, as Satan, confronts Death (George III)
and Sin (Queen Caroline) wielding the mace and a shield bearing the Woolsack and
the Lord Chancellor's Purse. Pitt, Dundas and Grenville, the leading figures in the
government, form a three-headed Cerberus. The date is 1792, shortly before
Thurlow's final dismissal.   *By courtesy of the Trustees of the British Museum*

CHAPTER THREE

The Chancellor and the Law

From the thirteenth to the seventeenth centuries

Origins

BY THE middle of the fourteenth century the chancellor had become, with all his other functions, an important judicial officer, and the chancery an established court of law. For both chancellor and chancery this was a development which was profoundly to influence their character and eventually to overshadow all other aspects of their work. It occurred in quite a short space of time: it is in the reign of Edward I that references first appear to a *curia cancellariae*, a court of chancery, and it was clearly well-established by the year 1327, when the condemnation five years earlier of Thomas of Lancaster was quashed on the grounds that it was reached without due process of law "even though the chancery and other places of the king's court were open". Though the way in which they inter-connect is complex and obscure, there are two basic reasons for the emergence of a judicial role for the chancellor and his office.

The first derives from the administrative work of the chancery. Men in the thirteenth century saw little distinction between the judicial and the administrative or executive functions of government. No medieval Montesquieu had come to teach them the separation of powers. All organs of government had alike originated in the *curia regis*, the royal court or household, and they retained, at least at this period, some of the "undifferentiated" authority exercised by the king himself. The king's justices dealt regularly with administrative matters and the exchequer had long had, besides its financial responsibilities, a role as a tribunal before which a variety of judicial issues could be tried. Subjects with a grievance felt themselves free to go to any royal official who they believed might be able to afford them a remedy. The ambiguous usage of the word *curia*, which could connote either a court of law in something like the modern sense or a court simply in the sense of the king's entourage, reflects the lack of any clear distinction recognised by contemporaries. The anonymous late thirteenth-century author of the legal treatise known as *Fleta* (because it is said to have been written in the Fleet prison) in a chapter entitled "The Different Kinds of Royal Court" enumerates at least ten different courts that had developed around the *curia regis*. Among them *habet enim curiam suam in cancellaria sua et in diversis locis hospicii sui*, "he [the king] has a court in his chancery and in various parts of his household".

Until the reign of Edward I the chancery did not benefit from this general tendency of medieval departments. It was too closely integrated with the itinerant royal household to have any independent attraction to litigants. But as it became more settled and better defined its advantages rapidly became apparent. It was an organised, accessible office with a large and literate staff. Its secretarial functions covered the whole range of government and public rights, so that many cases were already within its purview in so far as they concerned royal grants under the great seal or other documents emanating from the chancery. It was natural for disputes concerning such matters to be referred to the department which had already had some business with them.* More to the point still, the chancellor and his clerks were already closely associated with the judicial process by virtue of their writ-issuing functions. These functions were of course essentially administrative. It was not basically the clerk's job to investigate the merits of a claim, merely to formulate or select an appropriate writ to enable the issue to be decided by the established courts. But contemporaries, again, were not concerned with such a distinction. *Fleta* described the work of the clerks of the chancery in this way: "It is their duty to hear and examine the petitions and plaints of suitors and by means of royal writs to provide them with a remedy suitable to the nature of the wrongs they have revealed." In other words, the writ giving access to the king's courts was seen as a remedy in itself, an act of grace as important in its way as the final judgement. And it is clear from *Fleta's* words that the

---

*Cases coming before the chancellor specifically for this reason, as concerning, for example, the validity of letters patent, were regarded later as belonging to the "common law" or "Latin" jurisdiction of the chancellor, as opposed to the far more important "equity side". But for the Middle Ages the distinction is an unreal one. For a discussion of what is meant by "equity" and "common law" at this time see pp. 91-95.

provision of that remedy could require at least a preliminary investigation of the case and a degree of legal expertise. Writs could not always be simply taken off the shelf. For most of the thirteenth century there was no set limit to the writs available: as litigants came to the king with an increasingly wide variety of problems the chancellor or his senior clerks devised writs to cover them, writs which might well become standard forms — by the end of the reign of Henry III these amounted to some 120. In 1285 a provision of the second Statute of Westminster limited the creation of new writs to extensions from those already recognised, described as *in consimili casu*. This rule seems to have been designed in the interests of certainty in the law. At a time of increasing stabilisation and definition in the established courts, it was felt that there should be some limit on the classes of litigation coming before them. At any rate, the chancery regarded it not as a restriction but as an incentive to invention — by 1320 there were no less than 820 standard writs available.

Both before and after 1285 it is clear that the chancery had a vital creative influence in the development of the law through the formulation of writs. Its opinion carried real weight with the courts. On at least two known occasions it intervened when the abrasive chief justice of Edward II's reign, William Bereford, refused to assist a plaintiff whose writ was supposedly not apt to cover the facts of his case. In one case he quashed a writ on the grounds that it referred only to the rights of a remainderman and not those of a reversion holder (a technical distinction in the law of succession to land). Hauled before the chancery clerks, he had it pointed out to him that this was a plain case of *in consimili casu* under the Statute of Westminster. "Blessings on the maker of that statute," replied Bereford (ironically?): "Make out the writ and we will maintain it."

The chancery was thus well suited to take on the functions of a court of law. That it was already doing so during the reign of Edward I, and that the chancellor was already regarded as peculiarly able to give judicial remedies as an act of the king's grace, is clear from the surviving documents. A typical note from the king to the chancellor reads, "I pray and request you of your love for me to give to the bearer of these letters such remedy as the court will allow". But how and in what sort of case this jurisdiction was generally exercised is, for this early period, very obscure. The question can only be adequately answered when the second source of the chancellor's jurisdiction has been assimilated.

This second source derives from the chancellor's growing executive role in connection with the royal council. This was a time of strong discontent with the established courts of King's Bench and Common Pleas, the "two benches". These had been in existence as courts of law separate from the *curia regis* since early in the reign of Henry III, and in fifty years they had inevitably been through a process of definition and self-limitation. The professional royal judges no longer took any case that might have been heard by the king. Guided by a new set of treatises and handbooks, they were becoming increasingly rigid in the procedure and law that they applied in their courts: this indeed is the attitude embodied in the *in consimili casu* provision of the Statute of Westminster. Litigants were quite liable to find their cases ignored because the judges regarded them as outside their jurisdiction. Besides this, the courts were becoming more and more ineffectual at giving speedy justice or justice which could be properly enforced, as the old system of itinerant justices began to break down under the weight of business with which it was expected to cope.

In these circumstances, litigants naturally turned elsewhere. The reign of Edward I shows an enormous increase in the volume of petitions addressed to the king and his council by suitors who saw better prospects of success with them than in the courts. The flow was especially great at times when a parliament was meeting, for then the king was notionally specially available to hear the grievances of his subjects. There was however no question of the king being able personally to attend to even a fraction of the petitions coming before him. The burden, as of so much else, had to be shouldered by his ministers and council. In the parliament of 1280 regulations were made for dividing the load between different officials: the chancellor, not surprisingly, was to be sent petitions *ke tuchent le sel*, arising from the use of the great seal. In 1293 he received the potentially wider category of petitions "concerning the chancery". But far more important was the gradual development, not definitely apparent until well into the fourteenth century, of the council's practice of referring the great bulk of petitions coming before it to be dealt with by the chancellor, whether or not the subject-matter could be regarded as in any way his particular responsibility. This no doubt partly reflects the growing pre-eminence of the chancellor in the council. It is also evidently connected with the prior existence of the chancery as an efficient court and the legal work the chancellor was already doing in that capacity. Essentially, however, it represents the "executive" council, itself only another aspect of the *curia regis*, coming in to repair the inadequacies of the courts.

The chancellor's judicial jurisdiction in the fourteenth century and later was thus rooted in both the chancery and the council. But this is a distinction which becomes clear — or at least visible — only in analysis. The different authorities derived from the royal *curia* were as capable of coalescing as they had been of dividing. The king's officials and councillors, the professional justices of King's Bench and Common Pleas, and the chancellor and chancery are found throughout the century working not only singly but in a variety of combinations. A case in 1293 between the King of Scotland, John Balliol, and his unsuccessful rival for the throne, John Hastings, was heard "before the chancellor and the justices of both benches in the chancery": is the chancery here simply a location or is it an institution? and if an institution what does it lend to the proceedings that the chancellor and the judges do not already provide? Such questions cannot now be answered with any certainty. In 1357, even more confusingly, the chancellor and the treasurer were jointly commissioned to hear complaints about exchequer decisions "in any chamber of the council near the exchequer . . . taking to them justices and other men of wisdom as they think fit". The interpenetration was especially close between chancery and council. Throughout the fourteenth century the two are often, in their judicial functions, hardly separable: it is often impossible to say whether a given tribunal is properly to be described as the chancery sitting as a court with the advice of several councillors, or as the council, under the presidency of the chancellor with the secretarial assistance of some of his clerks. Though there was un-questionably a distinct court "of chancery", its limits were shadowy and the chancellor's judicial activities should not be seen as limited to any one context: he was too important an official to be bound by restrictions of mere form.

A very wide variety of business came before the chancellor and the chancery in their judicial roles. The contemporary category of matters *ke tuchent le sel* was capable of almost infinite extension in view of the range of business that required the application of the seal. And petitions coming in to the chancellor through the council were likewise of unlimited scope. Many, of course, required no judicial process at all, being merely requests for favours of one sort or another, and many more were on the borderline between administrative and judicial action. But two areas in particular became regarded as peculiarly the responsibility of the chancellor and his court; they are now discussed.

The Chancellor and Enforcement

Throughout the fourteenth century the most common type of case coming before the chancellor was concerned with the problems of enforcing legal rights. The chancellor was repeatedly invoked in cases where a plaintiff or petitioner was unable to bring his opponent to court or to enforce judgement on him because of his superior wealth or power. Violence and "maintenance", the browbeating or manipulation of justice, were perennial features of medieval society, with which the common law courts* were ill equipped to deal. A typical story is told in a petition of 1398. It is addressed to "the chancellor of our lord the king":

"The humble petition of Hugh de Bisley shows that Thomas Walweyn, John Hickokkes, Richard Monmouth and Thomas Sodegrove, with many others unknown, came to Stroud in the hundred of Bisley armed with swords and bucklers and bows and arrows while an inquest was in progress, at the orders of the sheriff of Gloucester and the bailiff of Bisley, with the authority of a royal writ, to establish the extent of the lands of Sir Richard de Talbot in respect of a debt owed by him to Sir William Heron and others. There they threatened the jurors so that they dared not continue with the inquest. They assaulted Hugh, the petitioner, and Thomas Walweyn told him that if he should be so bold as to prosecute or otherwise meddle or sue further in that case, or to bring any action at law against a certain Richard Greenhill, then he had better not be so foolish as to go on living there, for he would be killed if he did.

*"Common law" is a phrase with a variety of meanings according to context. It here refers to the system of law and procedure applied in the old courts of King's Bench and Common Pleas, as opposed to that employed in other, less formal tribunals. See further pp. 91-95.

And the petitioner and Sir William Heron will be greatly harmed if they cannot have your gracious remedy. May it please your lordship to grant writs directed to the evil-doers commanding them to come before you at a certain day to answer in this case, for otherwise no writs or orders of the king will be obeyed and no jurors will dare to do their duty in these parts."

Such cases came to the chancellor or to the chancellor and council partly because he represented the supreme executive authority in the kingdom. Men who might be able to bribe, bully or ignore the local officials or the king's justices on their occasional visits would think twice before disobeying the king's chief minister. But the chancery had other advantages. The chancellor and his court were bound by no procedural rules, and the elaborate techniques of delay that could be deployed before the professional judges were not available. Unlike the two benches, there were no paper pleadings in the chancery: the parties appeared in person and were examined orally. This was achieved by means of a writ of *sub poena*, commanding the attendance of a defendant on pain of punishment if he defaulted. A full hearing was only one possible course. The chancellor could dismiss the matter unheard, or refer it to a commission of local justices or other officials either for final decision (a commission of "oyer and terminer") or for a report on the facts; or he could order the case to be dealt with by the normal courts. The chancellor was applying no settled corpus of law, simply acting as seemed just or expedient. If a technical question of law was involved, one or several judges might sit with the chancellor or otherwise advise him: indeed at the beginning of the fifteenth century there were complaints that the judges were being distracted from their proper functions by the need to attend on the chancellor. The essence of the chancellor's jurisdiction was flexibility, in both procedure and remedy.

This jurisdiction was of course popular with those who benefited from it. Inevitably too it had its enemies. Local magnates might resent interference with their convenient control of the local courts and justices. More respectably, there was also concern that too easy a resort to the rough-and-ready jurisdiction of the chancellor was liable to prejudice the often complex and delicate patterns of rights to land.

Thus in 1378 the commons petitioned that no writ should issue from the chancery or the council concerning a man's freehold — *mais soit la commune Loi de la terre maintenu d'avoir son droit cours.* The council of the infant king agreed that no final judgement should be made on landed rights, but it reserved the right of the king to intervene where *pour maintenances, oppressions et autre outrages . . . le commune Loi ne pourra avoir duement son cours.* This was only one aspect of a continuing concern, no doubt fostered by common lawyers anxious at encroachment on their territory, that the chancellor and the executive authorities generally were too cavalier in their attitude to the courts. There are repeated complaints in the late fourteenth and early fifteenth centuries that the chancellor is by-passing or over-ruling the authority of the common law; indeed in 1437 an act was passed requiring petitioners in chancery to pay damages to their opponents if their actions were decided to be proper cases for the common law courts. But the very frequency of the protests makes it clear that the chancery was too popular a court to be repressed.

The Chancellor in the Court of Chancery

It was only in the fifteenth century that the chancery began clearly to acquire a distinctive jurisdiction of its own rather than existing chiefly to support the common law. The established courts were failing to meet the needs of litigants in two areas in particular. One was the law of contract. The over-rigidity and the cumbersomeness of the common law was especially irksome in its attitude to binding agreements. The common law courts of the fifteenth century recognised only such agreements as were embodied in sealed covenants, a restriction that was quite unrealistic in ordinary commercial transactions. Further, once an agreement was so sealed they would allow no defence of mistake, duress or fraud to prevent its enforcement. The common law had other disadvantages. Contracts made outside England were not considered to fall within the jurisdiction of the courts, a serious matter at a time when European trade was becoming both more complex and more extensive. A more widespread problem was that the only remedy awarded for a breach of contract was of money damages: "specific performance", i.e. requiring a party actually to fulfil his part of the agreement, was not available. On top of these particular defects there were the general failings of the common law courts — technicality of procedure, extreme dilatoriness, an insistence on paper pleadings to the exclusion of oral evidence, inadequate machinery for enforcement, and expense.

The chancellor had no such inhibitions. He was not a judge and had no reason to follow the technicalities of the law. He represented the king's grace and was willing to grant, or at least to consider, the petition of anyone who claimed to have been defrauded or otherwise taken advantage of, whatever the precise nature of the contract. A petition that came before Chancellor Stafford in about 1433 illustrates two of the problems with which he had typically to deal. The petitioner was the chancellor of the University of Cambridge who had agreed to acquire from Sir William Bingham a piece of his land convenient for the founding of a college, "adjoining on every side to the ground of the said chancellor and university"; but the knight defaulted on the bargain. The university could not sue at common law, it was claimed, because there was no written agreement; and even if they could have, damages would have been no compensation — what was wanted was the particular piece of land contracted for. They accordingly petitioned that Bingham be ordered to appear before Stafford in the chancery and "be compelled to do what truth, good faith and conscience require in this case". Not all contracts coming before the chancellor were so sober in their circumstances: a pathetic fifteenth-century petition asks for a bond and a sale to be set aside which the defendant had obtained by making the petitioner drunk and taking advantage of his "weakness of intellect while absent from his wife and friends".

But the chief defect of the common law related to the new practice known as "feoffment to uses". A "use" was essentially a trust: by it land or other property was formally conveyed to "feoffees" who were to hold it not for their own benefit but for that of named beneficiaries, who might be anyone whom the "feoffor" chose. The main purpose of the use was to give landowners greater control of the descent of their land after their deaths and to avoid the rigid rules of inheritance imposed by feudal custom and law: it was thus in the fifteenth century that the passing down ("devising") of land by will became a practicable possibility. Widows were a common class of beneficiary, for their rights at common law were meagre; daughters and younger sons might also benefit. To this extent uses promoted flexibility in the descent of landed property. Uses could also be employed to prevent estates being broken up or alienated (i.e. sold out of the family), for no current beneficiary, the "life tenant", would have an absolute interest of which he could dispose. They had the further advantage that, since the feoffees, who could be a self-renewing body, need never die, the estate did not become liable for the dues that were normally incurred on the death of a feudal tenant, and need never be subject to a wardship when the heir was a minor.

The use was a popular and valuable device, but it had the serious disadvantage that it was not protected by the common law. The courts of King's Bench and Common Pleas never came to terms with the concept of land that was formally held by one man who was nevertheless legally bound to hold it for the benefit of another: no more than one man at a time could be recognised as having an interest in a piece of land. This left feoffors and beneficiaries very vulnerable to dishonest or incompetent feoffees, or indeed to any legal problem affecting the ownership of the land. The law recognised no obligation on the feoffee to use the land entrusted to him in any other way than he chose; the only sanction was his own conscience. This gap came in the fifteenth century to be filled by the chancellor. Free of the narrow thinking of the common lawyers, he was willing to recognise the rights of the beneficiaries and to enforce them by calling an offending feoffee before him by a writ of *sub poena*, and if he found against him, ordering him to execute his trust. In one early case, for example, from the reign of Richard II, a certain Peter at More enfeoffed three feoffees with land to the use of Joan, his widow, and, after her death, of his brother. If his brother died without issue the lands were to be sold and the proceeds expended on masses for his soul. But one feoffee, a parson aptly named John Profit, persuaded his colleagues, using his influence as their confessor, to make over the lands to him, whereupon he promptly sold them and left the widow without the wherewithal to live. The chancellor is asked to order the feoffees to come before him "so that the said Joan may have her right in the said lands and tenements". We seldom learn the outcome of these early cases, for the petitions alone survive; but the case shows the circumstances in which it was expected the chancellor might act.

By the 1450s litigation relating to uses was providing the bulk of the judicial work of the chancellor and rapidly replacing the enforcement-orientated jurisdiction that had been his main concern in the fourteenth century; the chancery was finally coming to be recognised specifically as a court of law rather than merely an administrative office whose chief officer did judicial work. The stability of John Stafford's eighteen-year chancellorship probably did much to encourage these trends. It was a development of great social importance, and of no less significance in the history of the chancery and of the office of chancellor. The flexibility and the control which the use gave to the landowning class in their management of their estates was a potent factor in the final decline of the old feudal attitude to land, which was increasingly regarded as a commodity not essentially different from any other and available to be bought and sold freely. This was a change that in its turn contributed fundamentally to the social instability of the later sixteenth and seventeenth centuries. On a more mundane level the use seriously diminished royal revenue from the exploitation of feudal rights. Henry VIII's government attempted to restore the situation by forcing through a very reluctant parliament the Statute of Uses of 1536. The statute was based on the simple foundation that, in the most common forms of use, the beneficiary would henceforth be regarded for all purposes as the legal owner of the land, and thus subject both to the traditional feudal rights of the king and to the authority of the ordinary courts. But the Statute of Uses imposed only a temporary and partial limitation on the chancellor's jurisdiction. The Court of Chancery had already become established as the chief court of the kingdom dealing with the law of succession to land, and this was to be the root of its importance in later centuries. The consequence for the chancellor was to impose on him an ever heavier burden of judicial work which eventually became the principal preoccupation of the office.

The Court of Chancery did however continue to deal with other sorts of judicial business — quite apart from the redundant, but still lucrative, remnants of its administrative work — and some of the other services it offered were popular. Chancery's jurisdiction to relieve the victims of fraud went beyond the bounds of contract to cover all the areas in which fraud could operate unrestricted by the common law. At a procedural level, the court was willing to order litigants at common law to make discovery of relevant documents, an elementary power not exercised by the common law courts. And, the source of much trouble, the chancellor might issue injunctions in certain circumstances preventing a party from enforcing his full legal rights.

A large part of the original attraction of the chancery as a court had been the simplicity and accessibility of its procedures. These features did not survive the court's growing popularity in the sixteenth century. It was still possible in the reign of Henry VIII for Thomas More "every afternoon at his house at Chelsea to sit in his open hall, to the intent that, if any person had any suit unto him, they might the more boldly come to his presence, and therupon bring their complaints before him; whose manner was also to read every bill himself, ere he would award any subpoena: which bearing matter worthy of a subpoena, would he set his hands unto, or else cancel it". Wolsey's administration of his Court of Chancery was in the same informal spirit, even though the cardinal doubtless had less time to show a personal concern for litigants. But by the reign of Elizabeth procedure had become considerably more formal and more complex. It had not become more efficient. The trouble was that the medieval chancery had been an administrative department, and its conversion into a court of law was never planned. Chancellors and their subordinates did not come to grapple with the problems of its organisation until the main lines of its structure had already become set in the warped form that it was to retain into the nineteenth century. Its most fundamental failing was that it had only one judge, the chancellor himself, whose many other concerns did not allow him to devote his full energies to the work, even after his real political and governmental importance had declined. Partly in consequence of this but more, one suspects, simply because they were there, left over from an earlier system in which they had had a genuine purpose, the subordinate officials of the chancery came to play a disproportionately large part in the judicial process, spinning a complex tissue of interlocutory proceedings which, while they might achieve by a side-wind the result sought, too often wound the litigant in a cocoon of expense and delay. The characteristic proceedings of the Court of Chancery in the sixteenth century were not the final substantive hearings before the Lord Chancellor on his marble chair in Westminster Hall* but the endless self-perpetuating procedural formalities before the Chancery Masters. The history of the Court of Chancery at this period is institutional and not legal history.

An exposition of the complexities in which a Chancery action could become entangled is outside the scope of this work. But the basic structure can briefly be indicated. A plaintiff began his action by presenting a petition, a "bill", setting out his complaint and asking for a specific remedy—discovery of documents, enforcement of his rights under a trust, release from an oppressive contract, or whatever. The petition was heard by one of the twelve Masters, whose office derived from that of the twelve senior clerks of the medieval chancery. The Master would generally grant the plaintiff a writ of *sub poena* addressed to the proposed defendant, ordering him to appear in Chancery to answer the plaintiff's claim. At this stage each action was supposedly allotted to one of the "Six Clerks", subordinates of the Master of the Rolls who had somehow acquired, among much other miscellaneous business in the interstices of Chancery, the function of shepherding cases through the court and providing expensive and unnecessary assistance and advice to the unlucky litigant. What should ideally now have happened was that the defendant should have obediently appeared and both parties told their stories to the chancellor for him to adjudicate. Instead most of the remainder of the action was conducted on paper, with elaborate pleadings and evidence taken on oath from parties and witnesses by local commissions—a cumbersome and highly ineffective way of getting at the truth, though well adapted for incurring costs. The technicalities of procedure gave infinite scope for parties to raise objections by bringing a variety of motions before the Masters—claiming, for example, that pleadings were inadequate, that the collection of evidence by the commissioners had been corrupt or mismanaged or that some further remedy of the court, often an injunction to prevent other proceedings, was required. Far from every action survived this obstacle course eventually to come before the chancellor, often after an interval of years.

The attempts made to bring some order and proportion into this state of affairs were unable to effect any radical change. From the time

---

*Chancery cases were generally heard in Westminster Hall, where the common law courts were also based; though well into the seventeenth century it was not unusual for them to be heard on occasion at the chancellor's residence. The Master of the Rolls and the Six Clerks, however, operated in Chancery Lane, and the Masters' chambers were mostly in Doctors' Commons, by the river.

of Lord Chancellor Wriothesley (1544-7), a man anxious to rid himself of the burden of chancery work, chancellors sporadically promulgated sets of orders designed to regulate Chancery procedure in the interests of a degree of efficiency and expedition. Nicholas Bacon (1558-79) was active in this respect, reorganising offices, defining responsibilities and prescribing scales of fees. Thomas Egerton (1596-1617) in the early days of his tenure of office made an even more determined attempt to rationalise the Court of Chancery, retaining his previous post of Master of the Rolls in order to co-ordinate his programme. But all in vain: once even the most subordinate Chancery officials had acquired the lucrative perquisites of judicial business they proved impossible to dislodge.

Substantive law did not keep up with the growth of procedure. The principles on which chancellors decided cases in the Court of Chancery did not begin to be firmly settled until the second half of the seventeenth century, and much depended on the training and outlook of individual holders of the office. Certainly in what little is known about the fifteenth-century chancery there is evidence of the application of canon law*, especially in procedural matters. When in the sixteenth century the office came usually to be held by common lawyers they tended to apply the common law principles with which they were familiar, in so far as they were appropriate to the different subject-matter of the Court of Chancery; though the fact that the Masters were generally trained in the civil law* also had an influence. To attempt a more detailed analysis on the scale possible here would be futile: in the famous words of the seventeenth-century antiquary and polemicist, John Selden:

> "Equity [i.e. the law applied in Chancery‡] is a roguish thing: for law we have a measure and know what to trust to. Equity is according to the conscience of him that is chancellor and as that is longer or narrower so is equity. 'Tis all one as if they should make the standard for the measure we call a foot to be the chancellor's foot. What an uncertain measure this would be."

It is thus nonsense to talk, as Lord Campbell does, of such figures as the fifteenth-century Chancellor Rotherham as great "equity lawyers". Even the high judicial reputation enjoyed by, for example, Thomas

---

*"Canon law" is the law of the Church. It derives principally from late Roman ("civil") law.

‡ See pp. 91-95.

More would seem to be based on his personal qualities, of incorruptibility, humanity, conscientiousness, rather than on his attainments as a lawyer: these were not what the office needed.

The Chancellor in the Council

While the chancellor in his Court of Chancery became almost exclusively concerned with the limited class of civil litigation discussed in the previous section, he did not thereby lose touch with his more general judicial work. Petitions on a variety of matters continued to flow in to him and to the council, and if they were not considered to be business for the court of chancery it was in the council, under the presidency of the chancellor, that they were heard. The distinction between chancery and council in their judicial capacities was a fairly clear one by the middle of the fifteenth century, even though the personnel of the two courts might overlap. The jurisdiction of the council was very wide, but a number of specialist classes of litigation were dealt with peculiarly as council business: among the more important were commercial cases, or those with a foreign element, cases relating to personal status — questions of nationality, villeinage and so forth — and disputes within or between municipal corporations.

Most important, however, was the council's activity in the field of public order. Cases of riot, maintenance or intimidation came before the council in ever increasing numbers in the fifteenth century, from the humblest hedgerow tussles to the great Bedford riot of 1439, in which Lord Fanhope with forty or fifty men broke up the assizes and insulted the judges, or the near civil war in the West Country in the 1440s between Lord Bonville and the earl of Devon. This was essentially nothing more than a continuation of the "enforcement" jurisdiction which had gone primarily to the chancellor in the fourteenth century, but which was now gradually excluded by the growing specialisation of the Court of Chancery. Like the chancery, though, the council in its judicial capacity began to approach more and more closely the character of a court, with settled practice and procedure and an increasingly well-defined jurisdiction, which was eventually confined largely to offences against public order. This was a slow process, not complete until well into the sixteenth century: the court that finally emerged was the Court of Star Chamber. The "Star

Chamber" was originally simply the name of the room in the palace of Westminster in which the council used to meet, for both judicial and other business. Despite the amount of judicial work done by the council in the reign of Henry VII, it was not until the chancellorship of Thomas Wolsey that the term "Court of Star Chamber" seems to have come into common use to describe the council sitting judicially. Wolsey tended to monopolise to himself the ordinary administrative work of the council, while at the same time encouraging suitors to approach it as a court; it was this no doubt which led contemporaries to make a clear distinction between the two aspects of the council. The development was confirmed by the consolidation and re-organisation of the council as an administrative body into the later Tudor "Privy Council", a process begun by Thomas Cromwell in the 1530s and renewed under Elizabeth I. But such a separation of convenience between the council meeting to govern and the council meeting as a court did not mean any essential change in the Star Chamber's conciliar nature. This is reflected in the fact that it continued to be composed of the ordinary royal councillors, under the presidency of the chancellor in his capacity as the traditional head of the council and (usually) its most experienced lawyer. It should be mentioned, however, that the two chief justices continued to sit in the Star Chamber after they had ceased to be *ex officio* councillors in the reign of Henry VII.

The Star Chamber has been described as "the chancellor's court of criminal jurisdiction", in contradistinction to his court of civil jurisdiction, the chancery. This properly emphasises the central role of the chancellor in Star Chamber, but it is possibly misleading in two respects. Star Chamber, thanks to its separate origin, was never as closely linked to the office of chancellor as was the Court of Chancery: it was always the court of the council as a whole. Nor is it quite right to describe the Star Chamber as a criminal court in the modern sense. The great majority of its business was initiated by private petitioners concerned not for public order as such but for the protection of their own individual rights. Indeed many petitions to the court which alleged breaches of the peace or forcible entry or dispossession of land only did so in order to bring what would otherwise have been properly a suit at common law within the recognised scope of Star Chamber: often in reality no violence of any sort had occurred. Star Chamber was preferred by civil litigants in sixteenth-century England for the same reasons as the chancellor's court had been two hundred years earlier. It was quick, untechnical in procedure, and it had the authority of the king's council behind it. This last point was graphically described by the Elizabethan writer, Sir Thomas Smith:

> "If the riot* be found and certified to the King's Council, or if otherwise it be complained of, the party is sent for, and he must appear in this Star Chamber, where seeing (except the presence of the prince only) as it were the majesty of the whole realm before him, being never so stout he will be abashed; and being called to answer (as he must come, of what degree soever he be) he shall be so charged with such gravity, with such reason and remonstrance, and of those chief personages of England, one after another handling him on that sort, that, what courage soever he hath, his heart will fall to the ground . . ."

On the other hand, a sharp distinction between civil and criminal jurisdiction is a somewhat anachronistic concept for the sixteenth century. Governments that were anxious to enforce the king's peace preferred to do so not by direct action but by providing machinery for their subjects to bring such cases to justice. Public prosecutions are rare in this period, though Star Chamber was indeed where they were brought when they did occur. In 1487 Henry VII set up a special conciliar court, consisting of two of the great officers (i.e. normally including the chancellor), two councillors and two judges, before which he could bring cases of "unlawful maintenances . . ., giving of liveries . . . and retainders . . ., embraceries‡ of his subjects, untrue demeaning of sheriffs in making of panels and other untrue returns, taking of money by juries, great riots and unlawful assemblies". But this was a very exceptional example of government initiative, neither long-lived nor apparently very active; and it was in any event capable of being used by private petitioners as much as by the king. It was not until the seventeenth century that the Star Chamber came to be thought of — and even then unjustly — as a "government court".

Equity

The chancellor's jurisdiction had at first no jurisprudential basis. It did not need one, for no-one questioned the king's right, through his

---

*"Riot" in the sixteenth century could include any form of public disorder.

‡"Embracery" was the offence of influencing juries.

ministers, to act alongside his courts of common law to do justice. It was not necessary to define this right further. But as legal and constitutional thought became more sophisticated in the fifteenth century, and especially as the chancery acquired a definite sphere of judicial activity, the chancellors and other judges began to produce opinions about the theoretical justification for the existence of the court. The canon law training of most fifteenth-century chancellors made it natural that they should think in the terms with which they were familiar from the canonists. The prevalent theory was that the chancellor's court was a "court of conscience" in which moral laws were invoked to enforce rights not recognised by the established law. A feoffee to uses or a merchant who had made an agreement but not executed a formal deed were not bound in law, but they were under an obligation as a matter of conscience. In 1475 the common law judges stated: "In the chancery a man shall not be prejudiced by mispleading or by defects of form, but he shall be judged according to the truth of his case: and we must judge according to conscience and not according to things alleged by the parties [i.e. the formal pleadings]." In 1489 Archbishop Morton declared: "every law should be in accordance with the law of God; and the law of God is that an executor who fraudulently misapplies the goods and does not make restitution will be damned in hell, and to remedy this is to accord with conscience as I understand it".

The "conscience" theory of the chancellor's jurisdiction remained influential well into the seventeenth century. Interestingly, however, it lost much of its specifically moral or religious implication, partly no doubt as a consequence of the disappearance of the clerical chancellor. "Conscience" came to be understood less as a reference to the spiritual health of the litigant and more as an abstract notion of justice existing in the court. The transition is marked by a *dictum* of Mr Justice Fenner in 1595, who declared: "uses . . . are ordered and guided by conscience, either by the private conscience of the feoffee, or the general conscience of the realm, which is Chancery". It is in the latter sense that the idea that the chancellor was "keeper of the king's conscience" became current: Sir Christopher Hatton (1587-91) was the first chancellor to express it. It is a fine phrase, generally quoted without any notion of its specific meaning: it certainly has nothing to do, as is sometimes said, with the earliest chancellors having supposedly acted as the king's confessors.

Parallel with this change "conscience" came to be supplemented by, and to some extent absorbed into, a new concept, that of "equity". Equity is a very difficult word. Its natural sense, still alive in English usage, is that of fairness or, simply, justice. From this it is a short step to the notion of "natural" justice, unguided by formal rules or man-made laws. In this sense, often used by historians and commentators, the chancellor's jurisdiction had always been "equitable", since he answered petitions simply as he thought just, without reference to established rules of law. But it was not a word much used in this sense in the Middle Ages. It first appears as an important concept in *Doctor and Student*, a treatise by the early sixteenth-century lawyer, theologian and polemical pamphleteer, Christopher St German. He had a precise meaning for the term. In his chapter "What is Equity" St German wrote:

> "And for the plainer declaration what equity is thou shalt understand that sith the deeds and acts of men for which laws be ordained happen in divers manners infinitely it is not possible to make any general rule of the law but that it shall fail in some case. And therefore makers of laws take heed to such things as may often come and not to every particular case, for they could not though they would. And therefore to follow the words of the law were in some cases both against justice and the common wealth: wherefore in some cases it is good and even necessary to leave the words of the law and to follow that reason and justice requireth, and to that intent equity is ordained, that is to say to temper and mitigate the rigour of the law. And it is called by some men epicaia."

The last-mentioned term, the Greek *epieikeia*, gives this meaning of equity its academic credentials. It derives, through medieval writers, from Aristotle, who had defined just such a jurisprudential principle which would justify departures from general laws in the interests of justice in particular exceptional circumstances. *Epieikeia* was taken as the title of a work by the Elizabethan chancery official Edward Hake, and by his time this version of equity was the most common interpretation of the place of the Court of Chancery in the system of law. Lord Chancellor Ellesmere, who in 1615, in *The Earl of Oxford's case*, gave a famous and controversial apologia for the chancery's role, combined both *epieikeia* and conscience in his exposition: "The cause why there is a Chancery is for that men's actions are so divers and infinite that it is impossible to make any general law which may aptly meet with every particular act, and not fail in some circumstances. The office of the chancellor is to correct men's consciences for frauds, breach of trusts, wrongs and oppressions, of what nature soever they be, and to soften and mollify the extremities of the law . . .".

What, however, it is necessary to understand about sixteenth-century and later accounts of the purpose of equity is that they represent *ex post facto* attempts to justify to contemporaries an already long-established phenomenon. Historically the origins of the court of chancery had nothing to do with conscience, *epieikeia*, or equity as later understood, and these concepts always fitted it awkwardly. The scope of Chancery, once it had become a court at all, was far more specific and less wide-ranging than St German or Ellesmere would suggest. The chancellor had no roving commission to correct injustices wherever he might find them. His jurisdiction, in the chancery and elsewhere, developed pragmatically to cope with particular problems in response to the demands of the king's subjects, just indeed as the common law courts had themselves emerged. For the same reason any modern attempt neatly to categorise equity is unsatisfactory. It is, for example, often said that the principal advantage of the chancery as a court was procedural, that the chancellor offered few remedies that were not available at common law but was better able to see that they were effective; "equity was simply a way of working the common law". This corresponds to the view expressed in the later "equitable maxims" that "equity follows the law" and "equity acts *in personam*". These mean that the chancery could not alter or adjudicate on rights protected in the established courts of law: what it could do was to suspend or supplement their operation in particular cases by issuing an order binding on the defendant as an individual. This was indeed the technical legal position, which survived as an anomaly of much importance in the later history of the Court of Chancery. But historically the distinction is of little significance. All it means is that the courts of common law were first on the scene and had entrenched themselves in certain areas of the law, on which later arrivals should not encroach. There was no fundamental distinction, as lawyers tend to think, between law and equity as they actually developed. Equity covered matters both substantive and procedural as the need appeared. In the English legal system it is primarily a historical phenomenon rather than a principle of jurisprudence.

CHAPTER FOUR

The Rise of the Lawyer Chancellor

1529-1551: The Chancellorship in the Age of Thomas Cromwell

THOMAS More, who accepted the Great Seal on 29th October, 1529, is conventionally represented as the first of a new breed of Lord Chancellor.* He was a layman and trained in the common law, the son of a judge of the King's Bench. He did not have a strong political position either in his own right or as the instrument of others; nor, as Chancellor, was he allowed the commanding position in government that his medieval predecessors had enjoyed. This was to be the pattern followed by most of his successors. Nevertheless, his appointment is unlikely to have seemed revolutionary at the time. The shadow of Wolsey had discouraged the emergence of any obvious candidate for the position of chief minister to the king, and the field was further narrowed by Henry VIII's obvious reluctance to have an ecclesiastic as his Chancellor (though the office may have been offered for a second term to the elderly Archbishop Warham). In these circumstances, More was not markedly more or less distinguished than any of a number of courtiers and councillors. He had the important asset of a good knowledge of Parliament, having been a loyal and effective Speaker of the Commons in 1523: an alleged clash with Wolsey in that capacity can, if it occurred, only have redounded to his credit after the cardinal's fall. More had for many years occupied a vague but important place in the king's immediate entourage, as an auxiliary secretary, part-time diplomat, and general amanuensis. Henry valued his company for the opportunity it gave him to parade his pretensions as a scholar and a theologian, for Thomas More, the

---

*I use from now on the full title, which became firmly established in usage at about this time. As is often the case, the lesser the actual significance of the office the more elaborate become the formalities surrounding it. The title "Lord High Chancellor" came into use towards the close of the sixteenth century.

friend of Erasmus and author of *Utopia,* was unquestionably the most distinguished English humanist of the time: More's hand has often been seen, to a greater or lesser extent, in the king's famous *Assertio Septem Sacramentorum,* the attack on Luther which earned him the title of *Fidei Defensor.* The choice of More as Chancellor in 1529 was thus recommended by a long association with the king which had the advantage, at a time when Henry was determined to be his own master, of being more personal than political. His appointment was not intended to introduce a new sort of Chancellor, but in the circumstances it was unexceptionable.

In most respects, More did all that had been expected of him. He appears to have gained a good reputation in his judicial work. He put the king's views forcibly in Parliament, denouncing Wolsey in a powerful speech as "the great wether" who had to be expelled from the flock by the good shepherd (one of the more unlikely descriptions of Henry VIII) for having "so craftily, so scabbedly, yea and so untruly juggled with the king". Among his other parliamentary tasks were the scotching of rumours that Henry's motives for his intended "divorce" related to anything but theological scruple (a point on which More refused demands from the peers for his personal view) and a stern admonition to the Commons for their reluctance over taxation. There is no question that More was a committed member of the government on all issues save that of the divorce and the consequent attack on the Church, and these were matters on which both he and the king hoped that a collision could be avoided. This is an important point to emphasise, for More's admirers have tended to depict his entire period of office as dominated by his fundamental disagreement with the king, and indeed to suggest that he accepted the chancellorship only because he was compelled to, and that he had little stomach for the sordid business of court politics. This was not so. More's whole career had been in the sphere of public life and he knew the ways of the world as well as any man: his boyhood service in the household of that devious old politician Cardinal Morton, whom he always admired, was no training for a political innocent. Though he undoubtedly was concerned about compromising his views on the divorce there is no reason to suppose that he was not attracted by the office, as any courtier would be, and he had no qualms about leading the attack on his old patron, Wolsey, or defending in public a king with whom he was already in disagreement in private.

This view does nothing to detract from the courage and sanctity that More displayed in his resignation and the events that followed — rather the reverse. He stayed in office as long as he decently could, but he gave up the seal calmly and with dignity in May 1532 when the government had finally begun unequivocally on its attack on the Church. The story of his persecution and eventual martyrdom in 1535 is not appropriate here, but his last words on the scaffold, that he died "the king's good servant but God's first", accurately as well as movingly describe a man who attempted to apply principle in public life. There is an irony in the contrast between these words, from the first of the regular line of lay Chancellors, and those of Wolsey, the last of the medieval prelate Chancellors, who died lamenting that he had not served his God as he had his king.

More's chancellorship is perhaps deceptive as a turning-point in the history of the office. In 1529 there was no "obvious choice" for Lord Chancellor and the appointment of a lawyer of slight political influence is unsurprising. By 1532 Thomas Cromwell had emerged as the single most important royal minister, and he was confidently expected by such informed observers as Chapuys, the Imperial ambassador, to step into Wolsey's shoes. Instead More's successor was Thomas Audley, like him a lawyer, and a courtier and administrator decidedly of the second rank. There is no question that Cromwell could have had the position had he wanted it — if not in 1532 then certainly a year or two later. Professor Elton suggests that the principal reason for his preference for the humbler offices of Master of the Rolls and King's Secretary lay in his plans for the restructuring of the government. The chancellorship was too old an office and Chancellor and chancery were too encumbered with time-consuming traditional duties, above all their expanding judicial responsibilities. The less defined and restricted position of Secretary was more apt for the efficient and dynamic government that Cromwell hoped to create. Whether or not these arguments represent Cromwell's actual motives at the time — he may, more simply, have been anxious to avoid reviving the memory of Wolsey more than was necessary — they certainly reflect the actual effect of his decision. From 1532 onwards only briefly and by an accident of royal favour is a Lord Chancellor to be found as a minister of the first rank. For an office to attract men of ambition it must have functions that offer the holder access to real power. As a consequence of the administrative changes of the mid-sixteenth century, of which Thomas Cromwell is generally regarded as the catalyst, the chancellorship was left with a rag-bag of particular governmental functions surviving from its medieval past; some were not without importance but they were as a whole quite insufficient as a political base. The further demotion of the administrative role of the chancery was not perhaps a crucial change, for that was already far advanced, but under Cromwell and his successors the chancery was further by-passed by the creation of a series of independent committees, regional councils and administrative courts to which much of the work of government was devolved. Less and less administrative business passed under the Great Seal at all, though it still had to be used for formal grants and appointments and so forth. The central place in the administration, following Cromwell's re-organisation, was taken by the office of the Secretary, and the Secretary (or Secretaries, for there were sometimes two) was in the reign of Elizabeth finally established as the chief executive officer of the kingdom. This in itself might not have affected the Chancellor, but its corollary was a dominant role for the Secretary in the royal council, now slimmed down and formalised as a regular institution, the "Privy Council". It was this which struck at the real basis of the Chancellor's position. Shorn of his *ex officio* leadership of the council, the Chancellor might remain formally, in More's words, "the highest officer in this noble realm", but the dignity was a high-sounding sham; and the chancellorship had no means or reason to resist the pressures of business that were giving the office more and more of a judicial character.

It was perhaps to emphasise the shift in the balance of power between Chancellor and Secretary that Audley on his appointment received only the title of "Keeper of the Great Seal", though the king specified that he was to exercise all the functions of the Chancellor in chancery, Star Chamber and council. The only precedent for this was the period between 1500 and 1504 when the title of Chancellor does not seem to have been applied to Deane and Warham; it is not known why. In 1532 there was apparently a deliberate intention to diminish the status of the office, although the next year, when Parliament was about to re-assemble and Audley would have important public duties, he was given the full title of Lord Chancellor.

Audley was Lord Keeper and Lord Chancellor for twelve years, eight of them as the right-hand man, or — to more hostile critics such as Chapuys — the tool, of Thomas Cromwell. It was a position of which he was himself very sensible and which sometimes rankled. There survives a petulant letter from Audley to Cromwell complaining that he had none of the rewards of patronage that as Chancellor he was entitled to expect:

> "I was a poor honest man before it pleased the King's Majesty to call me to mine office, and more better accepted then for my poor degree than I am now with all mine estate. And yet I have served his Grace well and his people indifferently. I meddle with as few things as ever did Chancellor, I am not so chargeable to the people as Chancellors have been. I think never Chancellor less set by . . . And if a Chancellor of England when he dieth have not 200 marks land, it is to be noted, when a merchant and one of the law will not be so satisfied . . .".

This unlikeable letter sums up Audley's relationship with Cromwell, dependent but resentful. It is not surprising that the Chancellor lifted not a finger to help his patron on his sudden fall in 1540. Yet the two worked well together. Cromwell made much use of Audley's undoubted legal abilities, employing him particularly on the drafting of the copious and revolutionary legislation of the 1530s. Audley's responsibility as Lord Chancellor for the justices of the peace and for the commissions of assize made him a principal channel through which the Secretary both received information and issued instructions in his ceaseless campaign to detect and suppress dissent in the country. Audley was also the appropriate man, as a lawyer and as nominally the king's leading minister, to preside at the numerous state trials of Cromwell's regime. In these various capacities he incurred a popular odium second only to Cromwell: as "the greatest thieves and traitors living in this realm" they were the chief targets of the Pilgrimage of Grace of 1536.

Audley, like More, had been Speaker of the House of Commons, and his successor as Speaker, Richard Rich, was another future Chancellor. This highlights the one area, apart from his judicial duties, in which the importance of the Lord Chancellor was growing. The 1530s, with the revolutionary Reformation Parliament lasting an unprecedented seven years from 1529 to 1536, were a period of decisive advance in the political importance of Parliament. The role of the Chancellor as traditionally the royal spokesman in Parliament took on a new significance and a new definition. Although he continued to address both Houses at the opening of a session, he became specifically associated with the House of Lords. To call the Chancellor the "Speaker" of the Lords in the same sense as the Speaker of the Commons is misleading, but he presided over their meetings and acted as intermediary between the House and the king. A sign of the new self-consciousness of the Lords was the Statute of 1539 which regulated the order of precedence among peers and gave a formal recognition to the Chancellor's pre-eminence—as well as ordaining his traditional seat on the woolsack.*

Thomas Wriothesley, who became Lord Chancellor on Audley's death in 1544, was politically more ambitious than his cautious predecessor. The son of a minor courtier, he had made himself both rich and useful by a career at court as diplomat, predator of monastic lands and protégé of Cromwell. A courtier's adaptability enabled him to survive Cromwell's fall in 1540 and in the confused period that followed he emerged as one of Henry's most influential councillors and a leading member of the reactionary anti-Protestant faction which dominated the king's last years: some of the most unpleasant religious persecution of an unpleasant reign must be considered his responsibility. No-one's position was entirely secure in these years, under the shadow of the king's unstable caprice. Henry, with sinister bonhomie, liked to call his Lord Chancellor "my pig"; and on one occasion, when Wriothesley and his colleague Bishop Gardiner had obtained the king's consent to the arrest of his last wife, the Protestant Catherine Parr, he arrived with an armed band to take her to the Tower only to find her walking lovingly in the garden with Henry and to be sent away with violent abuse—"knave! arrant knave! beast! fool!". He was lucky it was no worse. In 1547 Wriothesley was granted the Earldom of

---

*A woolsack was the most comfortable form of seat available in the Middle Ages. The idea that it came into use as a symbol of the dependence of the English economy on wool has no foundation.

Southampton in Henry VIII's will, and by virtue of his office as Chancellor took the leading part in the proceedings surrounding the accession of the young Edward VI. But in barely more than a month he had been dismissed by the Protestant Protector Somerset, who no doubt shared the view of a contemporary that the Lord Chancellor was self-seeking and intolerant — "he was an earnest follower of whatsoever he took in hand, and did very seldom miss where wit or travail could bring it to pass . . . I never was able to persuade myself that Wriothesley could be great but the King's Majesty must be in the greatest danger". Besides, Somerset's constitutional position as Protector was extremely shaky and it was essential that he have undisputed access to the Great Seal. The Seal was still the supreme symbol of royal authority and its control was unusually important when the king was a mere boy with a divided council, and what his official will was and how it was to be confirmed were far from clear: Wriothesley seems to have hinted that he would not be content merely to affix the Seal on the say-so of the Protector. Though the ex-Chancellor continued to intrigue against both Somerset and his successor, Northumberland, his death in 1550 forestalled any possible return to power. Wriothesley is something of an oddity among sixteenth-century Lord Chancellors. He was neither a lawyer nor a professional administrator. It is appropriate that the occasion (though hardly the reason) for his fall in 1547 was his establishment of a commission of four professional civil lawyers to take over the hearing of cases in Chancery; this concerned the common lawyers, who saw it as an insidious attempt to increase the amount of business coming to the Court of Chancery, but Wriothesley almost certainly intended only to shake off the unwelcome burden of judicial work. But without a functional basis for his position, Wriothesley as Chancellor could owe his power only to his standing at court in the peculiar conditions of Henry VIII's old age.

Somerset did not at once select a successor for Wriothesley, and the Great Seal was kept for six months by William Paulet, an able and influential royal servant who survived to be Elizabeth I's Lord Treasurer for fourteen years and to earn the title of Marquis of Winchester. In October 1547, however, the Seal was passed to the lawyer and courtier, Lord Rich, who remained Lord Chancellor until 1551. None of the civil servants of the early Tudor period have traditionally been historians' favourites, but Richard Rich has had probably the worst press of all, largely because of the ignoble part he played in the trial of Thomas More. It was Rich who gave the vital evidence of a friendly conversation with More in the Tower in which he supposedly uttered the words on which his conviction for treason was based. More's snub to him at the trial was memorable:

"In good faith, Master Rich, I am sorrier for your perjury than for my own peril. And you shall understand that neither I nor no man else to my knowledge ever took you to be a man of such credit as in any matter of importance I, or any other, would vouchsafe to communicate with you. And I, as you know, of no small while have been acquainted with you and your conversation, who have known you from your youth hitherto, for we have long dwelled in one parish together, where . . . (I am sorry you compel me so to say) you were esteemed very light of your tongue, a great dicer and of no commendable fame . . . Can it therefore seem likely unto your honourable lordships that I would, in so weighty a cause, so unadvisedly overshoot myself as to trust Master Rich . . . so far above my sovereign lord the king, or any of his noble councillors that I would unto him utter the secrets of my conscience touching the king's supremacy, . . . a thing which I never did nor ever would . . . reveal to the king's highness himself or to any of his honourable councillors?"

It is bad luck on Rich that this speech will always remain his epitaph. But he and Audley and their colleagues are men whose careers are now being re-assessed. Their indifferent service through periods of wild fluctuation in politics and religion—Rich, for example, was a councillor successively of Henry VIII, Edward VI (under both Somerset and Northumberland), Mary and Elizabeth—tends now to be regarded as a sign not of lack of scruple but of balance and good sense, or even of dedication to the art of government. Paulet's admission that he was sprung from the willow and not the oak is treated with respect, for his contribution and those of the other lesser statesmen of the period to the development of a national administration is now better appreciated. Rich was, in his way, a man of vision, who while still an unknown barrister wrote to Wolsey outlining a scheme for the wholesale reform of the common law; and as chancellor of the newly-created Court of Augmentations from 1536 he organised one of the most effective and efficient financial institutions of the century. Though they are not especially attractive characters, these men were not the monsters of treachery and turpitude described by Lord Campbell and historians of his outlook.

Audley and Rich do indeed represent the new type of Chancellor — laymen, common lawyers, political second-rankers. But the change may seem sharper than it actually was. The differences between a fifteenth-century clerical administrator-chancellor of the type of Kemp or Stafford and his lay sixteenth-century successors were mostly superficial. Both were in the business of government first and foremost (though on a more humble level after the fall of Wolsey and the rise of Cromwell), a business requiring an essentially secular mentality.* As for the common law, with the first post-Reformation Chancellors this was as much a means of access into government as a profession in its own right, just as the Church had been in the Middle Ages. Not till Thomas Bromley (1579-87) was there a "pure" lawyer-chancellor, one who had not already made himself useful in other areas of government. Nor of course had all medieval Chancellors been figures of political significance — the crucial difference however being that they at least had the institutional base, in chancery and council, on which power could be established.

1551-1603

Rich resigned the Great Seal on grounds of ill-health in 1551. The next three Lord Chancellors, Thomas Goodrich (1551-3), Stephen Gardiner (1553-5) and Nicholas Heath (1556-8) were all bishops. It is not likely that this reflects a conscious reaction against the appointments of laymen which had begun with More. Certainly in Goodrich's case it is more an indication of the way in which the internal politics of Edward VI's reign were expressed in terms of religious differences. It seems to have been as a deliberate stroke of policy that the duke of Northumberland appointed Goodrich, a leader of the advanced Protestant faction which he favoured, rather than an uncommitted civil servant in the mould of Paulet or Rich. Goodrich continued to support his patron to the bitter end, serving as Lord Chancellor to

---

*Like their medieval predecessors, they liked to devote a prudent part of their wealth to good works. Audley put his money into Magdalene College, Cambridge, while Rich founded Felsted School in Essex, among the estates he had acquired from the dissolution of Leighs Priory.

Lady Jane Grey, Northumberland's Protestant rival to the Catholic Queen Mary. In the case of Nicholas Heath, Mary may well have been disposed to appoint an ecclesiastic, for her advisers were nothing if not clericalist. But again Heath's credentials were not so much simply that he was a prelate but in particular that he was one of the firmest and most committed — though also one of the most moderate — Catholic activists. He had been deprived of his see of Worcester in 1551 for refusing to accept Cranmer's new form of the service of ordination; Mary restored him and in 1555 promoted him to the see of York. Heath's most important duty as Lord Chancellor was also his last, when in November 1558 he announced Mary's death to Parliament, and recommended the proclamation of Elizabeth. He was nevertheless deprived of the Great Seal. Heath co-operated as far as he conscientiously could with the new government, but after he had insisted on opposing the Act of Supremacy in the House of Lords he was deprived of his see and was allowed to go into a prosperous retirement.

Stephen Gardiner was a far greater figure than either of these and was a politician of the first importance, irrespective of his cloth. His principles may have been firmer than theirs but his background was essentially that of a Rich or an Audley. A trained lawyer and distinguished humanist scholar, he had made his career not principally in the Church but in the royal service, as one of that remarkable group of able men who flourished under Wolsey and Cromwell. He had been an elder contemporary at Cambridge of Wriothesley and of William Paget, Henry VIII's last Secretary, and had played opposite them in Plautus — in more light-hearted parts than any of them was later to have to take. Gardiner negotiated with the Pope as Wolsey's agent, became King's Secretary in 1529 (gaining the see of Winchester as a reward in 1531) and was a leading anti-Papal controversialist in the 1530s: his *De Vera Obedientia* ("On True Obedience") was the most formidable defence of royal supremacy in the Church. His experience of public affairs was further widened by three years as Henry's representative in France and by a mission to Germany in 1540-1. It is small surprise that with Cromwell out of the way it was he who, with a small group of friends including Lord Chancellor Wriothesley, dominated Henry VIII's council and government. But unlike most of his contemporaries, he was more than a mere politician. His defence of the royal supremacy did not preclude a committed doctrinal conservatism, and much of his energies were expended in theological controversy and in promoting a rigorous persecution of English Protestants. The religious revolution caused by the accession of Edward VI in 1547 spelt the end of Gardiner's influence and he spent the years from 1548 to 1553 as a prisoner in the Tower of London.

Gardiner's appointment as Mary's Lord Chancellor in August 1553 meant that he had to come to terms with the Papal supremacy whose overthrow by Henry VIII he had so passionately defended. The process does not seem to have caused him any difficulty — to do him justice, his support for Henricianism had been waning even before 1547 — but it infuriated the Protestants: *De Vera Obedientia* was re-printed in Germany with such subtle marginal notes as "Hearken to your own reason, my Lord Doctor Doubleface" and with a preface describing him as "now Lord Chancellor and common cut-throat of England". Mary and her Papalist advisers, however, could not afford to resent Gardiner's tainted past, for he was unquestionably the ablest and most experienced politician, diplomat and administrator in the Catholic party. Nevertheless Gardiner was in an unhappy position. His own chief concern was to restore a Catholic doctrine and liturgy, and, while Mary and her advisers would certainly have agreed so far, they attached an equal importance to the return of Church lands and to the queen's marriage to Philip II of Spain. Gardiner, who had a better sense of what was practicable, managed to persuade the queen into a reluctant compromise at least on the issue of Church lands. But as Lord Chancellor he was the natural front-man for the government and its spokesman in Parliament and elsewhere, and his critics made no distinction between his own policies and those insisted on by the queen. His chief opponent was his old friend Paget, who organised a formidable and largely successful opposition in Parliament to Gardiner's doctrinal measures by playing on the fears of holders of Church property, even though Gardiner had expressly renounced any intentions in that direction. The falseness of his position was increased by the growing influence of the returned expatriate Cardinal Pole. It was Pole and not Gardiner who initiated the calculated campaign of burning heretics which did much to alienate sympathy from the government: Gardiner was personally concerned only in the first handful of examinations for heresy. He was not opposed to burning in principle, but he regarded it as a dangerous weapon if applied injudiciously — heresies were "like boils in a man's body which oversoon lanced wax sorer and in time putrify their matter". Proud, choleric and overbearing as he was — his examinations of heretics tended to degenerate into abusive shouting-matches — he was far from "the bloody, butcherly bishop of Winchester" of Protestant legend. When he died in November 1555 Mary's government was deprived of its most valuable support.

The chancellorship of Stephen Gardiner was an anachronism in the history of the office. Elizabeth I reverted to the trend established in her father's reign when in December 1558 she entrusted the Great Seal to Nicholas Bacon, a lawyer and for the last ten years Attorney of the Court of Wards under both Protestant and Catholic regimes. Bacon was a far from undistinguished man, shrewd, honest, cultivated and a good lawyer; he also had the considerable advantage of being the brother-in-law of William Cecil, soon to emerge as Elizabeth's most trusted minister. In his twenty years of office he wielded a considerable though unspectacular influence as a councillor, particularly in his implacable Protestant opposition to Mary, Queen of Scots, and his hostility to the ambitions of the earl of Leicester. He earned the deep respect of both the queen and his contemporaries. His successor, Thomas Bromley, declared "I shall succeed one in whom all good qualities did abound . . . whereby my want and insufficiency shall be made more manifest", and when swearing in Lord Keeper Egerton almost forty years later the queen broke into tears at the memory of her first Lord Keeper. Bacon's hand can be seen in, among other things, Elizabeth's re-coinage and in the Statute of Artificers of 1563, the first in a programme of restrictive social legislation initiated by Elizabeth's government, policies which reflected his serious-minded humanist approach to the theory and practice of government.

Bacon was nevertheless a councillor of the second rank, more noted by his contemporaries as a lawyer than a statesman. His appointment was a return to the line of lawyer-administrators. Cecil, as Secretary and later as Lord Treasurer, occupied something of the same dominant position in the administration under Elizabeth as had Cromwell in the 1530s, with the same depressive effect on the status of the Chancellor.

This was even more true of Bacon's successors, Thomas Bromley (1579-87), John Puckering (1592-6) and Thomas Egerton (1596-1617), later Lord Ellesmere and Viscount Brackley. These were professional lawyers and, though all three had as law officers made themselves useful to the government in state trials, their political importance was slight. It is true that the very nature of their work meant that they could not be complete non-entities. Nicholas Bacon, banished from court for his supposed part in the authorship of a pamphlet advocating the adoption of Lady Catherine Grey as Elizabeth's successor, contrary to the queen's own policies, was told henceforth to stick to his work in Chancery. That was quite impracticable. His duties in Parliament ensured the Lord Keeper or Chancellor a place in the public eye, and in Star Chamber it had become customary for him, at the end of the judicial term, to deliver to an assembly of judges and justices a review of the policies of the government and a general exhortation to obedience. These were important tasks in a regime well aware of the values of publicity. His judicial functions were also occasionally of political importance: Bromley, for example, presided over the special commission appointed to try Mary, Queen of Scots. The Chancellor could be a valuable ally in the factional politics of the reign, for his patronage was extensive, although there is little evidence that such exploitation was widespread under Elizabeth. The earl of Essex, who was quite unrestrained in his attempts to accumulate political influence, apparently thought he could rely on Lord Keeper Puckering: on one occasion a request that Puckering appoint one of his followers as a justice of the peace in Pembrokeshire has the sinister ending: "I shall reckon it for a special courtesy, and add it to many others whereby your Lordship continually by satisfying my like requests doth tie me unto you". But the Lord Keeper was evidently responsive to other pressures: in 1595 Essex's retainers in Wales appear to have been dismissed wholesale from the commissions of the peace, probably at the prompting of Cecil, now Lord Burghley. Egerton, Puckering's successor and a far more considerable character, was friendly with Essex, but he was appointed by the queen on her own initiative and refused to allow himself to become attached to the earl's party at court. It was to his custody that Essex was committed on his unauthorised return from Ireland in 1599 and he presided over the commission which stripped Essex of his offices early in the next year.

Although a general pattern can be observed at this period in the declining status and political importance of the office of Lord Chancellor, and its increasing preoccupation with legal business, the fact is that the chancellorship was in an anomalous position. Its status rested on history rather than on the solid foundation of any job the Lord Chancellor actually had to do, and it was therefore possible for the general trend of the office's development to be interrupted by some erratic variations. As late as the reign of Charles II there were Chancellors who were not lawyers but career politicians, even, in the case of Clarendon (1660-1667), a "prime minister". The notorious aberration of Elizabeth I's reign was the choice as Bromley's successor in 1587 of Sir Christopher Hatton, a royal favourite and court politician with only the most vestigial legal background. Hatton was one of the queen's closest intimates and accomplished in both the social and political skills required at court. He was among the many rumoured to have been Elizabeth's lover, and while this was certainly untrue their relationship was very fond. It was Hatton who produced the memorable observation that "the queen doth fish for men's souls, and has so sweet a bait that no one could escape her network". By the 1580s he was one of the three or four most influential Privy Councillors. No entirely satisfactory explanation of his appointment to the chancellorship has ever been offered. It is true that Hatton was a man of intelligence and ability, who in the event — despite the initial shock to the profession — performed his judicial duties creditably and seems indeed to have shown an imagination and good sense that the professionals did not always share. Sir John Neale has drawn attention to his excellence as a parliamentary orator and in particular to the fine speech he delivered when opening the Parliament of 1589, celebrating the defeat of the Armada and calling for full commitment to the war against Spain. On this sort of occasion the Chancellor was a figure of immense importance. Hatton was certainly not the frivolous "dancing Chancellor" of popular myth. It is true also that there was no obvious candidate among the lawyers; and it has recently been pointed out that Hatton had political rivals who may have wished him to see him kicked upstairs. But these facts do not really explain why he was chosen. In any event it is clear that the office had no such pronounced character that Elizabeth felt constrained from offering it as she liked. It is worth noting that no successor to Hatton was appointed for over six months, a fact which in itself emphasises the lack of any indispensable role for the Chancellor.

The same ambivalence appears in the titles by which these men were known. Bacon and Puckering were never raised to the chancellorship proper; nor was Egerton until the next reign. They remained, as Audley had briefly been, Lord Keepers of the Great Seal. Elizabeth was notoriously mean with honours, and she may have borne in mind the comparatively humble origins of these men — Bacon's father was a sheep-farmer and Egerton was illegitimate. There was undoubtedly too an intention to avoid the political, and probably also ecclesiastical, connotations of the older title. But for no apparent reason Sir Thomas Bromley was made Lord Chancellor, and so, more understandably, was Hatton. The distinction was purely honorific: Bacon had an Act passed in Parliament in 1563 which confirmed that the powers and duties of a Lord Keeper were equivalent to those of a Lord Chancellor.

1603-1621: The Chancery under Attack

In the early years of the seventeenth century the office of Lord Chancellor and the Court of Chancery emerged from the backwater down which they had drifted in the previous fifty years, to become deeply involved in political controversy. A bitter dispute developed between Thomas Egerton, now Lord Chancellor Ellesmere, and the great common lawyer, Edward Coke, Chief Justice of the Court of Common Pleas and from 1613 Chief Justice of King's Bench, culminating in an open confrontation in 1615-16. The chief supporter of Ellesmere's position, Francis Bacon, succeeded him as Lord Keeper in 1617, but in 1621 he was condemned by the House of Lords for corruption and forced to resign his office. James I added a strange twist to the episode when, to the general astonishment, he appointed as Bacon's successor Bishop John Williams, the last clerical Chancellor and almost the last not to be trained in the law. These events have been variously interpreted. Notionally Coke and Ellesmere were arguing about the rival jurisdictions of their respective courts, and Bacon's impeachment was, apparently, the result of his personal conduct as Chancellor; but both issues in fact contained a strong political and constitutional element. In the politics of the early Stuart period the law occupied a central position. The ultimate crisis came under Charles I when the courts came to be used in an attempt to give legitimacy to the enforcement of policies that had not been endorsed by Parliament. James I (1603-25) was sensible enough to avoid any such substantial confrontation, but nonetheless the immediate political conflicts of his reign tended to be accompanied by a vigorous two-sided display of constitutional shadow-boxing, in which the law and the monarchy each sparred with images of the other. The concept of the common law, of which Parliament was itself in some sense a product, as an alternative source of authority to the king was a useful weapon for men who opposed James on quite other grounds. Coke's famous remark that "Magna Carta is such a fellow he will have no sovereign" typifies the slogan-value of the common law tradition: it is a good rule in history never to take at face value any statement purporting to be based on Magna Carta.* Meanwhile James himself, a keen constitutional theorist, was intellectually attracted to absolutist ideas in which the law was the chief embodiment of royal authority—a provoking but harmless notion which was loyally upheld by Ellesmere, Bacon and Williams. Equity and the Court of Chancery were especially important to the debate because James believed that equity (as either *epieikeia* or his royal conscience or both) represented that part of the law that was still reserved to the king, his residual power to see that the administration of law in his kingdom, the common law, conformed to absolute justice. "In the court of equity," said Ellesmere, "the king governs (like God himself) by his own individual goodness and justice, though placed (during his royal pleasure) in the breast of another." It was in accordance with these fanciful theories that James I appointed Bishop Williams. He had had his fill of professional lawyers; and who better than a bishop to mediate pure and unsullied natural justice? This was more theory than reality, since, as we have seen, Chancery was by the end of the sixteenth century simply another court, not different in its essentials from King's Bench or Common Pleas; but statements of this sort drew king and Lord Chancellor together at a time when Chancery was already coming under severe attack.

For Chancery was, quite separately, engaged in a stern struggle with the common law courts over jurisdiction. The main bone of contention

*Cf. Archbishop Stratford's propaganda in 1341.

was the long-established Chancery practice of issuing injunctions, writs which ordered cases that were proceeding, or indeed had been decided, at common law, to be brought before the Chancellor to be heard afresh. The justification for this practice was that conscience required that litigants the justice of whose case had been defeated by the technical rules of common law should nevertheless have a remedy elsewhere. Injunctions had been a natural weapon as long as there had been a Court of Chancery. Indeed they were inevitable, for if Chancery could not, as it accepted it could not, alter the rules of common law it must have instead some way of preventing a litigant who was in the wrong from the point of view of conscience from actually enforcing those rules. This is what the injunction, an order binding only on the individual and not purporting to affect his rights as such, provided. Common lawyers, though some with better grace than others, recognised this; but there was always bound to be scope for disagreement about what was and what was not a proper case for depriving a man of his legal rights, particularly where the injunction re-opened a case that was apparently settled. Wolsey, with his enthusiasm for plain equity, had aroused much resentment by his liberal use of injunctions; it was among the principal charges brought against him at his fall. Thomas More had had a hard time smoothing ruffled common law feathers over the far fewer injunctions that he himself issued as Chancellor. His son-in-law recalls that More invited the judges to his home and after dinner "showed them both the number and causes of every one of them [i.e. his injunctions] in order, so plainly that, upon full debating of those matters, they were all enforced to confess that they, in like case, could have done no otherwise themselves". He also pointed out that injunctions would be unnecessary if the judges themselves tempered the rigour of the common law; but this hint received little response — in More's view because the judges were frightened of the responsibility of exercising their own discretion. After More's time there are no records of serious trouble over the use of injunctions until the end of the sixteenth century, probably because the common law training of most of the Chancellors, and their close relations with the judges (who often sat in Chancery), encouraged them to find a *modus vivendi*. Indeed, it could happen that judges who felt compelled by law to find for one party would recommend that "notwithstanding the said verdict is passed, there is great cause why the said plaintiff should be relieved in the Court of Chancery". Nevertheless, occasional grumbles persisted and the precise line of demarcation between courts remained negotiable. Quite apart from injunctions, cases that did not belong in Chancery would often drift into its orbit because a Chancery process had been required at some stage in proceedings, such as discovery of documents (often used deliberately as a device to bring a case into Chancery), or because of an allegation that an apparently valid document was in fact fraudulent; and once there litigants tended to stay. Strong-minded Chancellors, notably Nicholas Bacon and Thomas Egerton, anxious as much about their own work-load as about the resentment of other courts, attempted to keep these truant cases out of Chancery, but they were never wholly successful.

The confrontation between Chancery and the common law courts built up gradually from the last years of Elizabeth's reign. In a series of *habeas corpus* cases beginning with *Finch -v- Throgmorton* (1598) the common law judges declared unlawful the imprisonment on the Chancellor's orders of litigants who had been imprisoned for disobeying injunctions and insisting on enforcing judgements obtained at common law. Chief Justice Coke was the most outspoken critic, often carrying his strictures on Chancery far beyond what the case itself called for and questioning the whole basis of the Chancellor's right to "intermeddle" in any matter triable at common law. Ellesmere replied with the classic exposition of the Chancellor's jurisdiction in *The Earl of Oxford's case* (1615). The crisis came when in late 1615 two disreputable jewellers obtained judgement against their debtors in the Common Pleas under a highly oppressive contract. Their victims applied to Chancery and an injunction was issued preventing the judgement being enforced: it was a plain case for equitable relief. Coke took up the gauntlet. He encouraged the jewellers to bring against all the Chancery officials involved an indictment for *praemunire*, the old offence, designed to exclude Papal jurisdiction, of appealing from the king's courts to an outside authority. The indictments failed, to Coke's chagrin, because the grand jury refused, despite shameless bullying from the Chief Justice, to have anything to do with so unmeritorious a case; but things had now reached such a pass that the king, advised by his Attorney-

General, Francis Bacon, resolved to settle the dispute himself. In a speech in Star Chamber in June 1616, whose effect was embodied in a subsequent decree, James upheld the right and duty of the Court of Chancery to "give unto our subjects upon their several complaints such relief in equity (notwithstanding any former proceedings at the common law against them) as shall stand with the true merits and justice of their cases, and with the former ancient and continued practice and precedency of our Chancery". Coke was firmly slapped down: "I thought it an odious and inept speech and it grieved me much that it should be said in Westminster Hall that a *praemunire* lay against the Court of Chancery and officers there. How can the king grant a *praemunire* against himself? The Chancery is called the dispenser of the king's conscience. And therefore, sitting here in a seat of judgment, I declare and command that no man hereafter presume to sue a *praemunire* against the Chancery." The content of James's statement was unimpeachable. Coke's attacks on Chancery had been contrary to all precedent and bad in law. The king was simply restoring the *status quo*; and he was careful to enjoin the Chancellor as well as the common law judges to stay within the bounds of his jurisdiction. But what was questionable was the way in which he chose to justify his decision by emphasising the special relationship between himself and the Chancery: "The Chancery is undependent of any other court, and is only under the king. There it is written *Teste meipso.** From that court there is no appeal. And as I am bound in my conscience to maintain every court's jurisdiction, so especially this, and not to suffer it to sustain wrong . . .". That such notions were founded more in James I's scholarly imagination than in reality did not make his pronouncements less harmful to the public image of Chancery. At a time when questions of law and absolutism were under constant debate it was unhealthy for any court to be publicly associated with the royal prerogative. The bad reputation of Chancery with parliamentarians almost certainly owes much to this episode.

Why so violent a confrontation between Chancery and the common law courts occurred is something of a mystery. Bacon was probably nearest the truth when in 1617 he told the judges that "the former discords and differences between the Chancery and other courts was but flesh and blood: and now the men were gone, the matter was

---

*This is a reference to the formal witness-clause on a writ (which of course emanated from the chancery). It means "witness: myself [i.e. the king]".

gone . . .". Bacon was no doubt thinking of Coke, who had always been his own principal enemy and rival and whom he had just been instrumental in having dismissed from the Bench. Coke was volatile, aggressive, quite without judgement and liable to destructive obsessions. But Ellesmere was little better, a sour, unforgiving, neurotic man, like Coke highly intelligent and articulate but without Coke's genuine creativity as a lawyer and politician. He had approached areas of possible conflict with utter insensitivity and the harshness of his sentences on those who flouted his orders in Chancery, and indeed on defendants in Star Chamber, was out of all proportion. The combination of the two men was explosive. But there was accordingly no reason why saner successors should not co-operate effectively, as indeed it proved: the issues of 1616 were quiescent for many years.

The confrontation must also however be seen against the background of contemporary financial pressures on courts and their officials. The late Elizabethan and early Stuart period was marked by a rapid upward spiral of expenditure and expectations among courtiers and officials; these had to be met from a limited number of sources of official income. The courts were as much subject to this trend as other parts of the king's service, and indeed the distinction between judicial and administrative functions was still only painfully coming to be recognised, especially in the Chancery with its peculiarly mixed origins. In any event an intensification of competition for business was inevitable in the new circumstances. Cases meant cash, since judges, officials and counsel alike depended for a living not principally on fixed salaries but on the fees they received from litigants. Men fight more bitterly to protect a threatened standard of living than they do for jurisprudential principle. Chancellor and judges, despite huge incomes, felt perpetually insecure. Ellesmere pathetically compared himself to the cripple by the pool of Bethesda, always left behind when the waters were stirred — a happy, if unintentional, image of the diseased throng of Jacobean courtiers desperately scrambling into the turbid waters of official patronage. In fact, the Chancellor received some £3,000 in salary and official fees, with more than twice as much again from recognised but unofficial gratuities. A five-figure income was well within reach. Nicholas Bacon, fifty years earlier, had received perhaps £2,500 a year in all.

The economic pressure, real or supposed, on Chancery officials did not simply promote rivalry with other courts. As elsewhere in the administration, it led to the development of a complex structure of sinecurism and venality. Not only were fees, presents and gratuities being exacted in far greater amounts, but the offices to which they belonged were being systematically exploited and marketed by men whose careers were quite outside the Chancery but who needed the security of an official income. The two most notorious groups of offenders were the Masters and the Six Clerks. The Masters at least mostly did their own work, but they took care to see that they profited handsomely from it. The long and involved interlocutory proceedings in Chancery gave plenty of scope for the charging of fees for unnecessary services. "Those rackers and tormentors of causes" Lord Keeper Williams called the Masters, referring to their supposed habit of prolonging cases purely in order to gain extra revenue; and other critics noted such features as orders copied in triplicate, pleadings ordered to be re-written because of trifling scribal errors, and documents covering forty pages that could have been put on to six — for Chancery charged by the page. Figures exist for the annual income of the Master of the Rolls, though he is admittedly a more exalted figure than his colleagues. Worth under £300 p.a. in the 1530s, his office had risen in value to between £1,100 and £1,500 by 1603 and was by 1610 bringing in over £2,000 a year. These were very substantial figures; but what is most noticeable is the steepness of the rise. The Six Clerkships meanwhile were becoming sinecures of immense value. While the actual work was done by underclerks who themselves no doubt exacted further under-the-counter fees, a Six Clerk himself might expect to recover well over £1,000 a year, and in the 1620s a Clerkship might be bought (from the Master of the Rolls, who had the right to appoint) for some £6,000 down.

Such practices did not encourage efficiency. Chancery had by the early seventeenth century lost its earlier virtues of speed and cheapness, though it remained popular for the alternatives it offered to the limited common law. Some 1,500 cases a year entered the court under James I, an impossible burden for a single judge, even with the partial assistance available to him from the Master of the Rolls and the common law judges. By 1621 a backlog had built up that Coke claimed totalled 35,000: the real figure was probably nearer half that. Statistics are, however, apt to mislead. By no means all Chancery litigation was intended to produce a result. It was often no more than a tactical "kick into touch", designed to relieve pressure on a disputed cause or estate and to protect the *status quo*; or an action might be started only to obtain a particular interlocutory decision — discovery of documents, or a temporary injunction. Bacon claimed to have cleared the whole of the immediate backlog within six months of his appointment, though the respite did not last long. But whatever the precise position, genuine litigants could be faced with delays, technicality and expense as daunting as those at common law. Discontent was widespread, and critics often read corruption or malice into what was in truth a less sinister, though equally unsatisfactory, situation. The Chancellors and their senior subordinates were in fact men of professional integrity. Under pressure of criticism Bacon and Coventry at least — if not the prickly Lord Ellesmere — made attempts at reform, but they were defeated by the recalcitrance, not of individuals, but of the system. Venality and sinecurism were necessary to the survival of the political and governmental classes, just as ecclesiastical patronage had been to the royal service in the Middle Ages. But it did Chancery's reputation no good to be harnessed to a feckless and profligate court which was increasingly the target of a strong "country" movement among members of the Commons shocked by the immorality and the waste of their money which flourished under the favourites Somerset and Buckingham.

The most prominent victim of such sentiments, hostile to the administration in general and Chancery in particular, was Francis Bacon, Lord Keeper from 1617 and made Lord Chancellor and a peer (as Lord Verulam and later Viscount St Albans) the next year. The Parliament that met in January 1621, after over ten years without a full parliamentary session, was determined to make its criticisms felt. But there was no reason why it should pick especially on the Lord Chancellor, and in the opening days Bacon carried on with ordinary parliamentary business, presiding and speaking in the Lords and acting as the spokesman of a conference of both Houses in a petition to the king for the stricter enforcement of the laws against Papists. A cloud no bigger than a man's hand appeared when the Committee of

Grievances in the Commons, which had been investigating the grant of monopolies, turned its attention to the role of the "referees" to whom patents of monopoly had to be referred for a confirmation of their legality. The most notable referee for the most notorious monopoly, that for gold and silver thread, was none other than the Chancellor — a fact of which Coke, a member of the committee, was doubtless well aware when he raised the issue. Bacon was indeed doubly implicated since all patents of monopoly (being simply a form of letters patent) had to bear the Great Seal and he was theoretically in a position to have refused to seal this as indeed any other grant. Ellesmere had occasionally exercised this power of veto, though he only acted when he was sure of political support, as when he refused to seal a pardon for the disgraced earl of Somerset in 1615; he was in any event acting more from personal malice than constitutional scruple. For Bacon to have done anything of the sort would have been to fly directly in the face of his patron, Buckingham — a very different matter. Bacon was not unduly perturbed, for the attack on himself seemed merely incidental to the general campaign against monopolies. Nevertheless, once the spotlight, whether fortuitously or by Coke's direction, had settled on him it was all too easy for the opposition to regard the Chancellor as typical of the court corruption at which they were aiming. Thus it was a serious matter when in March 1621 it was reported that a Chancery official had confessed to the Committee of Grievances that he had regularly received bribes from litigants; and when a zealous Commons seized on the admission, further confessions and complaints of corruption in Chancery quickly emerged. On 19th March a joint conference of Lords and Commons was held to decide what procedure should be followed to prosecute the charges against the Lord Chancellor; it was decided that the Lords, where there was as strong an anti-court opposition as in the Commons, should take over the investigation. Bacon was appalled. Whatever he had or had not done, it is certain that he had no conception that he was open to any such charge: on the contrary, he believed himself "the justest judge that hath been in the five changes since Sir Nicholas Bacon's time". Genuinely prostrated by the shock, he was unable to attend the Lords to hear or contest the evidence given against him. He wanted only to make a general confession of guilt and be left alone. Deserted as he immediately was by his court associates, who were happy that the opposition had found so dispensable a scapegoat, any defence that Bacon might have made would almost certainly have been fruitless; yet it appears from the particularised confession which the Lords insisted on him making that none of the twenty-eight charges against him revealed genuine corruption. Almost all were cases where Bacon had received presents or gratuities from litigants, as was customary (though the amounts were often very large), after a case had been heard. In only a handful was litigation still in progress, and in those Bacon admitted only to carelessness in not checking the true position; he denied that his judgement had been in any way influenced. If this was all he had done, few contemporary judges could have escaped condemnation. As it was, the case went by default. Bacon was fined £40,000, deprived of all his offices, banned from the court and imprisoned in the Tower. The king and Buckingham soon had him released and part of his fine remitted, but his political career was over.

As a result of his fall Bacon has tended to be regarded as a man of genius fatally flawed. He had it in him to be as great a Lord Chancellor as any in history, a fact of which he was himself only too well aware. The son of Lord Keeper Bacon, he was born in the purple, and his connections at court and ability in the law gave him a flying start on the course to the Woolsack. But he was more than a lawyer and politician. Intellectually Bacon was the most distinguished figure of his generation and the most influential of the century, a revolutionary and far-sighted philosopher, an enquiring scientist and an acute historian and essayist — quite apart from any claims to be the greatest English playwright. His devotion to the cause of natural philosophy is poignantly illustrated in the manner of his death. On a snowy day in 1626 on Hampstead Heath he caught a fatal chill while performing an *ex tempore* experiment in refrigeration on a dead chicken he had found in the road. Bacon was opposed to purely theoretical and abstract philosophy, advocating the use of experiment and inductive method. His dominating philosophical ambition, expressed in the *New Atlantis* and the projected *Instauratio Magna*, was no less than to organise the entire corpus of scientific knowledge into a coherent whole that could be practically mobilised to the benefit of mankind: to his impetus are owed the discoveries of Harvey and Boyle and the eventual foundation of the Royal Society. Though these ideals did not of course involve him in a particular political programme, they were an essential background to his political career and deeply affected his outlook. Bacon longed for the position of power that he knew he would use to such good effect. The chancellorship was inevitably his goal, both from filial piety and because of its suitability to his talents. His ideals for the office appear from two sources, a letter he wrote to the king in 1616 recommending himself as successor to Ellesmere, then apparently dying, and the fine speech he made at his first appearance on the Chancery bench in May 1617. These are worth detailed mention as evidence of how the most intelligent of seventeenth-century Chancellors regarded his office.

Bacon begins his argument in the letter of 1616 by pointing out that most recent Chancellors had earlier served as Solicitor- or Attorney-General, both of which offices he had held. He claimed that judges were too exclusively committed to the law, "whereby your Majesty will find your prerogative pent" — the implication being that the law officers were able to take the broader view of the law needed in a Chancellor, who was to be a minister as well as a judge. Bacon had done much to enhance the importance of the law officers, and particularly the Attorney-General, not only in their traditional roles as government prosecutors but as legal and constitutional advisers in the sensitive boundary area of law and politics; it was to Bacon and not to the judges that James I turned for advice in the Chancery controversy of 1615-16. Bacon had also played a busy and controversial part as Attorney-General in the short-lived Parliament of 1614. It was his tenure of the office that confirmed it as the natural stepping-stone to the chancellorship which it has since been. Bacon next explained that his chief value to James would be not so much in Chancery, with whose judicial functions the king need not be closely concerned, as in his duty as "a moderator amongst your Council, an overseer of your judges, a planter of fit justices and governors in the country". This last is a reminder of the important functions the judges and the justices of the peace played in government and administration. Both were expected to foster loyalty to the regime in their counties or on assize and to report disaffection back to Westminster. This channel of communication was controlled by the Chancellor, who appointed the justices and customarily addressed the judges as they left on their circuits. Bacon continued by claiming to have the favour of the House of Commons and to be able to wield much influence there. The Chancellor's parliamentary functions still brought him into contact with both Houses, as the king's principal spokesman. Finally Bacon hoped "that by my care the inventive part of your Council will be strengthened, who now commonly do exercise rather their judgments than their inventions . . .". This was the long-term imaginative statesmanship which Bacon hoped to promote at a court preoccupied by expediency; as an *ex officio* Privy Councillor the Lord Chancellor was well placed to influence policy.

The inaugural speech of 1617 was more purely legal in its concerns. The new Lord Keeper declared his intention to contain the jurisdiction of the Court of Chancery within its "true and due limits". He would deal personally with all sensitive cases that might infringe the rights of other courts. Claims for injunctions would be treated on their merits — "I do not mean to make it a matter of a horse-race or posting who shall be first, in Chancery or in courts of law." He would consult with the judges and keep a stern eye on the Masters. Bacon further pronounced that his justice would be both cheap and speedy, and he propounded specific measures by which these ends would be achieved, including morning and vacation sittings. He also stated that the king had empowered him carefully to consider all letters patent passing the Great Seal — "it was one of the greatest parts of my trust if I saw any scruple or cause of stay that I should acquaint him [of it] . . .". This sentiment however was little more than a constitutional platitude, for no Chancellor who obstructed the king's — or his favourite's — use of patronage was likely to last long. Even these ringing commitments did not exhaust the Lord Chancellor's projects, for he had also an ambitious scheme for the complete rationalisation and codification of English law. The first steps towards this end had already been taken in Parliament at the time of Bacon's fall; but it lapsed thereafter.

It was, however, precisely such consciously high ideals that constituted Bacon's weakness. His genius was indeed flawed, but by something more subtle than avarice. Unlike many intellectuals in power, he knew the facts of political life. "Honour," he wrote "hath three things in it: the vantage ground to do good: the approach to kings and principal persons: and the raising of men's fortunes." The three were necessarily connected in his mind. Only with power and worldly success could he achieve anything. Thus in forty years at or around the court he did not disdain to dirty his hands in political intrigue. Historians have found unedifying his desertion of his patron Essex in 1601 to become his principal prosecutor, and his later attachment to Buckingham; but if a man is destined, as the uniquely gifted son of Sir Nicholas Bacon clearly was, to occupy the highest office in the kingdom, he convinced himself that he must not scruple to consort with those who would have to be his colleagues. Besides, Bacon believed in his power to influence for good. In 1616 he wrote Buckingham a pathetically confident letter of excellent advice on a comprehensive range of governmental issues — quite wasted. In his dealings at court, Bacon was complacent in the knowledge that his heart was as pure as Job's. But such complacency is a doubtful advantage. Other politicians who did not appreciate his own conception of his exalted motives were antagonised to an extent he never thought it necessary to consider. They were not to know that despite appearances he was a man quite unlike themselves. It was complacency that was behind the incidents that supposedly demonstrated his corruption. Bacon took it for granted that everyone was as sure as he of his integrity and that there was no need for discretion in accepting the lavish gifts that were of course his due. It is no surprise that he was shattered by the utterly unexpected charges against him. In the words of his biographer Spedding: "For a man who believed himself to be setting an example for all others to follow of zeal, integrity and fidelity in the discharge of all his public duties, to find himself suddenly convicted, on evidence which could not but seem conclusive, of corruption in the highest seat of justice, and condemned to serve for the example which all men were hereafter to shun — and this without any warning from within of the danger in which he stood — was such a fall as neither guilty ambition nor injured innocence ever suffered". Bacon's fall was an Aristotelian tragedy.

1621-1660: The Failure of Reform

The next twenty years were a quieter period for the chancellorship. Bishop Williams was a forceful and ambitious Welshman who had

been chaplain to Lord Ellesmere and later attached himself to
Buckingham — a shrewd move, for, as Bacon observed: "He hath crept
far, as I may say, for ground-ivy . . . but he must clasp upon this tree
or none to climb". Despite his legal inexperience, Williams was an
adequate judge in Chancery, thanks to his service with Ellesmere and
his own wit and energy. He lasted four years until Buckingham
decided that he was too independent-minded. His career following his
dismissal in 1625 was eventful. In the Lords he was an irksome thorn in
Buckingham's side, and in the 1630s his hostility was transferred to the
new power at court, Archbishop Laud. Imprisoned in 1637 after a
trial in Star Chamber for refusing to implement Laud's ecclesiastical
policy, he was in 1640 released at the instance of the Long Parliament,
and by an astonishing twist of fortune was created archbishop of York
the next year by a king anxious to conciliate parliamentary opinion.
In the Civil War he set himself up as the king's commander in North
Wales, conducting a series of feuds against his fellow royalist generals
from his headquarters in Conway Castle. But, remarkable though he
was, as Lord Keeper Williams was too much in Buckingham's shadow
to have much impact in his own right.

Williams' successor was Thomas Coventry, an able lawyer of no
political preferences who by dint of doing what he was told remained
Lord Keeper* until his death in 1640. Lord Campbell had little time
for him. One side-note‡ in his *Lives of the Lord Chancellors* goes so far
as to state "Coventry responsible for misgovernment of Charles I, and
for the civil war". Campbell's thesis was that "as the only adviser of the
king on legal and constitutional questions" the Lord Keeper could
have prevented Charles I's attempts to rule without Parliament, and
that as the principal judge of the Court of Star Chamber he was
responsible for its use as an instrument of political repression. The
first charge is quite unrealistic. The Lord Keeper, or Chancellor, was
not by virtue of his office more influential than any other councillor
and he certainly had no special brief to guard constitutional propriety.
Though he was a loyal and busy administrator, Coventry's independent
political importance was slight. The second charge is nearer the mark.
Although it continued to be invoked primarily by private litigants who
were the real or alleged victims of violence, fraud or perjury, Star
Chamber in the 1630s was being used increasingly by the government

---

*Charles I, in conformity with the austerity of his administration, raised none of his
Lord Keepers to the chancellorship proper.

‡Campbell's side-notes are sometimes very curious. Alongside his account of
Archbishop Laud appears the single word "Puseyism".

for its own purposes. Star Chamber had always been the court in which royal proclamations were enforced, and this hitherto insignificant part of its work took on a new significance as proclamations became the government's substitute for parliamentary legislation. Most prosecutions were fiscal in intent: the threat, or more rarely the actuality, of trial before Star Chamber brought in large sums to a desperate treasury from offenders against a wide variety of proclamations, ranging from that restricting the right to residence in London to those giving legal force to monopolies. But there were also overtly political prosecutions, based on the court's ordinary "criminal" jurisdiction: ex-Lord Keeper Williams was tried for allegedly tampering with witnesses in an earlier case, a typically Star Chamber offence because it concerned the due execution of justice, and the Puritan pamphleteer, William Prynne, was condemned for libel, another Star Chamber offence. Prynne's sentence — he had his ears cropped and his nose slit, and he was branded on the forehead — is notorious, but far from unique. Judgements in particular cases could have the force of decrees of general application. It was by such a Star Chamber decree that one of the government's most resented controls, the imposition of a system of licensing on press and publishing, was achieved.

Over this important organ of government Coventry, as Lord Keeper, formally presided, and it was he who announced some of its most savage sentences. But in fact Charles I's Court of Star Chamber was dominated by other councillors. Notable among its legal members was John Finch, who was to succeed Coventry as Lord Keeper. Finch had served as Speaker of the Commons in the Parliament of 1628-9 and had been finally committed to the king's party as a result of the famous incident in which he had been pinned in his chair by the opposition leaders, who were determined to prevent him announcing the dissolution before they had made their protest at the king's policies. As Chief Justice of Common Pleas (the office by virtue of which he sat in Star Chamber) Finch delivered the leading judgement in the Ship Money case of 1637, the highwater mark of judicial support for the government's constitutionally very questionable attempts to raise taxation without recourse to Parliament: he was free in his advocacy of the royal prerogative and expressed a decidedly limiting view of the role of Parliament. Though that case was heard in the Court of Exchequer Chamber, and did not involve the Lord Keeper judicially, it is worth noting that Coventry also had an important, if less publicised, part in the enforcement of the collection of Ship Money, for it was his job to instruct the judges departing on circuit to encourage the prompt and willing payment of the tax: the judges were essential agents of royal propaganda in the counties, and it was for Coventry to give them their scripts.

Coventry died in January 1640. Finch was a disastrous choice of successor. In the spring of that year, financial necessity finally forced the king to recall Parliament; and though the "Short Parliament" was prematurely dissolved one of the first acts of the "Long Parliament", which assembled in November, was to put in train the impeachment of the Lord Keeper for his conduct as Speaker eleven years earlier and for his support of Ship Money. Finch wisely fled the country. His successor, Edward Littleton, had already succeeded him as Chief Justice of Common Pleas. Though less objectionable to the opposition than Finch, he was not a success. As was observed by Clarendon (later himself Lord Chancellor and sympathetic to Littleton's political dilemma), "from the time he had the Great Seal he seemed to be out of his element". Littleton was one of the many conscientious men of Charles I's reign who were quite unable to decide where their loyalties lay. A busy member of the opposition in the king's early Parliaments, he had become Solicitor-General in 1634 and conducted the argument on the government side in the Ship Money case. On the woolsack his *forte* was prevarication. Illness, feigned or real, kept him from presiding, as he should have done as Speaker of the Lords, at the impeachment of Strafford, the chief scapegoat for government policies in the 1630s; and he spent the next twelve months vainly attempting to avoid displeasing either a demanding king or a militant Parliament. In March 1642 the king left London and set up in York: civil war was imminent. This was one of the few situations in which the Lord Keeper's custody of the Great Seal had genuine political significance. An anxious Littleton told Clarendon (then Edward Hyde) after Charles's departure that he knew war was coming: "I often think with myself of what importance it will then be which party shall have the Great Seal, the *Clavis Regni*,* the token of supreme authority". As not since the Middle Ages there were rival powers each claiming to

*"The key to the kingdom".

represent lawful authority but not yet in open conflict. Parliament especially, being, so to speak, the challenger, was very concerned with the appearance of legality, and that appearance was precisely what control of the seal offered. Without it much of the work of the administration would be irregular. With it the opposition leaders could make the crucial appointments to local office which could determine the outcome of the pre-war jockeying for tactical advantage. They could also issue the writs to call a new Parliament: in fact the Lord Keeper was himself obliged under the new Triennial Act to issue the writs if no Parliament assembled after an interval of three years, a power which indicates the importance of the function, though it would be of little use in the immediate crisis. Such considerations were of course ultimately unreal. When Littleton eventually plucked up the courage to slip away from Parliament's jealous watch and join the king in York, the opposition was angry but it was not seriously hampered; and in 1643 Parliament had its own Great Seal made, to legitimise the administration and the law-courts operating in London. The Great Seal might give legality but it could not give power.

The long suppression of Parliament had prevented discontent with the courts from being voiced over the previous decade, but it remained strong and re-emerged in full force in the Long Parliament. Star Chamber was the principal target, despite its popularity with litigants, because of its recent political role. Parliament abolished it at once in 1641. It was never revived, a fact which has led commentators to overlook the extent to which Star Chamber occupied the energies of the Lord Chancellor in the sixteenth and early seventeenth centuries: in fact it had as much as to do with the Chancellor's development as a predominantly judicial officer as had the Court of Chancery. In the meantime, Chancery was hardly less unpopular than its sister court. The abuses of the 1620s had persisted through the next decade substantially unchecked. Coventry, as conscientious as Bacon if less idealistic, had produced several sets of orders aimed at reform and made attempts to investigate and regulate the taking of fees by court officials; there was also at the beginning of his tenure of office a commission issued empowering the common law judges and the Masters to hear cases in Chancery on their own. These measures were ineffective, defeated as much by the government's own efforts to lay its hands on lucrative official patronage as by the venality of the officials themselves. Not until after the final victory of Parliament in the Civil War was there an opportunity for the sort of radical re-structuring of the court system that was needed. Meanwhile Chancery struggled on, in the absence of a Lord Chancellor, under three "Lords Commissioners of the Great Seal" — Chancery lawyers who took over the Chancellor's judicial functions; they also kept and applied the seal as instructed by the Speakers of the Lords and the Commons. The availability of three full-time judges should have had a real impact on Chancery's backlog of cases. But, as occurred repeatedly, changes at the top were irrelevant. Cost and delay were built into the system, in the tortuous interlocutory proceedings of a Chancery action among the Masters, Six Clerks, cursitors and all their train. These men represented deeply entrenched interests, and reform met stiff resistance. The energetic and professional law reform committee set up in 1652 by Parliament under Matthew Hale — a successor to more dilatory and ineffectual committees — produced constructive proposals for Chancery reform, but their enactment was forestalled by the dissolution of the Rump Parliament in April 1653. Later the same year the erratic Barebones Parliament resolved to cut the Gordian knot, and voted for the total abolition of the Court of Chancery; but bills to implement this fine ambition foundered on the rocky fact that no-one knew how to replace it — though laymen expressed their usual happy belief that with sense and goodwill a body of law could be produced that would be "easy, plain and short". In 1654 an exasperated Cromwell, without any professional advice, promulgated an ordinance imposing reform on Chancery. The Chancery Ordinance replaced the Six Clerks with three Chief Clerks on a salary and cut their subordinate staff to sixty. There were to be a fixed scale of fees, a ban on sale of offices, rigorous procedural time limits and harsh sanctions against those who brought frivolous or vexatious proceedings. Procedure generally was to be simple and open. The Ordinance was impressive, but it had a troubled history. Pressure in Parliament managed to get it suspended until the next year, and when it was eventually partially implemented its operation was disrupted by the resignation of two of the Lords Commissioners, the non-co-operation of the Master of the Rolls and the refusal of the new Chief Clerks, who were simply three of the old

Six Clerks, to give up their fees and other perquisites. Between 1655 and 1660 the work of the Chancery was hopelessly confused, especially after constitutional disputes between Parliament and Protector had cast doubt on the legality of the Ordinance and opened the new Chancery officials to counter-attacks from the men they had replaced. The old court was still kicking vigorously when the Restoration came to re-establish the *status quo* of the pre-Civil War period.

The failure of Chancery reform was the failure of the English Revolution in little. Office and its profits were seen in the seventeenth century less as paid public service than as private property, a lucrative set of rights (never mind the duties) for which the holder had paid a commercial price. Chancery officials might well agree that the court needed reform, but they could not be expected to acquiesce in any proposals that deprived their investment in their office of its value. They could not therefore agree to the abolition of the sale of offices nor to the regulation of fees or, still less, to their replacement by fixed salaries. John Lenthall, a displaced Six Clerk and son of the Master of the Rolls, protested in a petition to Cromwell that "the property of your petitioner (and the people in their freeholds and estates) is not only warranted and taken care for by the Law of God himself, written twice over with his own finger, but by our Magna Carta* thirty times over confirmed by several Acts of Parliament attended by the common law . . .". This sort of rhetoric struck a responsive chord among men who had no direct interest in Chancery. Property owners showed admirable class solidarity. As a contemporary noted in one of the flood of pamphlets on the state of Chancery: "So many men of quality and estate immediately concerned and so many others mediately concerned on account of friendships and the like account that this of itself will be a great bulwark against reformation." And of course the law administered, however inefficiently, in Chancery was an essential part of the system of landholding and property. Abolition or radical reform of the Chancery might be the prelude to an attack on the rights it protected. Cromwell told a friend in 1650: "The sons of Zeruiah are yet too strong for us, and we cannot mention the reformation of the law but they presently cry out we design to destroy property; whereas the law as it is now constituted serves only to maintain the lawyers and to encourage the rich to oppress the poor." The sons of Zeruiah were too strong in the end.

*See p. 112.

CHAPTER FIVE

1660-1667	Sir Edward Hyde, Lord Hyde 1660, Earl of Clarendon 1661
1667-1672	Sir Orlando Bridgeman [Lord Keeper]
1672-1673	Anthony Ashley Cooper, Earl of Shaftesbury 1672
1673-1682	Sir Heneage Finch, Lord Finch 1674, Earl of Nottingham 1681 [Lord Keeper 1673-5]
1682-1685	Sir Francis North, Lord Guilford 1683 [Lord Keeper]
1685-1688	George Jeffreys, Lord Jeffreys 1685
1693-1700	Sir John Somers, Lord Somers 1697 [Lord Keeper 1693-7]
1700-1705	Sir Nathan Wright [Lord Keeper]
1705-1710	William Cowper, Lord Cowper 1706 [Lord Keeper 1705-7]
1710-1714	Sir Simon Harcourt, Lord Harcourt 1711 (Viscount Harcourt 1721) [Lord Keeper 1710-13]
1714-1718	Lord Cowper (see above) (Earl Cowper 1718)
1718-1725	Thomas Parker, Lord Macclesfield, Earl of Macclesfield 1721
1725-1733	Peter King, Lord King
1733-1737	Charles Talbot, Lord Talbot 1733
1737-1756	Philip Yorke, Lord Hardwicke, Earl of Hardwicke 1754
1757-1766	Sir Robert Henley, Lord Henley 1760, Earl of Northington 1761 [Lord Keeper 1757-61]
1766-1770	Charles Pratt, Lord Camden (Earl Camden 1786)
1770	Charles Yorke
1771-1778	Henry Bathurst, Lord Apsley, Earl Bathurst 1775
1778-1792	Edward Thurlow, Lord Thurlow. [Seal in commission April-December 1783]
1793-1801	Alexander Wedderburn, Lord Loughborough (Earl of Rosslyn 1801)
1801-1806	John Scott, Lord Eldon
1806-1807	Thomas Erskine, Lord Erskine
1807-1827	Lord Eldon (see above), Earl of Eldon 1821

Lord Erskine, looking as Ciceronian as he would have wished — a statue by Westmacott in Lincoln's Inn Library.   *By courtesy of the Masters of the Bench of Lincoln's Inn*

Lord Eldon, by Lawrence.   *National Portrait Gallery*

"The Lord Harry Playing the Duece with the Six and Eightpenny Gentry." Brougham
in 1830, shortly after his elevation to the Woolsack. This cartoon illustrates his
reputation as scourge of the abuses of the law.

"Paul Pry's Peep into Chancery" (1826), a popular view of the backlog of work under Lord Eldon. The various piles of papers, representing the different areas of the Lord Chancellor's responsibility, are marked Speaker's Papers, Cabinet Papers, Causes of Equity, Appeal Causes, Trustee of Bankruptcies, Doubtful Causes, Civil Appointments, Legal Appointments, Ecclesiastical Appointments, Guardian of Wards and Lunatics. Part of the caption reads:

> Relinquish all I hold most dear,
> Full Sixty Thousand Pounds a Year,
> Such Power! such Patronage I doubt,
> If I could live a year without."

A rather idealised early (1821) portrait by Lonsdale of Henry Brougham, the earnest
young radical.   *National Portrait Gallery*

Lord Lyndhurst.

A philosophical Lord Haldane, by de Laszlo (1928).   *National Portrait Gallery*

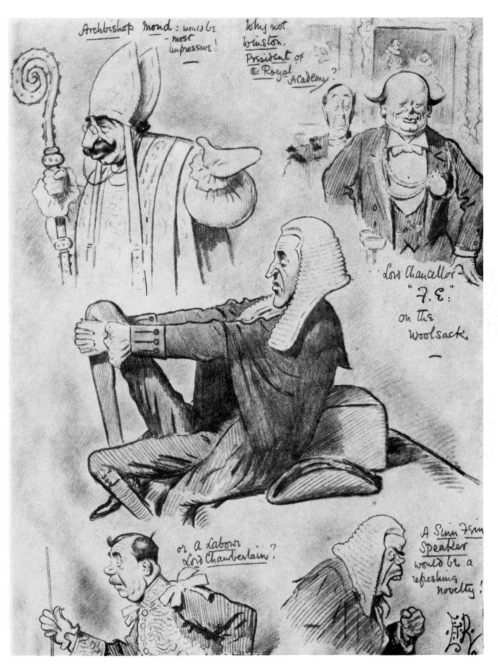

"Some Missed Opportunities", a cartoon from *The Bystander* by E. T. Reed. This **was** a fairly typical reaction to Birkenhead's appointment in 1919.

By courtesy of the Masters of the Bench of Gray's Inn

The procession of the judges from Westminster Abbey to attend the Lord Chancellor's breakfast at the beginning of the legal year. The procession is led by the Lord Chancellor (here Lord Simonds), preceded by his Mace and Purse.

The Lord Chancellors in the Ancien Regime 1660-1827

1660-1705: Transition

THE Lord Chancellors of the period between the Restoration and the Revolution of 1688 are a motley collection. Edward Hyde (1660-7), created earl of Clarendon in 1661, and Anthony Ashley Cooper, first earl of Shaftesbury (1672-3), were politicians of the first importance. Clarendon was Charles II's chief minister in the first years of the reign. A serious-minded and high-principled man (qualities he was rather too well aware he possessed), he had been prominent in the opposition to the nascent absolutism and disregard for property and the social order evident in Charles I's government in the 1630s. He had much to do with the reforming programme enacted by the Long Parliament in 1640-1 and the attacks on Strafford and Lord Keeper Finch. But he regarded these measures as constituting a complete settlement of the issues between Parliament and king, and he did not share the mistrust of Charles I which led many of his colleagues into extreme attempts to protect themselves against a royalist *revanche*. Clarendon was that rare phenomenon, a genuine constitutionalist, who deplored Parliament's "absolute, arbitrary, voting tyranny" as much as he had the policies attributed to Strafford and Laud. He joined Charles I in 1641 and in the next nineteen years of defeat and exile he was the principal adviser of the king and his heir. Clarendon's influence was crucial in preventing Charles II from trying to return to England with a French army or associating himself with any absolutist anti-Parliamentary reaction. Charles's uncontested restoration in 1660, accompanied by political amnesty, religious toleration (intended if not achieved) and a confirmation of the achievements of 1640-1, was

Clarendon's triumph. He was also the author, in his *History of the Rebellion and Civil Wars in England*, of the most intelligent and least unreliable contemporary account of his times. As for Shaftesbury, his chancellorship was only a brief episode in a mercurial career that ran from his active parliamentary opposition to Cromwell in the 1650s to the brave and brilliant demagoguery which created the Whig party in the Exclusion Crisis of 1679-81. No figures of such political eminence had held the office since Stephen Gardiner. Neither had had any legal training to speak of.

Other chancellors of the period, however, Orlando Bridgeman (1667-72), Heneage Finch (1673-82), created earl of Nottingham (by which name he is usually known) in 1681, and Francis North, Lord Guilford (1682-5) were professional lawyers carrying comparatively little political weight. Something will need to be said later of Nottingham's very important contributions to the law, but Bridgeman and Guilford were non-entities: Bridgeman's only good claim to be remembered is as the patron of Thomas Traherne.* Guilford has a minor celebrity as the hero of his brother Roger's writings, notably the gossipy *Lives of the Norths*. The index to Roger North's *Examen* gives the essential flavour of the author's critical approach:

> "NORTH, Francis: Mr. North modest to a weakness; His skill in the law inferior to none; Never guilty of an error to his disadvantage; General Scholar and Virtuoso; . . . His inclinations always to loyalty; Never retrograde; Allowed to be a good Judge even by his Enemies; His Affability and Patience; Never committed any Error but one, and that was taking the Great Seal."

Guilford, though probably indeed a likeable and cultivated man, was no such paragon but a timid and undistinguished lawyer who soon bitterly regretted the moment when he resigned the Chief Justiceship of Common Pleas to accept the Great Seal, "that accursed lump of metal" as Roger North called it, and its attendant cares. The insignificance of these men is indicated in their official status. Clarendon and Shaftesbury were both Lord Chancellors. Bridgeman and Guilford were only Lord Keepers, while Nottingham, who was rather more consequential, only became Lord Chancellor after two years with the inferior title. The last Lord Chancellor of the period

---

*Another Metaphysical poet with a Lord Chancellor for patron was John Donne, who was for a few years the secretary of Lord Keeper Egerton.

was George Jeffreys, the notorious "Judge Jeffreys" who held the office from 1685 to 1688. He too was a professional lawyer; and, though his forceful character and record of service to the government gave him a greater influence at court than his immediate predecessors had either desired or attained, he was never a figure of the same importance as Clarendon or Shaftesbury.

This diversity reflects the anomalous and unstable position of the chancellorship at this time. Since the administrative changes of the mid-sixteenth century the Lord Chancellors' only genuinely useful function was judicial. Thus when there was no special reason otherwise the office tended to go to career lawyers. This had been the dominant tradition since the reign of Elizabeth I, the tradition of an Ellesmere or a Coventry. It was obviously good from the point of view of the law. While the occasional non-legal Lord Chancellor was able to perform adequately in the Court of Chancery by accepting the guidance of his professional subordinates (as Clarendon did from his experienced Master of the Rolls, Sir Harbottle Grimston, and as the self-assured Shaftesbury at first would not) they could not make the sort of constructive contribution to the development of equity as a rational and consistent body of law which was now needed. But even "mere" lawyers could not in the seventeenth century be wholly apolitical. Nottingham and Guilford had both been in the Commons and had been Law Officers, in Nottingham's case for over thirteen busy years. Bridgeman and Guilford both, as Chief Justice of Common Pleas, had to preside over political trials, including, in Bridgeman's case, the trial of the regicides in 1660: on these occasions they were not expected to be unmindful of the fact that they were royal servants. The best-known example is Jeffreys' conduct, as Chief Justice of King's Bench, of the Bloody Assize of 1685 — his last task before his promotion to the chancellorship — in which the remnants of Monmouth's rebellion were tried and sentenced with appalling severity.

Something should be said of Jeffreys, if only by way of digression, for his atrocious reputation probably over-rates his real political importance. The undoubtedly very nasty episode of the Bloody Assize and Jeffreys's implication in the regime of James II provoked his Whig enemies into the creation of an utterly unbelievable Jeffreys-bogeyman, a monster of depravity, oppression and all the vices; and this ludicrous caricature was sanctimoniously endorsed by the pernicious Macaulay. But, as often happens, attempts to rescue some part of Jeffreys's reputation have been generally tendentious and hardly more convincing than the picture they are intended to overturn. Certainly no judge of the time would have been expected to come back with an armful of acquittals from such an operation as the Bloody Assize; nor would he have been expected to be over-nice in distinguishing the exact degrees of guilt of admitted rebels. But the thing could have been done with less despatch and with more dignity and discrimination than Jeffreys — quick-witted, quick-tempered, and possessed to a high degree of that hatred of "rebellion" that was so common after the Restoration — was able to command. Whatever the distortions in contemporary and later accounts of Jeffreys's behaviour on the bench, it is clear that he was temperamentally quite unsuited for judicial work. He felt no constraints on saying on all occasions exactly what he felt (which was usually shrewd and to the point) and saying it with a characteristic vehemence; and he almost certainly did have a streak of cruelty. Jeffreys was a loud, vigorous man, hard-drinking and opinionated. But, like many bad judges, he had been an exceptional advocate and was a very good lawyer, qualities indicated by his early success — he was Lord Chief Justice at thirty-nine and Lord Chancellor at forty-one* — and he earned a high reputation in Chancery. Jeffreys was one of the inner circle of James II's counsellors, but his influence was less than might have been expected: James paid limited attention to his few intelligent advisers, largely because none of them was willing to give the advice he wanted to hear. Jeffreys's only important part in the momentous events of the reign was as *ex officio* president of the Commission for Ecclesiastical Causes, the new instrument with which the king intended to subdue the Anglican Church. In this capacity he was closely involved in the *cause célèbre* of James's attempt to impose a Catholic President on Magdalen College, Oxford; but when the recalcitrant seven bishops came before the Privy Council in May 1688 he managed to ensure that they were tried not by the Commission but in King's Bench. By the end he was increasingly sceptical about James's command of events: the king, he told a friend sardonically, "would yield nothing . . . The Virgin Mary was to do all". Jeffreys's detachment in the last period of the reign was not enough to save him at the

*Not forty, as was once thought.

Revolution. Narrowly escaping being lynched by the London mob, he was imprisoned in the Tower and died in April 1689.

But to say that lawyers and judges were necessarily to some extent involved in politics does not help to explain why such men as Clarendon and Shaftesbury should voluntarily have taken an office whose functions were primarily in the Court of Chancery. The truth was that, though the proper destiny of the office may appear now to have been manifestly judicial, this was to a greater or lesser degree obscured by the clouds of glory that it trailed from its medieval past. Both the ancient dignity and the varied accumulation of particular powers that the chancellorship still commanded gave it some attraction to the ambitious politician—especially to those, like Clarendon or Shaftesbury, with a somewhat romantic view of ancient institutions. Shaftesbury, an admiring son-in-law of Lord Keeper Coventry, demonstrated a bizarre antiquarianism by reviving an obsolete ceremony whereby the Lord Chancellor at the beginning of the legal term led a procession of the judges on horseback from the Temple to Westminster Hall—an unhappy experiment, since few of the judges were practised horsemen. On a more sober level, Clarendon gives an interesting reason for his acceptance of the Great Seal as Charles II's Lord Chancellor in exile in 1658. The king was already coming under pressure from his loyal companions and from supporters in England to give lavish grants of land and money, which, Clarendon felt, would be dangerous and divisive when the restoration came. Since all grants had to be passed under the Great Seal he would be well placed as Chancellor to impose restraint, as Charles himself in his more judicious moments wished. "It was," he later wrote, "the principal part or obligation of my office to dissuade the king from making any grants of such a nature [i.e. diminishing the king's personal resources] . . . and even . . . not to suffer them to pass the Seal until I had waited upon the king and informed him of the evil consequences of these grants." The control of the Great Seal could be turned to advantage in a number of ways. Clarendon, for example, was accused in 1667 of making grants under the Seal to himself and his family, of calling in town and city charters for expensive and unnecessary confirmation and of passing illegal patents* and then protecting them from challenge in the courts by the use of injunctions in Chancery.

*i.e. letters patent, which would include all important grants under the Great Seal. The most controversial of Clarendon's grants was the "Canary patent", granting to a group of merchants a monopoly in the import of wine from the Canaries.

Shaftesbury, in a typical piece of chicanery, correctly issued a writ authorising the election to a vacant parliamentary seat, but notified only his own candidate, who was, not surprisingly, returned unopposed.

These powers were valuable; and in particular Clarendon's supervision of patronage assisted considerably in the delicate construction of the Restoration settlement. But in normal circumstances there was really no reason why a chief minister need himself have custody of the Seal to make use of its powers. Most of Clarendon's successors toed a line laid down by their political masters. The exceptions prove the rule. In 1672 Lord Keeper Bridgeman refused to apply the Seal to Charles II's proposed Declaration of Indulgence and soon after proved unco-operative over the grant of injunctions to protect from their creditors the bankers who had been embarrassed by the government defaulting on its debts. His scruples were an inconvenience, certainly, since the political situation made it difficult to dismiss him forthwith: but it was not long before Shaftesbury, the dominant figure at court, was able to step into Bridgeman's shoes. Similarly when Nottingham in 1679 refused to seal a royal pardon for the earl of Danby, the king's chief minister then in the process of being impeached, a simple compromise was reached whereby he handed the Seal over to the king, who had it applied to the pardon and at once graciously handed it back. This charade apparently salved Nottingham's conscience; what may be more to the point, it, surprisingly, also deflected from the Lord Chancellor most of the criticism of the Commons. It did not save Danby. The complete ineffectiveness of these shows of independence by Bridgeman and Nottingham reveals the realities of the situation. The Chancellor's traditional functions still necessarily involved him at least on the fringes of politics, but they did not give him more than the opportunity to embarrass those who wielded actual power. It was typical of that utter lack of realism which has made his reign so attractive to constitutional historians that James II should have hoped to bring the government to a standstill by dropping the Great Seal into the Thames before fleeing from the invasion of 1688 — typical also of James's capacity for failure that it should have been retrieved shortly afterwards by a fisherman.

It was the type of Bridgeman, Guilford and Nottingham who represented the real character of the office of Lord Chancellor in the

seventeenth century. The chancellorships of Clarendon and Shaftesbury were an anachronism. The office gave nothing essential to its
holder. This was recognised by contemporaries. In 1660 Clarendon's
enemies attempted to suggest that the chancellorship must be in the
gift of Parliament, since it was a judicial rather than a political office;
and the next year his friends told him that the burdensome judicial
business of the Lord Chancellor prevented him from giving his full
attention to the affairs of the king and the kingdom. Clarendon did
not disagree that this was so, but he thought it positively desirable that
he should not appear to be trying "to engross himself the disposal of
the public affairs". The truth was that the political Chancellor was
redundant. After the Glorious Revolution there was from 1688 to 1693
neither a Lord Chancellor nor a Lord Keeper of England. The judicial
work of the Court of Chancery and the routine administrative
functions associated with the Great Seal were put into the hands of
Lords Commissioners, as under the Commonwealth, while the
Speakership of the Lords was entrusted to a senior judge. It is probable
that this arrangement was intended to be permanent. No adequate
raison d'être had emerged for the office of Lord Chancellor since the
Restoration, and its occupants had done little to recommend it to the
party of the Revolution: it was, thanks to the careers of Guilford and
Jeffreys, associated with a politicised judiciary and with subservience to
an absolutist and unparliamentary monarchy.

Nevertheless, the office did not disappear. It was resurrected in 1693
for John Somers, a rising Whig lawyer and politician who was shortly
to become the dominant figure in the ruling "Junto". In the course of
the eighteenth century the chancellorship acquired a stable and
important position in the English political structure, and the Lord
Chancellors include some of the leading statesmen of the period—
among them Somers himself, Hardwicke, Thurlow and Eldon. Why
was this?

There were of course particular immediate reasons for the appointment of a Lord Keeper in 1693. Appropriate promotion was wanted
for Somers both by the king and by the Whigs. There was widespread
discontent with the way in which the trinity of Lords Commissioners
was increasing rather than reducing the confusion and expense of
proceedings in the Court of Chancery: a single supreme tribunal began

to seem more attractive. And the Speakership of the House of Lords was too important a political position to be occupied by a non-partisan figure.

But there are reasons on a deeper level which go to explain the abiding influence of the office in the eighteenth century, reasons rooted in the political changes of the last third of the seventeenth century of which the Revolution of 1688 was the decisive turning-point. The fundamental change was the shift in the focus of political affairs from court to Parliament. Influential though the king remained, a minister could no longer in the aftermath of the Glorious Revolution rely for supreme power principally on favour at court: he must be able to command a Parliament. The change can first clearly be seen in the chancellorship of Clarendon. Although Clarendon became inevitably the new king's chief minister in 1660, his temper was not matched to the new times. Personally he was out of sympathy with the flippant and hedonistic atmosphere at Charles II's court, and his attitude was not softened even when the seduction of his daughter by the king's brother, the later James II, gave him the unique political asset of a royal son-in-law. Politically, his outlook was set in the conflicts of the reign of Charles I. Parliament, he believed, despite its necessary role as guardian of the rights and interests of the subject, had no business to take a hand in the making of policy or the control of ministers: that was for the king and his council. Clarendon told Charles "not to be dejected with the formidable power of the Parliament, which was more or less or nothing, as he pleased to make it . . .". And in an unguarded moment he described the Commons as "four hundred men only of use to raise money, but not fit to meddle with state affairs" — a remark later to be used against him. Clarendon, though a shrewd judge of parliamentary opinion, never thought it necessary or proper to become involved in the hard business of building a government party in the Commons. The result was a series of rebuffs — including the repressive legislation against religious dissent which, in plain contradiction to the actual facts, is known as the Clarendon Code — and the growth of an active opposition to his authority manipulated by a younger generation of courtiers who were willing to buy parliamentary support for the king and themselves by the management of public patronage. It was this group, Shaftesbury among them, who encompassed the impeachment of the Lord Chancellor in 1667 on a variety of implausible or exaggerated charges and induced Charles to withhold his protection from the minister whose ponderous integrity he was already finding irksome. Clarendon went into a bitter exile, and died in Rouen in 1674.

Clarendon's fall demonstrated the penalties of neglecting to cultivate parliamentary support. He was the last Lord Chancellor of note not to be attached to a parliamentary faction — or, as it was soon to be, to the Whigs or the Tories. In one way this development obviously diminished the importance of the chancellorship. Although the eighteenth century saw something of a revival in the House of Lords, it was in the Commons that political control had to be founded — but the Lord Chancellor was by virtue of his office confined to the Lords. It is true that many peers had an enormous political influence; but this rested partly on the opportunities automatically made available to a man of rank in the hierarchical society of the time, and partly on the patronage which as landowners they were able to exercise over seats in the Commons. The Lord Chancellor, as a professional lawyer, could not compete in either respect. From the Revolution onwards there are few, perhaps no, Lord Chancellors in the very front rank of politics, men who could command or destroy a ministry. They could take the role neither of a Pitt the Elder, "the Great Commoner", founding power on the support of independent interest groups in the Commons, nor of a duke of Newcastle, laboriously constructing a political empire out of aristocratic favour and patronage. Clarendon or arguably Somers was the last Lord Chancellor to be "prime minister".

But once the office was free from the random accidents of royal favour which make its status so variable in the early modern period, it was in a position to develop a more solid and rational role (though still a strangely various one) reflecting the Chancellor's actual functions in the new structure of politics.

In the first place the age of the Glorious Revolution and its aftermath was one in which political issues were habitually expressed by means of legal concepts. The complex constitutional problems that dominated public affairs from the Exclusion Crisis to the end of the Stuart dynasty in 1714 required essentially legal discussion and resolution. Governments needed lawyers to lead and advise in the perpetually acrimonious round of politico-constitutional debate. Nor was the role of the law purely intellectual. Governments and others made repeated political use of the courts and of judicial processes in parliament, often with devastating results, as in the Trial of the Seven Bishops in 1688 or the impeachment of Dr Sacheverell in 1710. This was a feature as much of the later part of the period, the age of Camden and Erskine, as of its early years. Enormous opportunities were thus opened for able and ambitious lawyers to make a political career. They were indispensable in court, in parliament and in the inner counsels of government. The Law Officerships—the posts of Solicitor-General and Attorney-General—gave the widest scope for political usefulness, for the government was in constant need of committed advocates for its political trials; but the Woolsack was clearly the only appropriate summit to such a career, being not only the highest politico-judicial office in the land but the most lucrative. From the time of Somers onwards the Lord Chancellor would be generally no longer a fortunate lawyer of limited political experience, willing to follow the line laid down by his masters—the redundant type of a Nottingham or a Guilford—but an able and energetic barrister who had risen by applying his forensic skills in the party political arena.

Somers himself is a case in point. A barrister who had produced some good Whig pamphlets, he came to prominence in 1688 as one of the counsel for the defence at the Trial of the Seven Bishops (his successor as Lord Keeper, Nathan Wright, being among his opponents). Following the Revolution he was elected to Parliament, and he played a leading part in the debates on the difficult constitutional questions raised by James's flight and in the discussions which produced the Bill of Rights. He was businesslike, clear-thinking and persuasive. He became Solicitor-General in 1689 and Lord Keeper in 1693, and in 1697 was given the full title of Lord Chancellor and, a few months later, a peerage. These were in recognition of the fact that Somers was now one of the so-called Junto of three or four politicians who directed the government. In the delicate management of the Junto's relations with King William and with its touchy lobby-fodder in the Commons Somers enjoyed a special influence by virtue of his professional background. He had none of the intransigence and obvious self-satisfaction that tended to characterise his lordly Whig colleagues. Swift noted: "I have hardly known any man with talents more proper to acquire and preserve the favour of a prince; never offending in word or gesture; in the highest degree courteous and complaisant, wherein he set an excellent example to his colleagues, which they did not think fit to follow". Men of Somers' background (his father was a country attorney) did not drift into politics. He had consciously developed his political ideals. He was a friend of John Locke, with whom he worked on economic matters, and founder of the Kit-Cat club, the social and intellectual centre of early eighteenth-century Whiggery. It is this combination of political commitment and personal acceptability that gave Somers both his influence in his own time and his special place in Whig hagiography. It did not of course protect him from partisan enmities. He survived, longer than the rest of the Junto, the revival of the Tories in William III's favour, but he was finally dismissed in 1700. The Tories attempted to follow up their success by impeaching the ex-Chancellor. They concentrated on Somers' part in the peace treaty of 1698 with France. Negotiations for the treaty had been handled by the king in Holland with the greatest secrecy, and Somers had co-operated by applying the Great Seal to the document while there were still important blanks to be filled in, by sealing certain secret clauses separately and by omitting to record any of it on the patent rolls; nor was he given a formal warrant from the king to authorise the use of the Seal on the main treaty, though William later supplied a retrospective one. The whole episode has a distinctly medieval ring, with William and his Chancellor conspiring to evade formal procedures much as Henry III or Edward II had done. It could be said that constitutionally this was quite proper, for Parliament had no right to dictate what the king did with his Seal, and any irregularities were no matter for them. In fact the issue was never decided, for the Commons did not press their charges and Somers was acquitted by default. He remained the leading figure in the Whig party throughout the reign of Anne, and died in 1715.

The increasing importance of Parliament, though reflected primarily in the Commons, was also evident in the Lords. The Commons might be pre-eminent, but every bill had to pass the Lords and it was as necessary for a government to secure the Upper House as the Lower. In this the Lord Chancellor's part was crucial. His powers as Speaker were in themselves insignificant. The functions of the Speaker of the Lords had developed quite differently from those of the Speaker of the Commons. Then, as now, only purely formal matters of procedure — putting the question, recording attendance and so forth — were within his competence. Other matters of order and procedure were decided by the House itself. But in these limitations lay the Chancellor's freedom: there was no need for him to be impartial and he was able, provided he was himself a peer, to take an active part in debate.* As a leading member of the government and, generally, an experienced speaker, he would be, at the least, one of the foremost figures in the House; and a Chancellor of sufficient authority and force of character could combine these advantages with an exploitation of the apparently empty dignity of the Speaker to remarkable effect. The sway that Hardwicke and later Thurlow exercised over their fellow-peers from their commanding situation on the Woolsack was notorious. The Lords was a very active political forum under William and Mary (1689-1702) and under Anne (1702-14). From then until after the middle of the century the overwhelming parliamentary strength of the Whigs reduced the value of the Lord Chancellor's role to some extent, but between the 1780s and the passing of the Reform Bill of 1832 it again assumed enormous importance, especially when the flood of new peerage creations begun by Pitt the Younger brought into the Lords a growing proportion of the most active politicians of the day.

The Lord Chancellor retained throughout the eighteenth century a very extensive patronage, which was ripe for political exploitation. One very important area lay in appointments to the judicial bench and to the Law Officerships. In 1693 Somers, newly appointed as Lord Keeper, wrote to William III: "The lawyers are 'spread out over every part of the kingdom' and have great influence among the people. The method used to unite them in their service to the Crown has been by obliging them to a dependence on the Great Seal for their promotion where they merited it, and this has always given weight to that office in public affairs; and, if I understand you aright, making the Great Seal thus considerable was one of the effects you expected from placing it in a single hand . . .". This clear statement of the Chancellor's responsibility for appointments, and its political value, was occasioned by Somers'

*The Chancellor's curious double role in the Lords was, and is, symbolised by the convention that the woolsack is not regarded as within the House. The modern practice is that when the Chancellor wishes to speak in a debate he leaves the woolsack and takes three paces in the direction of the Earls' Bench, where, as the lay subject first in order of precedence, he would be entitled to sit were he not Speaker.

objection to the kings having under Tory influence overturned the expected succession to two vacant judgeships and the office of Attorney-General. He was not attempting, in any crude sense, to secure a packed bench; but he intended these important promotions to stay in the hands of the governing faction.

The struggles between Whig and Tory from the Exclusion Crisis to the final Whig triumph in 1714 also saw an unashamedly partisan use of the Lord Chancellor's powers to make appointments to the commissions of the peace. Control of the appointments of justices of the peace was important to the government both as a means of rewarding or buying the loyalty of the influential county gentry whose support would be needed at election time and because the powers of the justices could themselves be used to electoral advantage. Thus Somers in the mid-1690s carried out a thorough purge of the justices, weeding out those who "act directly against the interests of their Majesties' government". The Tories who came to power in William III's last years set to with equal zeal to repair the damage: Lord Keeper Wright (1700-5) even removed his predecessor Somers from the commission of the peace in his native Worcestershire. George II was attractively blunt about the whole business. Shortly after his accession in 1727 he spoke to his Lord Chancellor, Lord King, in whose diary the interview is recorded: "He told me . . . that his pleasure was that I should put into the commission of the peace all gentlemen of rank and quality in the several counties, *unless they were in direct opposition to his government:* but still keep a majority of those who were known to be most firmly in his interest, and he would have me declare the former part as his sentiment." Methods became less blatant later in the century, but the Lord Chancellor's appointment of judges and justices remained a highly charged political issue.

Such appointments were recognised as the special responsibility of the Lord Chancellor by a convention going back to the Middle Ages. So also was the patronage of the very large class of ecclesiastical benefices in the king's gift of a notional value of under £20 a year. This too might be a political matter at a time when Church issues frequently dominated politics. But there was a far wider class of patronage that, while not really his responsibility, nevertheless passed through the Lord Chancellor's hands because the grant required authentication by the Great Seal. This gave the Chancellor the opportunity to oversee much of the distribution of patronage that was so important a part of the eighteenth-century structure of politics. This was not always a mere formality, for Lord Chancellors were known on occasion to refuse to seal grants of which they disapproved. Conversely they might be criticised for applying the Seal irresponsibly. Quite apart from the matter of the treaty of 1698, Lord Somers came under severe attack in Parliament for giving a royal commission under the Great Seal to suppress piracy to Captain William Kidd, who promptly turned pirate himself. It did not help that the commission required Kidd to hand over a great proportion of his takings to the men who subsidised his expedition, among whom Somers was prominent. The ensuing furore all but overthrew the government. The care of the Seal could still entail genuine responsibility.

These were the foundations that supported the continuing political importance of the office of Lord Chancellor in the Hanoverian century. Only with the growing impetus of reform in the second quarter of the nineteenth century was it seriously shaken.

The Chancellors of the Whig Ascendancy 1705-1756

The type of Lord Chancellor that was to predominate in the eighteenth century is well illustrated in a single episode, the impeachment in March 1710 of Dr Henry Sacheverell. Sacheverell, an intemperate High Tory clergyman, was impeached by the Whigs as a result of a sermon in which he had denounced, more or less overtly, the sacred principles of the Glorious Revolution. Though the impeachment was successful it aroused violent political passions and contributed to the expulsion of the Whigs from power. No fewer than five Lord Chancellors, past, present and future, were involved in this momentous business. They were Lords Somers, Cowper (1705-10 and 1714-18), Harcourt (1710-14), Macclesfield (1718-25) and King (1725-33).

Of these five, Somers was the most distinguished. Since 1708 he had been back in government, as Lord President of the Council, and his experience and influence were hardly equalled among his colleagues. But his part in the Sacheverell trial was peripheral. With characteristic perceptiveness and caution, he had opposed the move to impeach Sacheverell, regarding it as unnecessary and provocative. Though he voted against Sacheverell and supported his colleagues where necessary, he remained in the background. A similar view seems to have been taken by Lord Cowper, the Lord Chancellor, but he was involved whether he liked it or not, for he had to preside over the House of Lords in its capacity as a court. On the whole his duties were undemanding, for there was no blatant manipulation of the trial; but his authority was always in reserve, and had from time to time to be used, to keep the impeachment procedure on the rails. William Cowper was an able lawyer and a firm Whig. He came from a typically Whig background — his father a rich Home Counties landowner, his mother the daughter of a successful London merchant; and Cowper himself married a merchant's daughter. A valuable government prosecutor in the 1690s, he became the leading Whig speaker in the Commons in the Tory ascendancy after 1700. Cowper succeeded the non-entity, Sir Nathan Wright, as Lord Keeper in 1705, the first breach in the Tory monopoly of office under Anne: and he was made Lord Chancellor — the first Lord Chancellor of Great Britain — in 1707 following the Act of Union with Scotland, in whose negotiation he had played a central part. Cowper, though close to Somers, was never quite identified with the Junto, which dominated the Whig party under William III and Anne, and his conscientious political manner gave him something of a "moderate" reputation. This no doubt had much to do with his appointment in 1705, and it is also reflected in the way in which the queen and her new ministers attempted to persuade him to stay in office after the Tory victory of 1710. It would be mistaken to detect in this any trace of the idea, fitfully recurrent later in the century, that the chancellorship was a non-partisan office. What is perhaps true is that the ability and the sense of public duty evident in at least some of the Lord Chancellors of this period — certainly Somers, Cowper and Hardwicke — and partly attributable to their professional background, appealed to the strong element in eighteenth-century politics which despised "faction" and regarded government as principally "the king's service". Some Chancellors were thus apt to appear more impartial than they actually were. In the event Cowper refused to abandon his party in 1710 and resigned. His loyalty was rewarded by a second term as Lord Chancellor following the death of Queen Anne in 1714, when his level-headed and experienced advice helped to ensure both the acceptance of the new dynasty and the supremacy of the Whigs under the new king. His *Impartial History of the Parties*, a memorandum presented to George I, is characteristic of Cowper's approach. It is a carefully argued and ostentatiously impartial document which concludes that there is little to choose between the Tories and Whigs and that George can serve his interests equally by entrusting the government to either. The real sting of his argument is the apparently harmless insistence that the king should choose one party or another and not attempt a non-partisan government — for Cowper knew that a wholly Tory administration was impossible in 1714 because of the taint of Jacobitism. This is not to say that Cowper was not an honest politician, but he was necessarily a good party man.

Besides Cowper and Somers, the Whigs in 1710 were well equipped with legal talent from a younger generation. Two of the most powerful speeches by the "managers" of the case against Sacheverell were delivered by two future Lord Chancellors, Sir Thomas Parker, later Lord Macclesfield, and Sir Peter King, later Lord King. Parker in particular impressed his colleagues, and a recent authority has declared that his main speech "for intellectual quality and power of analysis can rarely have been matched in any British political trial". Both Parker and King were successful barristers of undistinguished family who had taken what was a conventional step towards judicial preferment by entering the Commons. Parker indeed received his reward even earlier than he could have hoped, being made Lord Chief Justice in the middle of the trial.

Sacheverell's defence, meanwhile, was conducted by Sir Simon Harcourt, who had been Attorney-General and was the only Tory lawyer of equal ability to those in the Whig camp. In fact, Harcourt's views were scarcely further from his opponents' than they were from those of his disreputable and extremist client. Sacheverell had deliberately set out to offend the official orthodoxy of the 1689 settlement, and any defence had to be ingenious and very carefully pleaded — Harcourt said that "his speaking was like dancing upon ropes; if he slipped, he was sure to break his neck". In a brilliant and thoroughly disingenuous speech Harcourt presented Sacheverell as a moderate constitutionalist who had never harboured a heretical thought; and in so doing expressed for the first time an up-to-date

Toryism that was neither Jacobite nor obsessively High Church — a path to be followed by Harley and later, Bolingbroke. Such support was much needed by Harley following the Tory victory of 1710 and Harcourt became his Lord Keeper (and later Lord Chancellor) and one of his closest allies. With the accession of George I in 1714 Harcourt was forced to resign, but after a few years he became active in the Lords once more as a moderate supporter of the Whig government, and was in his last years an elder statesman of considerable influence. Harcourt was a likeable man and a generous patron. The most distinguished of his friends was Alexander Pope, who did much of the translation of *The Iliad* at the ex-Chancellor's home at Stanton Harcourt.

The Sacheverell trial demonstrated exactly the sort of men to whom the office was to appeal and to whom it was to be offered during the eighteenth century. These were party men, parliamentarians of skill and commitment — no longer the courtiers or mere lawyers of the earlier period. It was this background that gave them their value as much as anything that could be done with the office. Indeed with many their chancellorship tended to be less distinguished politically than the careers that had led up to them. This was true of King, for example — as it was, later in the century, of Loughborough and Erskine. It could have been true also of Thomas Parker (created earl of Macclesfield in 1721) whose chancellorship was notable for the high quality of his judicial decisions but was not otherwise of interest until he was dramatically impeached for corruption in 1725. The background to the charges was the loss of enormous sums of litigants' money, invested for their own profit by the Chancery Masters, in the South Sea crash of 1720. Macclesfield was not himself directly involved, but he was implicated nevertheless, for the very large sums charged by the Lord Chancellor to Chancery Masters as the price of their appointment were among the pressures which forced them to misappropriate funds in court in this and other ways — even though there is little doubt that the traditions of Chancery would have encouraged such practices anyway. Macclesfield had raised the payments expected of Masters far above what appears to have been the accepted level — and the hard bargaining conducted by his secretary (who on being offered £5,000 for a Mastership replied, in a notorious phrase, "Guineas are handsomer") was, to say the least, unseemly. Further, when these abuses had threatened to come to light, Macclesfield had attempted to shield himself and his subordinates from inquiry. It is not clear now how far the Chancellor's personal knowledge of the abuses of his court went, but the evidence presented at his impeachment establishes that he certainly knew a fair amount and turned a blind eye to more. Parker had the sense of his own worth that often dominates those who have made their own careers (for his father was only a country attorney) and he could not afford a comfortable disdain for financial opportunities — the more hostile would simply say he was greedy. But what really condemned him was not exceptional corruptness of nature but the changing attitude to public office. It was not for another century that venality would finally be eliminated from the public service, but it was already becoming doubtfully acceptable as a private perquisite of high office. Cowper, who admittedly could afford such a gesture, had put a stop to the practice of the bar offering the Lord Chancellor lavish New Year gifts; and this was characteristic of a growing belief that the office should be renumerated only by way of salary (some £7,000 in mid-century) and recognised fees (very substantial), with a pension by negotiation. These sources could still provide a very large income, and those Chancellors who kept the office for any length of time generally amassed great fortunes. Following Macclesfield's impeachment the sale of the Masterships and the private exploitation of funds in Court were forbidden by Act of Parliament, and a Commons committee, followed by a royal commission, began a lengthy inquiry into the Court of Chancery; but by the time a report finally appeared in 1740 the issue had gone to sleep and no substantial reforms were implemented.

On King's death in 1733, there were two obvious candidates to succeed him. Charles Talbot, the leading figure at the Chancery bar and Solicitor-General, and Sir Philip Yorke, a younger man but already Attorney-General after an astonishing career of success at the bar in which he had become Solicitor-General at the age of twenty-nine. By an amicable arrangement it was Talbot who took the Great Seal while Yorke became Lord Chief Justice, that office also being vacant, and a peer, with the title of Lord Hardwicke. Talbot died four years later, after a chancellorship of professional distinction but political insignificance, and Hardwicke was his inevitable successor. Hardwicke held office for the next twenty years, from 1737 to 1756, and earned a greater reputation than any other Lord Chancellor of the century. He was a great lawyer, a man almost universally trusted and admired by his contemporaries, and throughout his chancellorship he was at the very heart of politics. Yet his influence and his real distinction are not easy to appraise. This is partly because his reputation was founded to an unusual extent on his personal qualities. Hardwicke was intelligent, eloquent, honourable, judicious and diplomatic — all the public virtues. It is perhaps inevitable that he was also more than a shade pompous. This combination of qualities was both rare and valuable in the tortuous court and Cabinet politics of the period. Hardwicke was the indispensable adviser of, and intermediary between, the jealous ministers of George II and had also to mediate between the ministers and the king himself. Hardwicke's relationship with the most consistently important of the king's ministers in these years, the duke of Newcastle, was especially close. Newcastle, for a man of such eminence, was ludicrously insecure, and was hardly capable of taking any decision without the acquiescence and reassurance of his friends. In Sir Lewis Namier's words, "to Hardwicke he turned like a child to its nurse" — occasionally, he adds, "receiving replies reminiscent of the nursery". It is scarcely credible, for example, to find a Prime Minister writing to a colleague to ask for advice on how to answer a speech from the Town Clerk of Bristol (a copy of which he enclosed) conferring on him the freedom of the city. On this occasion Hardwicke replied somewhat tartly: "I am very sure Your Grace can want no advice on the answer to be given to Mr. Town Clerk of Bristol." Mostly, however, the Lord Chancellor's replies to his friend's endless outpourings of his problems and uncertainties were patient, painstaking and sensible. But Hardwicke had little taste or talent for political leadership in his own right. He was a right-thinking and rather complacent constitutionalist who regarded political opposition as mere faction. As Chesterfield said, "Lord Hardwicke valued himself more on being a great minister of state, which he certainly was not, than upon being a great magistrate, which he certainly was. All his notions were clear, but none of them were great. Good order and domestic details were his proper department; the great and shining parts of government, though not above his parts to conceive, were above his timidity to undertake."

Hardwicke's chancellorship was probably decisive in establishing the convention that the Lord Chancellor should be a member of the Cabinet. The process whereby a "Cabinet council" of senior ministers became recognised as a necessary and acceptable organ of government was one which depended more on political realities than on constitutional theory, and had not Hardwicke's personal importance over two decades been so great, it is not at all certain that the Lord Chancellor would have been thought of as a necessary member of such a body.

The Age of Camden, Thurlow and Eldon

Hardwicke's successor, after an interval of a few months while the Seal was in commission, could hardly have been a more different character. Robert Henley was a bluff and prosperous barrister, with a prodigious capacity for port and an admiring West Country constituency, who had become Attorney-General in 1756 thanks to his loyalty to the party of the Prince of Wales. Henley was a far from bad lawyer, but neither his professional nor his political rank would have earned him the chancellorship had not both Chief Justices and Lord Mansfield (then still Sir William Murray) refused office. Perhaps because of this and also because though his friends were in power they were not in the king's favour, Henley was given neither a peerage nor the title of Lord Chancellor. Both these honours had been customary at least since 1718, and the peerage was an important matter since it enabled the Chancellor to speak in his own right in the House of Lords rather than simply exercising his meagre powers as Speaker. Henley was, however, given a peerage in 1760 so that he would be eligible to act as Lord High Steward* at the trial before his peers of Lord Ferrers, who had murdered one of his servants. With the accession of George III, his old patron, Henley became in 1761 both Lord Chancellor and earl of Northington; there has never again been a Lord Keeper, nor a Lord Chancellor who has not been made a peer on appointment — though it remains strictly unnecessary that the Chancellor should himself be a member of the Lords.‡ Northington also obtained the

*See p. 43.

‡It was, however, and is, not unusual for the Chancellor to sit for a day or two as a commoner before his patent of peerage had been drawn up. In this period he would be entitled to participate only as Speaker. Lord Birkenhead in 1919 committed the solecism of hearing an appeal to the Lords during this gap, although not then technically a member of the House.

valued concession from the king that the Court of Chancery need not sit in the evenings, in order that he might finish his bottle of port in peace.

Northington was a loyal king's man who survived successive reconstructions of the ministry until 1766, when he was replaced by the Chief Justice of Common Pleas, Charles Pratt, Lord Camden. Camden was an able and politically committed advocate who had cut his forensic teeth on radical causes and had, as a friend and associate of Pitt the Elder, succeeded Henley as Attorney-General. He had been kicked upstairs to the bench when Pitt fell from power, but the idea of removing this tiresome liberal from politics proved to have backfired when he gave a series of outspoken judgements against the government, then highly unpopular, in cases arising out of its attempt to suppress John Wilkes's scurrilous opposition newspaper, *The North Briton*. Camden was genuinely "a zealous asserter of English liberty by law", as the inscription read on his portrait by Reynolds commissioned by an excitable City of London; and if, as his enemies claimed, he enjoyed the staggering weight of public acclaim which was heaped on him by the opposition, that can surely be forgiven. But his chancellorship was an anti-climax. Pitt, who was responsible for his appointment, went mad in 1767, and the character of the ministry changed, leaving Camden in the unhappy position of having to support a set of measures, especially on the American issue, which starkly conflicted with his own liberal views. From 1768 he was virtually a passenger in the administration, and in early 1770 he finally resigned (as arguably he should have done much earlier) after making a violent attack in the Lords on his own colleagues' handling of the Wilkes affair.

It was not easy to find a successor. The outstanding candidate was Charles Yorke, the second son of Lord Hardwicke, who had had a brilliant career at the bar and had for many years been a Law Officer and powerful force in the Commons. The king was very anxious to recruit Yorke to a ministry seriously weakened by his own objections to most of the most able politicians of the day. The trouble was that Yorke had himself been closely associated with the Rockinghamite opposition, and office would mean deserting most of his colleagues. Under pressure both from the king and, no doubt, from his own tormenting awareness that he was suited for the office as no-one else was, Yorke gave in and accepted the Great Seal and the title of Lord Morden. Three days later he died — by suicide, said his enemies, or at least from the shock caused by his friends' condemnation of his treachery. The obvious alternative Chancellor, Lord Mansfield, again refused to accept an office so insecure and so exposed to political controversy. The government put the Seal into commission, but when that proved as unsatisfactory as it usually did, they settled for the blameless but wholly insignificant puisne judge, Henry Bathurst, who was created **Lord Apsley (later becoming Earl Bathurst in succession to his father).** Campbell's unkind side-note to his account of Bathurst's replacement of the commission reads "One incompetent Judge better than three". Bathurst survived as Chancellor until 1778.

The 1760s had seen the revival, after the comparatively placid decades in which Hardwicke had flourished, of vehement political controversy, often spilling out far beyond Westminster. As had been the case earlier in the century, this favoured the able political lawyer who could bring his forensic talents to Parliament and prove his usefulness in the frequent political trials of the period. Camden and Charles Yorke had been of this type and after Bathurst the chancellorship was held by a succession of such men. These were Edward Thurlow, who was Lord Chancellor from 1778 to 1792 (with an interval in 1783); Alexander Wedderburn, Lord Loughborough and earl of Rosslyn (whose changes of title were only less frequent than his changes of politics), Lord Chancellor from 1792 to 1801; John Scott, Lord (later earl of) Eldon, Lord Chancellor from 1801 to 1827, except for just over a year in 1805-6; and **Thomas Erskine, Lord Erskine,** who occupied that single gap in Eldon's twenty-five years tenure of office.

Thurlow and Wedderburn were both Law Officers for most of the 1770s and were by far the most forceful and effective defenders in the House of Commons of the government's policies in America. Both were also active in court, Thurlow's prosecutions including that of the publishers of Junius. But their chancellorships were very different. Wedderburn's ability and his political experience, not to mention his importunity for office, made his appointment as Lord Chancellor inescapable, but it was generally unwelcome, for his reputation for untrustworthiness meant that he was little respected by his colleagues, and he carried little political weight. His was in many ways a sad career, a classic case of how the undisguised lack of principle with which he pursued his ambitions turned them to ashes when achieved. Pathetically, in his retirement he bought himself a house near Slough in order to be near his supposed friend the king at Windsor. In fact George detested him: when Loughborough died he declared that "he has not left a greater rogue behind in my dominions". (When his old rival Thurlow was told this he commented characteristically, "then I presume His Majesty is quite sane at present".)

Thurlow was altogether a more considerable force. Nicknamed "Tiger", scowling, arrogant, sardonic and hard-drinking, he acquired a remarkable and fearsome reputation. Dr Johnson said that Thurlow was the only man in England for whom he would "prepare himself": "when I am to meet with him, I should wish to know a day before." He was formidable in court, in Cabinet, and above all in the Lords where he was held in terrified awe. He had established his hold on the House on his first day on the woolsack when the duke of Richmond, a descendant of one of Charles II's bastards, referred contemptuously to the position of a mere lawyer among the company of the hereditary peerage; Thurlow rose from his place, reminded the duke of the eminence of the lawyers already in the House and asked him whether he did not think it as honourable to owe a peerage to successful professional exertions as to being "the accident of an accident". This sort of aspersion on the members' ancestry was unprecedented in the Lords, but it was characteristic of the contemptuous savagery with which Thurlow treated his colleagues. Thurlow's central place in the politics of the 1780s depended partly on his complete dominance of the Lords, which was playing a more important part in affairs than it had for a century past, and partly on the support of the king. The Lord Chancellor's individuality, his overbearing manner and his impartial disregard for the common conventions of politeness — or indeed of anything else, for he lived openly with a mistress (a former barmaid in a Fleet Street coffee-house) as well as being generally believed to be an atheist — were interpreted by many, Dr Johnson and George III among them, as marks of integrity and deep wisdom. Those who had to work with Thurlow were unconvinced. His wisdom rarely manifested itself in constructive policies; his talents were purely, though magnificently, destructive. As for his integrity, it was difficult to see what principle allowed him to serve under three administrations of widely differing character — those of Lord North, of Lords Rockingham and Shelburne and of Pitt the Younger — and to contemplate an alliance with the Foxite Whigs in the notorious Fox-North coalition of 1783 and the Regency Crisis of 1788-9. In fact Fox refused to have him in 1783 and in 1789 George III recovered from his insanity before Thurlow's dealings with the party of the Regent-to-be had come into the open. Pitt never trusted Thurlow after this episode but it was not until 1792 that he was able to persuade the king to consent to his replacement by Loughborough, and then only by presenting a stark choice between himself and the Lord Chancellor. Yet Thurlow was not the mere opportunist that he is now usually regarded as. He probably did have a genuine commitment to the king's service — much ridiculed though he was for his rhetorical profession of loyalty to the king in 1789 at the very moment when he was negotiating with the Prince of Wales — and he reciprocated the loyalty and affection shown to him by George. And he derived a strong personal satisfaction from always saying exactly what he thought — which is an integrity of a kind; if he served with people he despised, he at least did not conceal his opinion. Thurlow was the type of professional champion whom the establishment is from time to time able to attract to itself but who professes no commitment to the supposed principles or privileges that he is defending. Party loyalties thus meant little to him.

Thurlow was capable of kindness and generosity. Among his benefactions was the loan of £500 to Boswell to pay for Dr Johnson to go to Italy for his health. One to whom he showed special kindness was the rising Law Officer, John Scott, the able son of a Newcastle coal-merchant who had begun his career promisingly by eloping with an heiress. Scott took the leading part in the series of prosecutions brought by Pitt's government against political dissenters and he also drafted much of the repressive legislation of the period, including the Habeas Corpus Suspension Act of 1794. These were duties he under-took with fairness but also with conviction, for his views were already set in the course of extreme reaction. His opponent in the most famous of these trials, that of the members of the London Corresponding Society, and counsel for the defence in a long series of cases concerning freedom of speech and assembly, was one of the greatest of English advocates (though, like Mansfield and Loughborough, Scottish by birth), Thomas Erskine. Erskine's extraordinary forensic power, assisted by a high degree of charm and wit, gave him an unprecedented success at the bar, and he was reputedly the first barrister to earn a five-figure income. It is, however, Erskine's commitment to libertarian causes which has made his reputation, above all for the episode in which he refused, despite great personal and political pressure, to reject the brief for the defence of Tom Paine, who was being prosecuted for the publication of his *Rights of Man*. Erskine's only public office was his brief chancellorship during the "Ministry of All the Talents". It is probably true that Erskine's real abilities were confined to those of an advocate. Despite the genuine depth of his convictions, he did not quite have the grit in his character needed to assert himself effectively in the political world. His appearances in Parliament were unconvincing. In this, as in much else (including a pronounced but not vicious streak of vanity), there is a striking resemblance between Erskine and Cicero.

In 1799 Scott claimed the reward for his services as Attorney-General and became Chief Justice of Common Pleas and a peer — to the annoyance of the king who wanted him as Lord Chancellor in place of Loughborough. George extracted a promise that Eldon (as he now was) would accept the chancellorship when it became vacant. Eldon was always a favourite with the king and, surprisingly, also with the Regent; he was known affectionately in the royal family as "Old Bags" (a reference to the purse in which the Great Seal is traditionally kept). Eldon's straightforwardness and independence of mind and his uncomplicated political outlook were just the qualities George III had admired in Thurlow. Legally his tenure of the office was of great distinction: of Eldon's qualities and importance as a lawyer more will be said elsewhere. Otherwise his enormous influence was baleful. Of course his political views were on the wrong side to have earned him the approval of liberal historians; but when every allowance has been made for the distorting effect of the Whig tradition, and for the reactionary temper of the times, Eldon's rooted and utterly un-imaginative response not only to social and political problems but to any proposed change, of any sort in any direction, is extraordinary. It is instructive to compare Eldon's obsessive, almost hysterical, views with the equally strong but realistic conservatism of the duke of Wellington. Bagehot's summary is famous:

> "He believed in everything which it is impossible to believe in — the danger of Parliamentary Reform, the danger of Catholic Emancipation, the danger of altering the Court of Chancery, the danger of altering the Courts of Law, the danger of abolishing capital punishment for trivial thefts, the danger of making land-owners pay their debts, the danger of making anything more, the danger of making anything less."

Yet Eldon was not an ogre. Like many of the best-known hanging judges, he was personally kindly and amenable, a noted raconteur and a good friend. These private virtues were not appreciated by his many enemies. Among his bitterest opponents was Shelley, who wrote a long diatribe against the Lord Chancellor, and put him second in *The Masque of Anarchy:*

> "Next came Fraud, and he had on,
> Like Eldon, an ermined gown,
> His big tears, for he wept well,
> Turned to mill-stones as they fell.
> And the little children who
> Round his feet played to and fro,
> Thinking every tear a gem,
> Had their brains knocked out by them."

The occasion of the poem was the Peterloo massacre of 1819. Eldon had no immediate personal responsibility for Peterloo, but he publicly defended the magistrates' actions (declaring that if they had erred, "their error had been rather on the side of remissness than of undue vigour") and he was the leading advocate in Cabinet and in Parliament of the repressive Six Acts. Shelley had personal reasons for his hostility to Eldon, who had deprived him of the custody of his children on the grounds of his atheism and immorality. Eldon also crossed Byron and Southey by refusing to grant injunctions protecting the copyright of their works which he considered dangerous and immoral.

Eldon was probably the most influential single figure in the government from 1807 until Lord Liverpool began in the 1820s to give his decisive support to liberal tendencies in the Cabinet. Eldon finally gave up office, at the age of seventy-five, in 1827, when Canning became Prime Minister. He put up a ferocious resistance in the Lords to both the legislation bringing in Catholic emancipation and the Reform Bills of 1830-2. He died in 1838.

The close relations between the king and at least three of his Chancellors — Northington, Thurlow and Eldon — is a marked feature of this period. George relied on them extensively, as advisers, informants on proceedings in Cabinet, go-betweens in the formation of governments, and, where possible, as Trojan horses in administrations of which he disapproved. Northington, for instance, was the instrument by which he was able to bring down the ministry of Lord Rockingham in 1766. The Lord Chancellor insisted on a hard-line policy on America, the principal issue of the day, and refused to make any compromise with his colleagues. "Old Tom was so cross and negative," wrote one, "that no business could be done with regard to the affairs of Quebec. He would neither lead nor be driven, and in short would give no opinion at all but that he thought all was wrong." When this splendid obstructionism seemed to be unproductive, the Lord Chancellor announced that he would "secede" from Cabinet; and when Rockingham looked likely to ignore that too he resigned outright, on the interesting grounds that "to keep the Seals and not attend [i.e. in Cabinet] would be indecent". This finally brought the government down — though Northington was a member of its successor, as Lord President.

To what extent was this relationship the product of an idea that the Lord Chancellor should be above party, owing his loyalty only to the king and thus in some sense to the state rather than a particular government? There was certainly something of this. A friend of Boswell's lamented that "Our Chancellors in England are chosen from views much inferior to the office. They are chosen from temporary political views". Dr Johnson's reply — "Why, Sir, in such a government as ours no man is appointed to an office because he is the fittest for it" — does not suggest that he disagreed in principle. The Lord

Chancellor's duties as a judge and his responsibility for the appointment of other judges set him apart from other senior ministers. The
title of "keeper of the king's conscience" had an aura of special
responsibility, and the custody of the Great Seal of the kingdom, by
which the will of the Sovereign could be authentically expressed even
without his actual consent, had a similar significance: it was especially
important with George III's repeated lapses into madness, when
Thurlow and later Eldon had to decide whether the king was fit to sign
such crucial documents as warrants for the application of the Seal or
commissions for giving the royal assent to bills. Besides these, there
were innumerable special links between the chancellorship and the
monarchy, having their origins in the medieval past when the
chancellor was the king's chief minister. These included the disposal of
much patronage that technically belonged to the Crown, notably
appointments in the Church and to the judicial bench. Correspondence
between the two was encouraged by the regular business of sending
and acknowledging warrants and commissions, and it is not surprising
that the Lord Chancellor came to act as domestic as well as constitutional adviser to the king when difficulties arose. Thurlow was
regularly consulted on the financial problems of the Prince of Wales,
even after he had left office — though he finally in exasperation asked
for the prince to be told that "I am always ready to offer His Royal
Highness the best advice I can, and I observe that His Royal Highness
is always ready to ask it. But before I give it again, it might be as well
to know if anybody means to follow it". Eldon mediated between
George III and the prince on the subject of the education of Princess
Charlotte. On all such matters the Chancellor was well placed to give
sympathetic, impartial advice.

But this aspect of the office should not be exaggerated. George III
was fortunate to have three Chancellors whom he liked and trusted.
This was largely because he had chosen them himself, in Thurlow's
case virtually over the head of the Prime Minister. Eldon himself
remarked "I was the king's Lord Chancellor, not the minister's". The
distinctive features of the office were less important to their position
than their personal rapport with the monarch: Bathurst and
Loughborough, for example, were on quite different terms with him.
In a time when the personal influence of the king in politics was less,

the chancellorship would clearly be (what even under George it had essentially remained) a party appointment.

The Chancellors and the Law 1660-1827

The period from 1660 to 1827 was one of gradual evolution in the judicial character of the chancellorship. It will be convenient to deal separately with the changes in the Lord Chancellor's jurisdiction in the Court of Chancery and his increasingly important judicial functions in the House of Lords.

The Court of Chancery

Before the middle of the seventeenth century there was no such thing as "equity" in the later sense of a developed and consistent body of law. Equity was either a jurisprudential principle of uncertain application to the English legal system; or it might loosely, and unhelpfully, be used to describe the congeries of separate jurisdictions exercised by the Court of Chancery. But this was beginning to change. Over the next century and a half there emerged a coherent system of related principles and precedents which to a large extent brought order and predictability to the way in which cases were heard in the Court of Chancery and removed the discretionary element from the Lord Chancellor's jurisdiction. Lord Eldon, whose twenty-five years on the Woolsack (1801-6 and 1807-27) are generally regarded as setting the seal on this process, once declared:

> "The doctrines of this court ought to be as well settled, and made as uniform, almost, as those of the common law, laying down fixed principles, but taking care that they are to be applied according to the circumstances of each case. I cannot agree that the doctrines of this court are to be changed with every succeeding judge. Nothing would inflict on me greater pain, in quitting this place, than the recollection that I have done anything to justify the reproach that the equity of this court varies like the Chancellor's foot."*

The growing rigidity of equity was inevitable. It is in the nature of laws and lawyers to seek definition and clarification: the common law, as we have seen, had gone through a similar phase in its earliest years, with unsatisfactory results. But there were other factors at work. One

*See p. 88.

was the reviving predominance of the Lord Chancellor's jurisdiction in trusts and land law, which for much of the sixteenth century had taken second place to the more general jurisdiction in fraud. The eighteenth century, and indeed the whole period following the Restoration, saw the consolidation of the power and wealth of the landed aristocracy. In the settled and ordered society of the time it was necessary for the landed classes to have a secure but flexible means of regulating the disposition of land and protecting the integrity and prosperity of their estates through successive generations. This the Court of Chancery provided. The machinery of the trust was put into use to create the so-called strict settlement, whereby the competing interests of the existing owner, his heir, his widow and his younger children could be provided for and reconciled as beneficial interests under a trust.

The Chancellors were quite consciously supplying this need. Lord Hardwicke (1737-56) in a long and interesting letter to the Scottish judge and jurist Lord Kames, wrote:

"Another source of the increase of business in courts of equity has been the multiplication and extension of trusts. New methods of settling and encumbering land-property have been suggested by the necessities, extravagance or real occasions of mankind."

He added a further area of development:

"But what is more than this, new species of property have been introduced, particularly by the establishment of the public funds and various transferable stocks, that required to be modified and settled to answer the exigencies of families, to which the rules and methods of conveyancing provided by the common law would not ply or bend. Here the liberality of the courts of equity has been found to step in and lend her aid."

Of almost equal importance was the Court of Chancery's jurisdiction over mortgages. Most men of property in the eighteenth century were involved in mortgages, either as lenders or as borrowers, and the mortgage was becoming an essential part of the economic structure underpinning the wealth of the ruling class. Again, it was Chancery which evolved a body of law which protected equally the reasonable rights of both parties to the transaction; for the mortgage, like the trust, involved the concept of two or more rights co-existing in a single estate, which the common law was unwilling to recognise.

From this solid base in the core of the English social structure, the Court of Chancery extended its jurisdiction into related areas which did not depend chiefly on trusts. One was the protection of the property of married women. Another was the guardianship of infants. The origins of this "wardship jurisdiction" have been said to be medieval, deriving from the Chancellor's exercise, on the king's behalf, of his rights and duties as *parens patriae* (a phrase used by lawyers with more confidence than precision). It is certainly true that on the hazy border between their administrative and their judicial functions the Chancellors of the fourteenth and fifteenth centuries did have to deal with disputes concerning the exercise of the king's feudal right of wardship, which allowed him to manage the lands of heirs whose fathers had died before they came of age. But this was in no sense a special responsibility of the office, and when Henry VIII decided that this lucrative right should be properly exploited it was entrusted to a separate court established for the purpose. It was only with the abolition of the Court of Wards and Liveries in 1660 that Chancery began to be regarded as the proper court for the protection of the rights of infants.

It was estimated in the eighteenth century that in a period of thirty years every estate in England could be expected to pass through the Court of Chancery. This was a powerful impetus to the settling of equitable principles at least in matters of family and land law. As Lord Hardwicke recognised, the jurisdiction in fraud was rather different. He wrote to Lord Kames:

"In the construction of trusts, which are one great head of equity, the rules are pretty well established. So they are in the case of mortgages, which makes another great branch of that business. But as to relief against fraud, no invariable rules can be established. Fraud is infinite, and were a court of equity once to lay down rules . . . the jurisdiction would be cramped and perpetually eluded by new schemes which the fertility of man's invention would contrive."

But fraud was, comparatively, of declining importance in the work of Chancery.

Three Lord Chancellors in particular are traditionally regarded as making the main contribution to the evolution of equity in its modern form — Lord Nottingham (1673-82), Lord Hardwicke and Lord Eldon. Each of these was anxious to promote certainty in the administration of equity, that is to say the establishment of, and consistent adherence to, known principles and precedents.

Nottingham's great contribution was his insistence that in working out the details of equitable rights to property, i.e. rights under a trust, the Chancellor should, as far as was possible, apply precisely the same rules as if they had been ordinary rights at common law. It was essential that this immensely important area of the law should be capable of precise understanding. His anxiety to restrict the scope of the discretion of the judge is expressed in the "great case of *Cook v Fountain*" (his own description):

> "With such a conscience as is only *naturalis et interna* this court has nothing to do; the conscience by which I am to proceed is merely *civilis et politica*, and tied to certain measures, and it is infinitely better for the public that a trust, security or agreement which is wholly secret [the concealed nature of a trust being the point at issue in the case], should fail than that men should lose their estates by the mere fancy and imagination of a Chancellor."

Nevertheless the influence of these Chancellors does not depend on any dogmatic expression of policy with which they approached their cases. All three (though Eldon only reluctantly) were willing to recognise that certainty could never be wholly achieved and that an area of discretion had to remain. Nor, anyway, were their attitudes unique. Nottingham was not, as is sometimes believed, the first Lord Chancellor to attach great weight to precedents. And between him and Hardwicke there were several Chancellors of high calibre — notably Macclesfield and Talbot — who gave important assistance to the definition of equitable principles. The influence of Nottingham, Hardwicke and Eldon is rather in the wealth of reported decisions of high intellectual quality, and enhanced by their judicial reputations, which they left behind them. The production of published reports of cases in Chancery was just beginning in the late seventeenth century; and in Nottingham's case there was, besides the published reports, a wide acquaintance among his successors with his own notes of his decisions, even though they were not printed until Eldon's time. It was the creation of a body of rational and accessible precedents, in which equitable principles were asserted and applied, which was decisive in establishing certainty in equity. In this regard it is fair to note that both Hardwicke and Eldon had exceptionally long tenures of office and may owe something of their influence to the sheer scope they had for making law. Eldon's reputation in particular has benefited from his being the right man at the right time. The (from the legal point of view) somewhat amateurish chancellorships of Hardwicke's successors, of whom only Northington, and perhaps Camden, had shown much distinction as equity lawyers, had created a need for a Lord Chancellor who could gather up the loose ends of a system which had been established in outline but never wholly worked through. This Eldon, with his defining, systematising intellect and his deep learning, was well suited to achieve. In applying, qualifying and reconciling principles Eldon was a master; he would have been incapable of conceiving or establishing them.

The undistinguished judicial careers of Eldon's immediate pre-decessors in office, Thurlow and Loughborough, reflect one conse-quence of the increasing definition of equity. By the middle of the eighteenth century there had developed a marked, though not unbridgeable, gap between those barristers who practised in the Court of Chancery and practitioners in the common law courts; equity had become a precise science which could not easily be acquired by an outsider. Chancellors with a common law background were thus at a disadvantage. It never became a rule that a common lawyer could not be appointed to the chancellorship, especially as there was a fortunate convention that the Attorney-General, whose office was held by many prospective Chancellors, should, if he did not already do so, practise in the Court of Chancery; but the appointments of, for example, Bathurst and Erskine caused great alarm in Chancery. The problem was of course only a particular aspect of the dangers attendant on the practice of appointing a senior judge for reasons which would at least in part have nothing to do with his judicial qualifications. This has necessarily been a perennial problem with the chancellorship, though more serious when, as was the case until 1851, the Chancellor had solitary control of his court without colleagues by whom he might be guided or overborne.

Two other growing areas of the Chancellor's jurisdiction should be noted, which are not equitable in origin. The less onerous of the two was the Chancellor's jurisdiction in lunacy. As in the case of wardship, the supposed medieval origins of this jurisdiction are accidental, and lunatics came for over a century within the purview of the Court of Wards. It was only after 1660 that the duty of providing for the administration of the property of those of unsound mind began regularly to be delegated to the Lord Chancellor by the king, to whom in each case a petition had technically to be made. The burden fell on the Lord Chancellor simply because he was there, a senior councillor of the king with a court and the beginnings of an analogous control over the rights of infants.

The other new jurisdiction was that in bankruptcy cases. Since the sixteenth century the Lord Chancellor had had responsibility in his administrative capacity for appointing commissioners to manage the affairs of bankrupts. Since Lord Nottingham's time the commissioners, or persons aggrieved by their actions, had begun to regard the Chancellor as the proper person to decide their legal difficulties. A series of statutes in the early part of the eighteenth century confirmed and regularised this practice, and by the chancellorship of Lord Hardwicke it was a very substantial part of the business of the Court of Chancery. Bankruptcies tend to increase in step with growing economic activity: they had more than tripled between the middle and the end of the century, and it has been computed that Lord Eldon was dealing with about four times as much bankruptcy business as Lord Hardwicke. The extra burden on the court was very great, but also very lucrative: fees in bankruptcy cases might bring the Chancellor as much as £4,000 a year, quite apart from his salary and the established perquisites of the office.

These were the new fields opened to the Court of Chancery in the eighteenth century, but the older work of the court continued, in cases concerning *inter alia* specific performance of contracts, agreements obtained under the influence of fraud or mistake, and discovery of documents.

If this was a creative period in the history of equity, it was one of stagnation in the court itself. Perhaps the only positive change was the movement in the mid 1750s of the court out of term (for Chancery did not observe the common law terms) to the Hall of Lincoln's Inn. Here it was close to the court of the Master of the Rolls in Chancery Lane, which reduced at least some of the inconvenience to litigants caused by the physical dispersal of the Court of Chancery. The special position of the Master of the Rolls among his fellow Masters had eventually resulted in his acquiring judicial functions of their own. The nature and validity of these were the subject of much controversy early in the eighteenth century, but the position which finally emerged was that he was entitled to hear most classes of Chancery business, subject to a right of appeal (often exercised) to the Lord Chancellor. This was the more necessary as the practice of the Chancellor sitting with the common law judges had declined and finally disappeared by the end of the century.

Otherwise little had changed. Chancery in the eighteenth century still suffered from the same superfluous and expensive staff and contortuplicated procedure which had excited the reformers of the previous century. For much of the century, however, its defects appear to have been acceptable. Much of the credit for this must go to Hardwicke, who worked with extraordinary diligence to keep down arrears of business. He sat regularly for five or six hours a day, with frequent special sittings (sometimes in his own house) in the evening,* a figure which is the more impressive when one appreciates that when the Lords were sitting there would be judicial business there on three afternoons a week, with the House meeting for its other work in the early evenings. This could mean a working day lasting from seven to midnight.

At the end of the century, however, a deterioration began to be evident which had become very marked by the 1820s. Calls for reform became insistent and loud. Delay was the principal problem. The proper interpretation of the statistics relating to Chancery litigation at this time was a source of bitter debate among contemporary critics and apologists of the existing system, but it is clear beyond doubt that very serious delays were being experienced by at least some litigants. By 1825 it could be claimed by one propagandist that the arrears in the

*These were the sittings discontinued by Northington—see p. 151.

Court of Chancery would at the current rate of progress take forty years to clear. The causes of the delays were as hotly disputed as their extent. Certainly the business of the court had grown enormously. Again, figures are unreliable, but the fact that money in court in 1820 amounted to some £34 million, as against about half that sum in 1800 and only £1½ million in 1750, is very striking — though it would not be suggested that the growth of work between those dates was in anything like that proportion. The increase in bankruptcy cases was the chief factor, but ordinary equity cases were also becoming both more numerous and heavier and more complex with the development of new forms of commercial enterprise and partnership which had to be regulated according to equitable principles.

Little could be done about these factors save to expand the court in order to cope. But many contemporaries were not convinced that the growth of business was the only or, for some, even the main cause of the congestion in Chancery. They blamed the Lord Chancellor. Eldon was notorious for the scrupulous hesitation with which he approached any decision, however marginal or insignificant. The slightest doubt over the law or the evidence in a case could be enough to produce a lengthy adjournment for re-consideration, research and re-argument. Eldon himself admitted to this inclination, but defended it:

> "With Lord Bacon, 'I confess I have somewhat of the cunctative,' and, with him, I thought that 'whosoever is not wiser upon advice than upon the sudden, the same man is not wiser at fifty than he was at thirty.' I confess that no man ever had more occasion than I had to use the expression, which was Lord Bacon's father's ordinary word, 'You must give me time.' I always thought it better to allow myself to doubt *before*, than to expose myself to the misery *after* I had decided, of doubting whether I had decided rightly and justly. It is true that too much delay before decision is a great evil; but in many instances, delay leads eventually to prevent delay; that is, the delay, which enables just decision to be made, accelerates the enjoyment of the fruits of the suit. . . [because an 'impregnable' decree deters appeal]."

Such principles (expressed with typically Eldonian laboriousness) do the Lord Chancellor credit, but it is not surprising that they were exasperating to bar and litigants alike. Yet the real charge against Eldon should not concentrate on his habits as a judge, which cannot have done more than aggravate other causes of delay, but on his uncompromising resistance to almost any change in the organisation or procedure of his court. He did indeed consent to the creation, in 1813, of a "Vice-Chancellor" to share the work with himself and the Master of the Rolls, and he made a generous personal contribution to his salary, but this change probably attracted more new cases than the Vice-Chancellor himself could hear. At any rate arrears continued to mount. Eldon refused to contemplate the more radical changes that were proposed, notably the separation of the bankruptcy and lunacy jurisdictions from the Court of Chancery; and when a commission of enquiry was finally appointed in 1825 he gave it so little genuine co-operation that its eventual report was quite ineffectual. It was only with the Lord Chancellor's resignation in 1827 that any kind of serious Chancery reform became possible.

The House of Lords

Parliament is a court, and at various stages of its history both Houses have claimed original or appellate jurisdiction in certain sorts of cases at law. Impeachment is a case of the House of Lords exercising an original criminal jurisdiction. The original jurisdiction of the House of Lords in civil matters was abandoned by the end of the seventeenth century; but its right to decide appeals (by means of writs of error) from the common law courts was always accepted, and so, after a sharp tussle with the Commons in the case of *Shirley v Fagg,* was that from the Court of Chancery. Throughout the eighteenth century, therefore, a considerable part of the business of the Lords consisted of such judicial matters. In fact, appeals to the Lords were a good deal more popular from the Scottish courts than they were from England, thanks to a rule applying in Scotland that an appeal brought automatic stay of execution of judgement. Though at this date there was no binding convention that lay peers might not participate in the hearing of cases before their House, common sense, and the disinclination of non-lawyers to waste time on matters they could not understand, meant that appeals were decided by those peers who were legally qualified. Of these the Lord Chancellor was generally the most eminent, and for long periods, when neither Chief Justice was ennobled and when there were no active ex-Chancellors, the Lord Chancellor might sit alone. For the full nineteen years of his chancellorship Lord Hardwicke was the only peer who was equipped to hear appeals, and effectively the same position prevailed for much of Eldon's time; for though Erskine did not die until 1823 he treated himself as virtually in retirement after relinquishing the Great Seal. This state of affairs was very un-satisfactory to Chancery litigants who, if they chose to appeal, found themselves doing so "from a judge in a tie wig in Lincoln's Inn Hall, to the same judge in a full bottom wig in the House of Lords, with a snoring bishop perhaps on one side and a Scotch peer on the other".

Apart from this appellate jurisdiction the House of Lords had from time to time other kinds of judicial and quasi-judicial business in which the Chancellor would necessarily be involved. Impeachments have been mentioned. With those of Sacheverell and Macclesfield, the most notorious of this period was that of Warren Hastings, the Governor-General of India, who was picked on by the Foxite opposition and charged with corruption as an oblique means of attack on Pitt's government. The impeachment lasted for 148 days, spread over a period of seven years, from 1788 to 1795. During most of it Thurlow, who was a personal admirer and political supporter of Warren Hastings, was Lord Chancellor and as such presiding at the trial. His scope for influencing the outcome was limited, for in an impeachment the issue was decided on a vote of all the peers present; and in any event it was in fact Loughborough who was presiding when Hastings was finally acquitted. But Thurlow firmly took Hastings' side when points of procedure had to be resolved, and he secured the important decision that the articles of impeachment should be heard and determined as a single indivisible whole, as in an ordinary court, and not, as was claimed by Loughborough (then in one of his opposition phases), "by law and custom of Parliament". Less spectacular but more frequent and, cumulatively, equally time-consuming were the complicated peerage claims which arose from time to time. Finally, there was in 1820 the unique proceeding of a "Bill of Pains and Penalties" against George IV's Queen Caroline, who had for several years been effectively separated from her husband but had returned to England after an exceedingly indiscreet and indecorous tour of Italy during which she had almost certainly committed adultery with one or more of her seedy entourage. The bill, nominally a piece of legislation designed to dissolve her marriage to the king, was in fact a trial of the queen for adultery, and as each party took sides it soon became a highly charged political issue. Eldon as Lord Chancellor presided and delivered a summing-up of the evidence strongly against the queen; but the bill was dropped before a final decision was reached.

The consequences of the involvement of the Lord Chancellor in this wealth of judicial business in the House of Lords were twofold. In the first place, it imposed a further heavy burden on an already heavily burdened office. Attendance in the Lords was one of the principal factors preventing the Lord Chancellor from keeping up with his work in Chancery: Lord Eldon, for example, sat some 48 days a year in the Lords on judicial business. It could of course as well be said that the Chancellor's duties in Chancery prevented his sitting longer hours in the Lords, where there was also a serious problem of arrears. A committee set up in 1811, on Eldon's motion, reported over 330 cases awaiting decision — though many of these will have been purely time-wasting Scottish appeals — and recommended that the Lord Chancellor devote more time to the Lords; and it was partly to facilitate this that a Vice-Chancellor was appointed two years later. In truth the only real solution to the problem was for one or other jurisdiction to be abolished, but though that was indeed suggested it was too radical to be acceptable.

The other consequence affected the Lord Chancellor's standing in the law generally. The Lord Chancellor was in the eighteenth century for the first time unquestionably recognised as the head of the law — not indeed in any precise sense of ministerial responsibility, but as the most respected and influential judge in the kingdom. Already in the later seventeenth century common law judges were being "promoted" to the chancellorship — Bridgeman was the first — and while several Chief Justices became Chancellor there are no instances the other way round. But there the promotion consisted more in the ancient eminence of the office, and no doubt also its rich patronage and perquisites, than in any specifically judicial superiority: Chancery was only one court among many, and something of an oddity where an ill-defined system of equity could still be applied by a layman. Only when the Lord Chancellor presided over the highest tribunal of appeal in the land could he be the judicial equal or superior of the Chief Justices. There are of course other things involved. The fact that the Lord Chancellor appointed the judges clearly served to set him above, and apart from, them, even if the origins of the practice were in his administrative rather than his judicial role. The respectability of Chancery under a superlative lawyer such as Hardwicke must have helped to remove the idea that equity was a science inferior to law. Nevertheless, Chancery was only a province of the law; in the House of Lords the Lord Chancellor ruled the empire.

CHAPTER SIX

1827-1830	John Singleton Copley, Lord Lyndhurst
1830-1834	Henry Brougham, Lord Brougham and Vaux
1834-1835	Lord Lyndhurst (see above)
1836-1841	Charles Pepys, Lord Cottenham
1841-1846	Lord Lyndhurst (see above)
1846-1850	Lord Cottenham (see above) (Earl of Cottenham 1850)
1850-1852	Thomas Wilde, Lord Truro
1852	Edward Sugden, Lord St Leonards
1852-1858	Robert Monsey Rolfe, Lord Cranworth
1858-1859	Frederic Thesiger, Lord Chelmsford
1859-1861	John Campbell, Lord Campbell
1861-1865	Richard Bethell, Lord Westbury
1865-1866	Lord Cranworth (see above)
1866-1868	Lord Chelmsford (see above)
1868	Hugh Cairns, Lord Cairns
1868-1872	William Page Wood, Lord Hatherley
1872-1874	Roundell Palmer, Lord Selborne
1874-1880	Lord Cairns (see above), Earl Cairns 1878
1880-1885	Lord Selborne (see above), Earl of Selborne 1882
1885-1886	Hardinge Giffard, Lord Halsbury
1886	Farrer Herschell, Lord Herschell
1886-1892	Lord Halsbury (see above)
1892-1895	Lord Herschell (see above)
1895-1905	Lord Halsbury (see above), Earl of Halsbury 1898
1905-1912	Robert Reid, Lord Loreburn, Earl of Loreburn 1911
1912-1915	Richard Haldane, Viscount Haldane
1915-1916	Stanley Buckmaster, Lord Buckmaster (Viscount Buckmaster 1932)
1916-1919	Robert Finlay, Lord Finlay (Viscount Finlay 1919)
1919-1922	Frederick Smith, Lord Birkenhead (Viscount Birkenhead 1922)
1922-1924	George Cave, Viscount Cave
1924	Viscount Haldane (see above)
1924-1928	Viscount Cave (see above)
1928-1929	Douglas Hogg, Lord Hailsham (Viscount Hailsham 1929)
1929-1935	John Sankey, Lord Sankey, Viscount Sankey 1932
1935-1938	Viscount Hailsham (see above)
1938-1939	Frederick Maugham, Lord Maugham
1939-1940	Thomas Inskip, Viscount Caldecote

1940-1945	John Simon, Viscount Simon
1945-1951	William Jowitt, Lord Jowitt, Viscount Jowitt 1947 (Earl Jowitt 1951)
1951-1954	Gavin Simonds, Lord Simonds (Viscount Simonds 1954)
1954-1962	David Maxwell Fyfe, Viscount Kilmuir (Earl Kilmuir 1962).
1962-1964	Reginald Manningham-Buller, Lord Dilhorne (Viscount Dilhorne 1964)
1964-1970	Gerald Gardiner, Lord Gardiner
1970-1974	Quintin Hogg, Lord Hailsham
1974	Frederick Elwyn-Jones, Lord Elwyn-Jones

CHAPTER SIX

Towards a Ministry of Justice

Brougham and Reform 1828-1876

O N THE 7th February, 1828, Henry Brougham, the member for Winchelsea, rose in the House of Commons to move the issue of a commission "for enquiring into the defects occasioned, by time and otherwise, in the laws of this realm of England as administered in the courts of common law, and into the measures necessary for removing the same". Refreshing himself from a hatful of oranges, Brougham spoke for over six hours, dissecting in destructive detail the decayed state of almost every part of the legal system; he omitted consideration only of "the bottomless pit of Chancery", because measures were already in hand for its reform. The speech contained an exhaustive survey of the courts, from the Privy Council and the courts of Westminster Hall to the jurisdiction of the justices of the peace, proposing remedies for the delays of the higher courts and the ignorance, incompetence and prejudice of the lower. There was an analysis of the deficiencies of the system of pleadings, with digressions into innumerable dark side-alleys of the tortuous maze of procedure. Brougham ended with a peroration that has become famous:

"It was the boast of Augustus . . . that he found Rome of brick and left it of marble; a praise not unworthy of a great prince, and to which the present reign also has its claims. But how much nobler will be the Sovereign's boast when he shall have it to say that he found law dear and left it cheap; found it a sealed book, left it a living letter; found it the patrimony of the rich, left it the inheritance of the poor; found it the two-edged sword of craft and oppression, left it the staff of honesty and the shield of innocence."

Brougham became Lord Chancellor, taking the title of Lord Brougham and Vaux, two years later, but it is his speech of 1828 which

173

set out the programme not only for his own policies as Chancellor but for half a century of radical reforms in which the English legal system was transformed, with an equally radical effect on the office of Lord Chancellor. Brougham is one of the most remarkable men of the nineteenth century and certainly one of the greatest to have held the Great Seal — which is not the same as to say he was a great, or even, by conventional standards, a good, Lord Chancellor. Co-founder (with Sydney Smith and other young alumni of the Athens of the North) of the great liberal quarterly *The Edinburgh Review,* an apparent expert in the law, in the classics, in political economy and in the natural sciences (at the age of eighteen he had a paper on optics published by the Royal Society), a successful advocate, a campaigner and propagandist for the abolition of slavery, for popular education and a variety of other radical causes — Brougham was a prodigy of energy and versatility. The poet Samuel Rogers summed him up at the end of a visit: "This morning Solon, Lycurgus, Demosthenes, Archimedes, Sir Isaac Newton, Lord Chesterfield, and a great many others went away in one postchaise". Brougham was also unusual as a reforming campaigner in that a fair amount of his causes were actually successful — among them the foundation of London University ("Brougham's Cockney College") and of the Society for the Diffusion of Useful Knowledge, a large proportion of whose literature he wrote himself. Brougham entered Parliament as a Whig in 1810 and was almost at once established as the most effective opposition speaker in the Commons and the figurehead of Whig popularity in the country. Nothing he did at the bar earned him greater popularity than his defence of Queen Caroline at her "trial", in which his opening speech was described by the diarist Greville as "the most magnificent display of argument and oratory that has been heard for years". The trial was an extremely powerful focus for popular hostility to the government and it was exploited to the full by the Whigs. But his colleagues were never at ease with him. Not only were his views uncomfortably radical, but he was the antithesis of a reliable party man. Brougham had most of the symptoms of a manic depressive. He was wildly excitable and when carried away he might (and often did) say or do almost anything, however injudicious, damaging or liable to give offence — though he was quite without intentional malice and never kept an enemy.

Historians have produced many pompous pronouncements about Brougham's lack of judgement, his shallow intellect, his insensitivity to others, the faults of temperament which vitiated his great gifts, and so forth. As Bagehot more succinctly put it, "If he were a horse, no-one would buy him". This is all true. Brougham epitomises that ultimate in donnish disapproval, "brilliant but unsound". But it is all quite insignificant compared with the immense impetus that he gave to the forces of change in the critical opening period of the Victorian reforms. It is too easy to dismiss Brougham as an erratic genius. Contemporary sources reveal how he captured the imagination of his time and inspired the radical movement; this sort of achievement, though difficult for later generations to assess, is usually the most important of all.

Brougham probably did more than any one man to secure the passage of the Reform Bill of 1832. His election for Yorkshire, the largest constituency in England, was the biggest triumph in the Whig victory of 1830. Grey's immediate offer to him of the chancellorship was a shrewd move. Brougham had to be in the government if it was to retain its popular support, but of all offices that of Lord Chancellor, cutting off this dangerous radical from his accustomed influence in the Commons, was best calculated to keep his excesses in check. But Brougham soon acquired in the Upper House much of the dominance he had had in the Lower, and his fame (or notoriety) was if anything increased. It was noted that the Commons emptied when Brougham was speaking in the Lords. He dominated the debates for the Whigs on the Reform Bill, and with Grey persuaded the king into the critical decisions which saved it — the hasty dissolution of Parliament in 1831 and the pledge to create new peers in 1832. But, valuable though he was in these crises, Brougham was an impossible colleague. After a series of incidents, including the alleged leaking to *The Times* of the news of the dismissal of the ministry in 1834, Melbourne, Grey's successor as Prime Minister, refused to re-appoint the Lord Chancellor when the Whigs returned to power the next year. After the usual unhappy experiment with a commission, the Great Seal was in 1836 entrusted to the insignificant Solicitor-General, Charles Pepys, who took the title of Lord Cottenham — a change, said Disraeli, from Master Shallow to Master Silence, from Humbug to Humdrum.

Brougham was never again given political office, but he remained for the next twenty years (he did not die until 1868) a public figure of enormous influence and popularity.

Brougham's chancellorship was too short and too hectic to allow the implementation of all his planned reforms in the legal system; but what mattered was that a start was made and the long log-jam of Eldon's tenure of the office broken up. And it was a substantial start. Brougham had legislation passed to set up the Judicial Committee of the Privy Council, introducing professional legal control to what had hitherto been a ludicrously incompetent lay tribunal of appeal from the colonial courts, and replacing the obsolete Court of Delegates for Admiralty and ecclesiastical appeals. (This reorganisation, incidentally, gave the opportunity for the famous judgement of Lord Chancellor Westbury in 1864 in the trial of the liberal theological *Essays and Reviews,* in which he "dismissed Hell with costs and took away from orthodox members of the Church of England their last of everlasting damnation" — an important blow for intellectual freedom in the Church). Brougham reorganised the outlying parts of his Chancery jurisdiction by means of Bankruptcy and Lunacy Acts: the Lord Chancellor was to be involved in bankruptcy cases only at the second stage of an appellate process. The Masters in Chancery were put onto a fixed salary, with criminal penalties for the taking of fees, and their duties were re-defined. Court fees were reduced and the abolition of the Six Clerks' office begun. Arrears in Chancery were drastically reduced, if only by means of long sittings and some very slapdash judgements from a Chancellor who was known to regard counsel's arguments as affording a useful opportunity to get on with his private correspondence. Unfortunately, the Local Courts Bill, designed to provide cheap hearings for small civil cases, was defeated. Brougham also had a hand in a variety of reforms in the substantive law — including the first bold surgery on the cancerous growth of real property law — and in the procedure of the common law courts. The period from 1830 to 1834 is one of the busiest in the history of English law reform.

Brougham continued to be active for reform when out of office. In 1844 he set up the Law Amendment Society, the first body of its kind. But one of the most important effects of his chancellorship was the association it created between the office of Lord Chancellor and the promotion of law reform. Successive Chancellors regarded this as an especial responsibility and few in the remainder of the century did not make important contributions to the restructuring of the legal system or to the substantive law. Even the High Tory Lord Lyndhurst, John Singleton Copley*, three times Chancellor (1827-30, 1834-5, and 1841-6), was converted to the cause of local courts, which he had strongly resisted in 1833, and in 1846 introduced the County Courts Act on which the modern system is based. He also adopted in 1841 a bill of his predecessor establishing two new Vice-Chancellors to assist in the work of the Court of Chancery; and in 1843 he finally abolished the Six Clerkships. Lyndhurst was the only peer on the Tory benches who was a match for Brougham; indeed in later years the two were close friends. He was a figure of commanding presence and sharp intelligence, as a pure lawyer considerably Brougham's superior. Unlike Brougham, he was urbane and easygoing and a philanderer of distinction.‡ Lyndhurst's abilities and his natural authority gave him a central place in the Tory party, but his politics were something of an enigma: too intelligent to associate with the Tory backwoodsmen, he was equally out of sympathy with the drab seriousness of Peel and his followers, against whom he idly intrigued. It is quite in character that he was a patron of the young Disraeli and shared a mistress with him.

Lord Cottenham, who survived as Chancellor until 1841, and held the office again from 1846 to 1850, was politically a non-entity, but he was as good a lawyer and judge as either of his predecessors, and he had his own views on law reform. Brougham's extraordinary chancellorship had driven home to many, including an exasperated Melbourne, the anomalous nature of the office. Quite apart from considerations of constitutional principle and the separation of powers—given vivid illustration by the sight of the kingdom's most eminent judge parading the country haranguing radical crowds—the multiplicity of the Lord Chancellor's functions meant that none of them was given proper attention. Valuable though Brougham's reforms had been, the root cause of the arrears which were already creeping back into the Chancery was the simple fact that the Chancellor could not cope with his judicial functions as well as his duties in the Lords and in Cabinet. Brougham himself was aware of this and harboured ill-defined

*Son of the American painter of that name. Lyndhurst was in fact born in America.

‡Though Brougham was one of the many victims of the society courtesan and blackmailer, Harriet Wilson.

ambitions to divide the Lord Chancellor's functions and set up a
Ministry of Justice. The problem was growing as parliamentary sittings
became more frequent and the responsibilities undertaken by
government became heavier. The interval after Lyndhurst's short
chancellorship, while the Great Seal was held in commission, provoked
several schemes to rationalise the office of Lord Chancellor in
accordance with good Benthamite principles. The most radical
proposal, that of the Master of the Rolls, Lord Langdale, envisaged a
threefold division — a Lord Chancellor so called to preside over the
Court of Chancery, an official called the Keeper of the Great Seal to sit
in Cabinet and have responsibility for the state of the law as a whole,
and a Lord President to preside over the House of Lords sitting
judicially. This last was of some importance, since high mortality
among the senior judiciary could reduce the numbers of legally
qualified peers almost to nil: at times Brougham was the sole Law
Lord. Cottenham was too cautious to accept this scheme, but within
three months of his appointment he introduced in the Lords a bill of
his own which simply removed from the Chancellor all responsibility
for the Court of Chancery, which was to have its own Lord Chief
Justice, leaving his other functions intact. It seemed that the association
of five centuries between Chancellor and Court of Chancery would
be broken. In fact Cottenham's bill failed, attacked equally by
those who wanted more radical reform and those who wanted none.
The traditional chancellorship was preserved.

Yet it was clear that something had to be done. Cottenham in 1839
estimated that there were then three years' arrears in Chancery, and he
believed that the overwork would have killed him had he not been put
out of office by the Tory victory in 1841. Lyndhurst's two new
Vice-Chancellors relieved matters temporarily, but delay and in-
efficiency were still built into the system. It was the Chancery of the
1840s that was represented in Dickens' *Bleak House*, which began to
appear in 1852. *Bleak House* revolves around the fictional Chancery
case of *Jarndyce v Jarndyce:*

"This scarecrow of a suit has, in the course of time, become so
complicated that no man alive knows what it means. The parties to
it understand it least, but it has been observed that no two Chancery

lawyers can talk about it for five minutes without coming to a total disagreement as to all the premises. Innumerable children have been born into the cause; innumerable young people have married into it; innumerable old people have died out of it. Scores of persons have deliriously found themselves made parties in Jarndyce and Jarndyce without knowing how or why; whole families have inherited legendary hatreds with the suit. The little plaintiff or defendant who was promised a new rocking-horse when Jarndyce and Jarndyce should be settled has grown up, possessed himself of a real horse, and trotted away into the real world. Fair wards of court have faded into mothers and grandmothers; a long procession of Chancellors has come in and gone out; the legion of bills in the suit have been transformed into mere bills of mortality; there are not three Jarndyces left upon the earth perhaps since old Tom Jarndyce blew his brains out at a coffee-house in Chancery Lane; but Jarndyce and Jarndyce still drags its dreary length before the court, perennially hopeless."

Jarndyce v Jarndyce (eventually finished when the whole estate had been swallowed up in costs) is of course a distortion, and Dickens' claims in the preface to the book (and in his articles elsewhere in the press) were wildly inaccurate: Atlay, the biographer of the Victorian Lord Chancellors, slyly observes that confidence in them "is somewhat shaken by their being bracketed with a defence of the doctrine of death by spontaneous combustion". But Chancery proceedings were indeed still vitiated by the antiquated and abstruse technicalities of Chancery procedure (especially in the system of pleadings and the wealth of interlocutory business) and by the dependence of the whole upon the Lord Chancellor, who was still expected to sit at first instance as well as having to hear appeals from his subordinates. The expense and misery caused to litigants should not be under-estimated. But salvation was at hand. Acting on the advice of commissions set up under his predecessors, Lord Chancellor Truro (1850-2) introduced legislation in 1851 removing the Chancellor's first-instance jurisdiction and creating two "Lords Justices" to share his appellate work. The next year a momentous blow was struck when an act initiated under Truro but carried by his successor, Lord St Leonards (who was Lord

Chancellor for a mere ten months in 1852), abolished the Chancery
Masterships, replacing them by a flexible system of proceedings in
chambers on the modern pattern. This was a decisive step which did
more than anything else to lift the Court of Chancery out of the slough
into which it had sunk. Lord Truro, who takes the credit for these
measures, had been a successful advocate, a run-of-the-mill Law
Officer and a modest Chief Justice of Common Pleas, whose surprising
appointment to the Woolsack—for he had no experience of Chancery
—had encouraged rumours of an impending division of the chancellorship along the lines proposed in 1836. Rumour did him an injustice.

It is unnecessary here to recount in detail the further reforms both
in the legal system and in the substantive law carried through by
Brougham's successors. Few were not active for some scheme or
another. But the reforms in the Court of Chancery discussed above
were very important in their effect on the Lord Chancellor's own
office. No longer sitting in Chancery at first instance, and under less
pressure to do so on appeal, the Chancellor was tending to shift from
his work in equity towards a more exclusive concern with the appellate
work of the House of Lords. This tendency was confirmed by the
Judicature Act of 1873 and the associated legislation of the next three
years, which marked the culmination of forty years of reform of the
court system. In the complete re-structuring brought about by the Act,
the Court of Chancery was integrated with King's Bench, Common
Pleas and a number of lesser courts into a single High Court subject to
a single undifferentiated Court of Appeal. The fusion of the courts
meant the fusion also, after over four centuries of separate existence
and development, of the systems of law and equity. The Lord
Chancellor was a member of both courts and retained the notional
headship of the new Chancery Division of the High Court, but in
practice it was extremely rare for him to sit in either. The last occasion
a Chancellor sat at first instance was in 1921, and not in Chancery at
all, when Lord Birkenhead assisted in the clearing of a backlog of
divorce cases in order to set an example to the judges. Since the new
Court of Appeal covered all sorts of business there was no longer any
specifically Chancery reason why the Chancellor should serve on it.
The House of Lords was left as the only judicial sphere of the Lord
Chancellor. That too might have been removed, with momentous

consequences for the office, had the original scheme of the Act been implemented, for it was intended that in order to remove the evil of double appeals the decisions of the Court of Appeal should be final. But the forces of conservatism proved too strong, and in 1876 the appellate jurisdiction of the House of Lords was confirmed. The Appellate Jurisdiction Act of that year also began to dilute the exclusiveness of the House of Lords in its judicial capacity by allowing for the creation of "Lords of Appeal in Ordinary" who would not be hereditary peers.

The genesis and passing of the Judicature Act and its sequels were the work of two of the most admired Lord Chancellors of the century, Lord Selborne and Lord Cairns. Roundell Palmer, Lord Selborne (Lord Chancellor 1872-4 and 1880-5), had been the most successful practitioner of his generation at the Chancery bar, and his intellect and application were fabled. His appointment as Solicitor-General in 1859 was a recognition more of his professional ability than of political services rendered or expected; indeed he was little enough of a politician to refuse the Great Seal in 1868 because of his disagreement with Gladstone's proposed disestablishment of the Irish Church, on which as a pious High Churchman he felt strongly. When he eventually became Chancellor he devoted his chief energies to the drafting and passing of the Judicature Bill. "It was," as he proudly claimed in his memoirs, "the work of my own hand, without any assistance beyond what I derived from the labours of my predecessors". Selborne might almost be the type of the High Victorian ideal — godly, hard-working, devoted to a great reforming cause, sensitive and generous-spirited. These qualities, with his excellence as a judge, explain his great reputation with his contemporaries. They are not, unfortunately, the sort to have earned him the place in national history that he deserves.

Lord Cairns, who took over from Selborne the later stages of his legislation when Gladstone's government lost office in 1874, had little in common with him save the fact that both taught in Bible classes. He was a dour Ulsterman and Evangelical whose political commitment, sureness of judgement and intellectual weight had raised him to the inner circle of the Conservative leadership. Unlike most of his colleagues, Cairns had neither an aristocratic background nor a vested interest to protect. He was thus prepared to take a greater interest than they in the task of establishing a national organisation for the Conservative party, with which he was closely involved. It is perhaps for this reason also that Cairns was Disraeli's most trusted adviser in every area of politics and government, even taking a major part in the conduct of foreign policy—a far wider participation than that enjoyed by any other Victorian Lord Chancellor. He held office in both Disraeli's administrations, in 1868 and from 1874 to 1880. He was an equally outstanding lawyer, a lucid, logical and forceful arguer and thinker, who continued to co-operate with Selborne over valuable measures of law reform after he had left office. Legislation introduced by Cairns in co-operation with Selborne began the massive work of reconstructing the law of property which was completed in 1925.

The Victorian Chancellors

Compared with their predecessors of the eighteenth or early nineteenth centuries, the Lord Chancellors of the Victorian period were politically insignificant. Probably only Lyndhurst and Cairns would have won a place in the Cabinet other than as Chancellor. Lawyers in Parliament were offered a private ladder of promotion that led either to the bench or, through the Law Officerships, to the Woolsack, and, as was appropriate, professional rather than political merit played the largest (if not the only) part in the distribution of the highest prizes. Many entered Parliament only in order to avail themselves of this ladder, and even those of real political conviction were, if they chose a career of this conventional pattern, cut off from their party colleagues who followed a quite separate *cursus honorum*. Lord Chancellor Herschell always advised young barristers to get into the Commons as soon as they justifiably could. Some Law Officers were appointed almost as soon as they arrived in the Commons—or even before, in the case of Hardinge Giffard (later Lord Chancellor Halsbury)—on the strength of professional reputation and often only a vague indication of political sympathies. No Lord Chancellor of this period had held, or was later to hold, any other office apart from a Law Officership; though Cairns was from 1868 to 1870 Leader of the Opposition in the House of Lords, a position which effectively made him Disraeli's deputy. It is not surprising therefore that the Law Officers and Lord

Chancellors were regarded as something of a race apart, ineligible for the offices which gave real power. Few, perhaps surprisingly, proved exceptional speakers in either the Commons or the Lords, though they were of course valuable on the many quasi-legal issues that confront a government. Both law and government had become more professional in the post-Brougham, post-Peel era. It was increasingly difficult to combine the two with success.

One consequence of the prevailing view that the winning of a seat in the Commons was a natural part of a barrister's professional career was that the Lord Chancellor was expected to provide appropriate preferment for such deserving backbench barristers, including those who were not Law Officer material. Some Chancellors were more amenable about this than others. Lord Chelmsford (1858-9 and 1866-8) claimed to be deeply shocked to receive this letter from Disraeli:

> "Dear Lord Chancellor, — After all, I regret to observe that Mr. Justice Shee is no more. The claims of our legal friends in the House of Commons, supported as they are by much sympathy on our benches, must not be treated with indifference, and therefore I venture to express a hope that you will not decide on the successor of Mr. Justice Shee with any precipitation,
>
> Yours very faithfully,
>
> B. DISRAELI"

But it is unlikely that Disraeli was in fact going any further than other Prime Ministers of the period. Chelmsford disliked Disraeli, who admitted he had "always snubbed him", and no doubt welcomed a chance to put him in the wrong. Chelmsford was in fact dismissed shortly afterwards to make way for Cairns. The Lord Chancellor with the worst reputation for allowing political considerations to affect his appointments* is Lord Halsbury (1885-6, 1886-92, 1895-1905). Out of thirty judges made in his chancellorships ten had been Conservative Members of Parliament or parliamentary candidates, six being actually in the Commons when appointed. The selection of three or four of these caused serious protest in the profession. When, for instance, Mr Justice Darling was appointed, the *Solicitors' Journal* commented: "The way to the High Court Bench is once more shown to be through

---

*Halsbury's reputation in this respect has been investigated and to a great extent cleared by Professor Heuston in his *Lives of the Lord Chancellors 1885-1940*.

contested elections and general service as a political hack. When these
claims are present, learning, experience in practice, and the moral
qualities which go to make an efficient and trusted judge, are
altogether unnecessary". The "dubious" appointments made by
Halsbury are of course only a small proportion of the total, and they
no doubt appear worse because of the length of time Halsbury was on
the Woolsack. Professor Heuston has further attempted to clear the
Chancellor's name by showing, convincingly, that the general level of
his appointments was at least respectable. But what was offensive was
that political factors should be considered at all, whether or not the
judge so chosen was in fact acceptable.

The fact that Victorian Chancellors carried little weight in Cabinet
or Parliament does not mean that they were non-entities. Some were.
Of Lord Hatherley (1868-72) it was unkindly said by Sir Richard
Bethell, later Lord Chancellor Westbury, that he was "a mere bundle
of virtues without a redeeming vice". The same might have been said
about Lord Cranworth (1852-8 and 1865-8). He was, like Hatherley,
an ineffectual man, though of great charm and popularity. He
had little judicial reputation. It was again the caustic Bethell who
attributed his habit of always sitting with both Lords Justices in the
Court of Chancery Appeal to "a childish fear of being left alone in the
dark". But others were of real distinction. Cottenham, Selborne and
Cairns have already been mentioned as lawyers and reformers. To
them should be added Lords Halsbury and Herschell (1886, 1892-5).
Halsbury was a good, if not an outstanding, lawyer of the type
generally described as "robust", that is to say straightforward and
impatient of legal technicalities. These qualities are apparent in the
principal piece of law reform for which he is responsible, the Criminal
Evidence Act, 1898, which finally gave the accused in a criminal trial
the right to give evidence on his own behalf. They are also apparent in
the uncomplicated, unquestioning conservatism which was his political
creed. Halsbury was the leader of the die-hard peers who opposed to
the end the Parliament Act of 1911. "Robust" is certainly the word for
Halsbury personally: no sooner had he left the Woolsack, at the age of
eighty-two than he undertook the general editorship of the massive
legal encyclopaedia that bears his name, and he did not deliver his last
judgement in the House of Lords until he was ninety-two. Herschell was

the anithesis of Halsbury. Immensely hard-working, where Halsbury was idle, dull, where Halsbury was forceful, an excellent lawyer who had become Lord Chancellor at the young age of forty-eight, Herschell was of the type of the great Victorian civil servants. Indeed he was set on a career of public committees, commissions and international arbitrations when he died unexpectedly in 1897.

Slightly outside this worthy catalogue comes Lord Westbury (1861-5). He had a legal mind as good as any and was a zealot for law reform. His projects were astonishingly radical. They included the fusion of law and equity (later achieved by the Judicature Act), a complete codification of English law, the conversion of the Inns of Court into a single legal university and the setting up of a Ministry of Justice to take responsibility for legislation and the improvement of the law generally. None of these ideas got anywhere. Westbury's actual achievement was limited to small steps towards divorce reform and the registration of land. The fact was that no plans so far-reaching could have been introduced without long and sensitive wooing of professional opinion. For this Westbury had neither the tact nor the time. He was utterly confident of the evident rightness of whatever he proposed, law reform or anything else. Anyone who disagreed was a fool, and probably also a knave, whose idiocy and dishonesty should be pointed out to him at once. This Westbury had a considerable talent for doing. He had duels, in which the swords were generally poisoned, with, among others, Gladstone, Bishop Wilberforce and Lord Campbell. He thought little of most of the other Chancellors of his time: his contempt for Cranworth and Hatherley has been mentioned above, but he had an equal disregard for Lords Truro and Chelmsford. It is not surprising therefore that his reforms made little headway. Westbury's career was in any event cut short when he was compromised by the activities of his spendthrift son, who had been recommending his creditors to his father for offices in the Lord Chancellor's gift. He had also shortly before been criticised for allowing the House of Lords to grant a pension to a retiring official whom he had himself required to resign from another office for dishonesty. And in the background was the unfortunate fact that both his sons had been appointed by their father to registrarships in bankruptcy. Westbury had too many enemies for the affair to be allowed to slip by, and his offer of resignation had to be accepted by Palmerston. Westbury had not been consciously dishonest: in fact both episodes had been brought to light as a result of his own investigations. But he had been misled by his imperviousness to the opinions of others into thinking that his own integrity would be taken for granted, as he took it himself. The comparison with Bacon is obvious.

Lord Campbell (1859-61) does not owe his reputation to his chancellorship at all, but to his authorship of the *Lives of the Lord Chancellors* and *Lives of the Lord Chief Justices.* His tenure of the office was something of an afterthought. He was aged eighty on his appointment and, though still perfectly fit, must have thought that his career had reached its culmination with his appointment as Lord Chief Justice in 1850. Clever, ambitious and energetic, he had been prominent in the law and in Parliament since the 1820s. Shallow, conceited and innocently unscrupulous, he was rightly mistrusted by his colleagues. Yet clearly he was not disliked. Brougham and Lyndhurst, who had had many opportunities to see him at his worst — as on the occasion when Brougham, who had given the Mastership of the Rolls to a rival, had to compensate Campbell by obtaining a peerage for his wife — treated him as a joke. Whether they would have been amused had they seen the last volume of his *Lives,* of which they were themselves the subjects, is another matter. The *Lives* have all Campbell's own faults and virtues. They were mostly written, at some speed, in the period after Campbell's relinquishment of the chancellorship of Ireland, a post he occupied briefly in 1841 after the previous Chancellor had been bullied out of office to make way for him. Shallow they certainly are: Campbell was no historian. The earlier part of the *Lives of the Lord Chancellors* consists chiefly of ill-digested gossip, often inaccurately derived from plainly unreliable sources, tricked out with some empty sub-Macaulay references to the development of the British constitution. Of course it would be unjust to expect of Campbell a twentieth-century standard of discrimination in his choice of sources or of insight into medieval or sixteenth-century politics and government: the necessary groundwork had not been done. Nor is it fair to take offence at the patronising Early Victorian self-satisfaction with which he distributes "the just censure/approval of history" to his subjects, though even by the standards of the time

Campbell had a high opinion of his own opinion. But inaccuracy, sheer fiction, and bias are bad by any standards; besides, Campbell persisted in these failings even when writing of his own contemporaries. Atlay, his successor as biographer of the Lord Chancellors but his opposite in charity, care and historical scrupulousness, found in a single episode in the life of Lord Chief Justice Ellenborough that "in something like two and a half pages he had committed almost every conceivable error of fact". And the errors were not just the result of sloppiness: they all too often reflected political partiality or personal malice. The lives of Lyndhurst, the arch-High Tory, and Brougham, whose career had so outstripped Campbell's own and who had passed him over for Master of the Rolls, were shocking examples of this. Lord St Leonards, who as a member of the bar appeared often and unflatteringly in these lives and had supposed himself Campbell's friend, at once produced a pamphlet attempting to correct his "misrepresentations", and began by quoting the wry comment that Campbell had "added a new terror to death". All this needs to be said, for although no historian would now think of trusting the *Lives,* their reputation among lawyers appears still to be high. Nor is their reputation in all respects undeserved, for it is impossible not to like the *Lives of the Lord Chancellors.* As a historical gossip column they are never dull, and it remains true that there is much genuine and interesting research and reminiscence in Campbell that is available nowhere else.

The abilities of individual Chancellors, as lawyers, biographers or otherwise, clearly have little bearing on the history of the office. What, however, was becoming of increasing importance in the aftermath of the reforms of the legal system made between the chancellorships of Brougham and Selborne was the role of the Lord Chancellor as an administrator. He had always had the central responsibility of appointing the judges of what was now the High Court, and he also appointed the justices of the peace throughout the country, even if that function was largely delegated to the Lord Lieutenants. The establishment of County Courts, the separation from the Court of Chancery of the lunacy and bankruptcy jurisdictions, and such miscellaneous reforms as the creation of the income tax commissioners, who were to be appointed by the Chancellor, gave him a wealth of new patronage in the appointment of judges and quasi-judicial officials; and with these necessarily went supervisory responsibilities. One of the more curious consequences of this was the provision enshrined in the Lunacy Act of 1890 that any inmate of an asylum might write, uncensored, to the Lord Chancellor — and be given pen and paper with which to do so. Many Lord Chancellors have testified that this was a right regularly and copiously exercised, and the practice, though not the right, has apparently survived more recent mental health legislation. Besides these duties, the Judicature Act, 1873, constituted the Lord Chancellor President of the newly created Supreme Court (i.e. the High Court and Court of Appeal) and Chairman of its Rules Committee, which had, and has, a continuing responsibility for the reform of procedure. The administrative burden imposed thereby was very great. The Lord Chancellor had to co-ordinate the business of some two dozen judges and their courts, in London and on assize, with all their subordinate staff of Masters, clerks and ushers, and within a structure of organisation whose details had to be worked out and applied.

When these administrative functions are considered with the Chancellor's role in law reform, Lord Selborne was right to describe the Lord Chancellor as "Minister of Justice for almost every purpose unconnected with the criminal law". But he was a Minister without a Ministry. The Lord Chancellor had no permanent staff. All he had were a Principal Secretary, a "Secretary of Commissions", who dealt with the appointment of justices of the peace, a "Secretary of Presentations", dealing with ecclesiastical patronage, and a number of officials who occupied various offices connected with the functions of the Great Seal which had survived the transformation of the chancery into a court. The secretaries were private officials who left office with the Lord Chancellor. The lack of a professional legal staff had irked Westbury. Asked to take charge of a reform in the Game Laws, he wrote back bitterly:

"The parsimony of former times has stripped the high office of Lord Chancellor of all that was requisite to act in a suitable manner as head of the law. Thus I have not a person in my service, nor the means of employing a person, to whom I could commit the preparation of such a bill and the duty of making such researches as are necessary before preparing it. If any amendment of the law seems to me desirable, I must beg for the approval of the Home Secretary, and, through him, the sanction of the Chancellor of the Exchequer. My secretary writes to Sir George Grey requesting him to move the Chancellor of the Exchequer to consent that the Lord Chancellor may have a small sum of money to pay the gentleman he may employ to effect the necessary reform. After weeks of delay, an official letter comes from . . . some subordinate, doling out some niggardly sum, as if it were a favour, and often with the most absurd stipulations."

It was only when Halsbury succeeded Selborne in 1885 that the offices of Principal Secretary and Clerk of the Crown in Chancery (an office with a long and varied history of its own) were combined to form the nucleus of a permanent staff. Selborne had already been anxious to create a permanent office, and he and Cairns had co-operated in securing some continuity over the transfers of office in 1874 and 1880. The new Permanent Secretary, as he was now to be called, was Kenneth Muir Mackenzie, who had been Selborne's Principal Secretary in his second chancellorship. It was under Muir Mackenzie that the Lord Chancellor's Office became established in the form it was to retain until 1971. At the same time the procedures surrounding the use of the Great Seal were rationalised and several redundant offices abolished by the Great Seal Act, 1884. Rules under this Act also lay down which documents require the application of the Seal, and of these which may be sealed without a royal warrant.

The Twentieth Century

The office of Lord Chancellor has in the twentieth century developed far along the course laid down by Lord Selborne. The great bulk of the Lord Chancellor's useful work has been in legal administration and law reform, and his other functions have diminished accordingly. The most important changes from the point of view of the history of the office have all been since the Second World War, when law reform has regained an impetus not yet as strong as but approaching that of the age of Brougham. But the more placid earlier part of the century was by no means stagnant, though the reforms made were mostly in the field of the substantive law rather than in the legal system.

Lord Loreburn, a politically active ex-Law Officer and friend of Campbell-Bannerman who was Liberal Lord Chancellor from 1905 until 1912, was sympathetic to change. He gave encouragement to the early stages of the movement for an extended legal aid system. In 1906 he set up the Public Trustee Office to provide an alternative to the services of solicitors as trustees, which were at that time very unsatisfactory. His most important reform was to propose and implement a radically new method of selection of justices of the peace. The old system, whereby the Lord Lieutenants put names forward to the Lord Chancellor which were all but automatically accepted, had become plainly anachronistic. Further, it had allowed the bench to become the instrument of local political jobbery as certain Lord Lieutenants had tended to approve only supporters of their own parties. In recent years this practice had favoured the Conservatives almost exclusively, and Loreburn had been considerably embarassed by pressure from his fellow-Liberals to go if necessary over the Lord Lieutenants' heads and appoint their own candidates. This he had firmly refused to do, partly because it was quite impracticable since the Lord Chancellor had no alternative channel of communication with the counties, but principally because he regarded the pressure as unacceptable political interference with judicial appointments. Loreburn with some courage rejected the argument that Conservative abuses of the system entitled the Liberals to abuse it also. His own scheme, which became effective in 1911, set up advisory committees, whose members were themselves appointed by the Lord Chancellor, to propose lists of candidates for the magistracy directly to him. Appointments were thus brought more closely within the Chancellor's supervision and the possibilities for political bias were limited. Loreburn's stand on this issue was not wholly consistent with his practice over the selection of the judiciary, where he continued to give weight to the Prime Minister's wish to reward Liberal lawyers in the Commons. But he did not like it, and it was in the chancellorship of his successor, Haldane, that it was finally agreed between Prime Minister and Lord Chancellor that, in Haldane's words, "in filling . . . vacancies we would appoint only on the footing of high legal and professional qualifications . . . It is a principle of great importance for the administration of justice". Strictly this agreement only referred to the High Court judgeships, for the convention whereby the Prime Minister accepts the Lord Chancellor's recommendation in such appointments does not extend to the case of Lords Justices of Appeal or Law Lords; but the distinction has for some time been largely academic.

It was Haldane, who was Lord Chancellor in a Liberal government from 1912 to 1915 and again in the Labour government of 1924, who began the process which eventually led to the momentous achievement of the Law of Property Act and its associated Acts in 1925. This was the most ambitious and extensive piece of law reform of the first half of the century, codifying and in some respects revolutionising a system of property law which, in the words of Lord Birkenhead (Lord Chancellor from 1919 to 1922), was "cumbrous and inadequate and required drastic treatment to bring it into conformity with the business needs of the community". Legislation drafted but not enacted under Haldane was taken up with enthusiasm after the First World War by Birkenhead, improved and expanded with the help of its original drafters and of Haldane himself, and was finally with much parliamentary labour on the part of the Chancellor passed into law in 1922. When Birkenhead went out of office later in the year it was again Haldane, in his brief chancellorship of 1924, who prepared the legislation necessary to complete what had been achieved in 1922; but it fell to Lord Cave, his sound but unimaginative successor (1922-4, 1924-8), to see the bills through the Lords. Cave was originally not in favour of the reforms, but he acknowledged that the job once started had to be finished. This, the work of three successive Lord Chancellors, was law reform in the spirit of the nineteenth century — painstaking, radical and comprehensive.

Haldane and Birkenhead are the outstanding Chancellors of the century, in their contributions to both the law and politics. They were ideally suited — unlike as they were — to complement each other's work. Haldane was a Scot who as a student had spent much time in Germany studying philosophy. His admiration for Germany, which was far from unqualified, was to cost him his first chancellorship, when in 1915 he was forced to resign by a vicious campaign in the Northcliffe press alleging that he had pro-German sympathies in the war. But it was

Haldane's philosophical training that was most to distinguish his career. It both made him intolerant of confusion and disorder and equipped him intellectually to deal with it. His first ministerial post was as Secretary of State for War, and he carried out a thorough reconstruction of the organisation of both army and War Office. Asked by the Army Council what kind of army he was trying to create, Haldane replied "a Hegelian army": as he dryly notes, after this remark "the conversation fell off". But strange as such concepts might sound in the mess, Haldane's army reforms were a brilliant success, and their contribution to the fact that the British army was equipped, organisationally if not in its tactical thinking, to fight the War of 1914-18 was acknowledged by Haig and by most thinking soldiers. It was, equally, as a philosopher and reformer that Haldane came to support the Labour party and to agree to be its first Lord Chancellor in 1924. Haldane was never a socialist, though he had close links with the Fabians; what he saw in Labour was a fresh-minded government who would be willing to adopt his schemes for the reform of education and of the machinery of government. But though he admired and liked many of his Labour colleagues, and was by virtue of his long experience of government of great value to them both as adviser and talisman of respectability, Haldane was disappointed in Ramsay MacDonald's government, whose priorities were only too plainly not his own. Haldane's detached attitude to party politics somewhat reduced his political influence, though he was by no means a reluctant politician and walked with confidence in the corridors of power. On the other hand, though he was a very good lawyer, it is certainly not the case that his importance was restricted to the legal work of the Chancellor. Haldane's greatest contribution was in the science of government. In more recent years he would have been the archetypal "think tank" man. His talent was in applying a logical, critical, cool and disciplined mind to all the operations of law and government with which he was concerned.*

Not all those adjectives could apply to Lord Birkenhead. As F. E. Smith he had been a loud, flamboyant, thrusting barrister and M.P., whose wit and audacity were celebrated in a wealth of anecdotes which, most unusually for such normally ephemeral stuff, have long outlived him.‡ He was a High Tory of the type most admired (at least

*See further pp. 195-6.

‡The best stories from the F. E. Smith legend are recounted, along with more serious analysis, in *Great Contemporaries* by his close friend Churchill.

in retrospect) by Conservative apologists — independent-minded and as unimpressed by the dogma of reaction as he was by that of the Left. He brought all his intellect, energy and boldness to achieving the changes he thought necessary: among them, apart from property legislation, were the reform of the Upper House and divorce reform. Birkenhead is one of those who is done an injustice by his brilliant reputation. He was indeed all the things that are claimed of him — daring, irreverent, arrogant, capable of inspired and dangerous demagoguery. By its lights *The Times* was quite right to condemn his appointment, at the age of forty-seven, to the Woolsack as "carrying a joke too far", for was not the Lord High Chancellor observed in a French café smoking a cigar, and did he not offend the king by wearing a soft hat to go to Windsor? Yet the F.E. Smith who crammed three years work at Oxford into two terms in order to win a fellowship and pacify his creditors was also as Lord Birkenhead one of the best lawyers to have occupied the Woolsack; the F. E. Smith who was Carson's right-hand man in Ulster was also as Lord Birkenhead the principal negotiator of the Anglo- Irish Treaty of 1921 and its passionate champion in the Lords. Churchill in his essay on Birkenhead draws attention to the sombre, reflective part of his nature, which is generally in evidence in his somewhat melancholic portraits. Among a fairly sober catalogue of twentieth-century Chancellors, Birkenhead is a valuable reminder that what glitters may be real gold.

Less spectacular but equally influential was the contribution made to the cause of law reform by Lord Sankey, Chancellor from 1929 to 1934. Sankey was a serious, conscientious lawyer who became con- verted to Socialism while chairing, as a King's Bench judge, a commission to investigate the state of the mining industry. When Ramsay MacDonald came to form his second government Sankey was the only possible candidate for the Woolsack, although his political experience was negligible. Labour lawyers were never thick on the ground, still less Labour judges. Sankey was of little use in the Lords, where his first speech, after no less than nine silent months, was laboriously learnt by heart, a whole hour's worth, or indeed in Cabinet, where his habit of bringing a pocket atlas with him to help him follow discussions of foreign policy was viewed with derision by his colleagues. His real and lasting achievement, besides many valuable piecemeal reforms, was the establishment in 1934 of a permanent Law Revision Committee to consider defective parts of the law referred to it by the Lord Chancellor. This body was succeeded after the Second World War by the Law Reform Committee. They constituted the main moving parts of the machinery of law reform in England until the setting up of the Law Commission by Lord Gardiner in 1964.

Law reform was, sporadically, the most vital area of the Lord Chancellor's responsibilities in these quiet years. But it was only a small part of his work. The Lord Chancellors of the pre-war period were immensely busy men. Their basic daily programme for most of the year involved judicial sittings in the Lords or the Privy Council between half-past ten in the morning and four in the afternoon for four days a week, followed, when Parliament was sitting, by sessions on the Woolsack which began at a quarter past four and would last until eight or later: though his primary role was as Speaker the Chancellor would be quite likely to have to take part in debate on topics where the government needed his legal expertise, or indeed himself to introduce legislation. Wednesday was Cabinet day. Even the most insignificant Chancellor was a full member of Cabinet (except in the War Cabinets of 1916-19 and 1940-5) and participated in general policy-making as well as fulfilling his specialist role as the government's chief adviser on legal and constitutional issues.* This could mean very heavy duties: Birkenhead was necessarily deeply involved in the 1919 Peace Conference, and Sankey was Chairman of the Round Table Conference on India — both as time-consuming as they were important. In the interstices of this densely-packed timetable the Lord Chancellor had to find time to do the research necessary for his judicial work, read Cabinet papers, attend a variety of public functions, including a heavy ration of ceremonial on such occasions as the opening of Parliament, and, most important of all, supervise the work of his understaffed office in legal administration. A bare dozen civil servants were responsible for the organisation of the Supreme Court and the County Court system and their judges, and the drafting and constant necessary revision of their rules; also for the Public Trustee Office, the Land Registry, institutions for the care of the mentally ill and the committees for the nomination of justices of the peace. They also disposed of the still enormous ecclesiastical patronage of the Lord

---

*What would have been one of the most difficult constitutional problems to face any Lord Chancellor, the Abdication Crisis of 1936, had to be dealt with without the advice of the then Chancellor, Lord Hailsham, who was seriously ill.

Chancellor—some twelve canonries and 659 other benefices. Much of this work had to be referred to the Chancellor himself. Even quite trivial complaints about the disposal of a living in rural Yorkshire might require his personal intervention. And judicial appointments were entirely the Chancellor's own responsibility, though he might consult senior judges. The relationship of the Chancellor with the judiciary—for whom, in so far as anyone was, he was constitutionally responsible—was one of great importance and occasionally also of some difficulty, as when the unfortunate Sankey had to try to cope with the hysterical reaction of some of the judges to the supposed threat to their independence represented by the National Government's imposed cuts in salary in 1931.

This was an enormous workload. A. P. Herbert summed it up:

> "Poor gentleman—he has to mix
> With barristers and lords;
> He is in charge of lunatics
> And coroners and wards;
> And what with listening to Earls
> And looking after orphan girls,
> And imbeciles of every sort,
> And judges of the County Court,
> And all that kind of thing,
> He gets extremely little sleep;
> And then of course he has to keep
> The conscience of the King:
> And sometimes at the close of day
> He gives a vicarage away . . ."

Haldane, characteristically, was the principal critic of this antiquated and irrational accumulation of functions. In the report, published in 1918, of a committee which he had chaired on the Machinery of Government, he produced a long analysis of the Lord Chancellor's duties, declaring that "successive holders [of the office] have testified that it is beyond the work of any one man to perform the work that ought to be done"; after a full nine-hour day in the Lords in its judicial and legislative capacities "only a man of very exceptional vigour can find either leisure or strength to cope with the many other duties of his high office". This account is followed by a rather less detailed set of proposals for the drastic reduction of the Lord Chancellor's functions. He should no longer act as a judicial member of the House of Lords nor as its Speaker. A Minister of Justice, sitting in the Commons, should take over the responsibility for the administration of the legal system as a whole, assuming both the Chancellor's functions with regard to the civil law and the Home Secretary's as administrator of the criminal law. He would also be responsible for the state of the substantive law generally and for the promotion of reforms. Haldane believed such a scheme would both introduce an important element of parliamentary responsibility to the administration of justice, and provide an efficient and unified organisation for the legal system. The Lord Chancellor meanwhile would be left as the Cabinet's expert on legal and constitutional questions, able in particular to give his attention to the preparation of government legislation. He would also retain the appointment of the higher judiciary: Haldane felt that this was a matter of exceptional importance and sensitivity which should be kept at a distance from the political pressures to which the Minister of Justice would be subject. Birkenhead soon declared himself against any such radical changes. Though he wanted a larger staff for the Lord Chancellor's Office — "the true Ministry of Justice as I see it" — and agreed that certain rationalisations of the Chancellor's functions would be brought about in the course of time, he opposed the creation of a Minister of Justice as such, on the grounds that the office could not effectively be filled by a layman but would not attract the best lawyers. Only a man respected by his professional colleagues could properly reconcile their interests and those of government:

"In every democracy there arise from time to time occasions of jealousy and difficulty between the judiciary and the executive. Our present system, under which the head of the judiciary is also a prominent member of the executive Government, has its disadvantages. But it has this great advantage — that it provides a link between the two sets of institutions; if they are totally severed there will disappear with them any controlling or suggestive force exterior to the Judges themselves, and it is difficult to believe that there is no necessity for the existence of such a personality, imbued on the one hand with legal ideas and habits of thought, and aware on the other of the problems which engage the attention of the executive Government. In the absence of such a person the judiciary and the executive are likely to drift asunder to the point of a violent separation, followed by a still more violent and disastrous collision." This remains the most cogent justification for the survival of the present structure of the office of Lord Chancellor, in defiance of the usual doctrine on the separation of powers. Indeed the second Lord Chancellor Hailsham (1970-4) has declared that "in the absence of a paper constitution the separation of powers is the primary function of the Lord Chancellor, a task he can only fulfil if he sits somewhere near the apex of the constitutional pyramid, armed with a long barge-pole to keep off marauding craft from any quarter". The metaphor may be mixed but the point is well made.

Haldane's recommendations made no headway, less because of the strength of any opposition than because of the depth of public apathy on the issue. Nevertheless much of what he advocated has in recent years been achieved, not by comprehensive legislation but by the gradual, even accidental, evolutionary processes preferred by Birkenhead and by all those who like to believe in the mysterious adaptive powers of the British constitution. The substantial disappearance of the Lord Chancellor's judicial role was brought about by the introduction of the black-out during the Second World War: in order to finish its business if possible in daylight the Lords began its sittings in its legislative capacity from half-past two rather than a quarter past four, forcing the Chancellor to choose between sitting judicially and presiding on the Woolsack. The effective divorce between the two aspects of the Lords' business was confirmed by the establishment in 1948 of a distinct appellate committee of the House, initially intended only as a temporary measure while proceedings in the main House were being disturbed by the installation of a new heating system — but the committee proved so convenient that it became permanent. As a result there has been a marked diminution in the amount of time that post-War Lord Chancellors have given to judicial work. Lord Gardiner (1964-70), who believed that "while the House is sitting my place is on the Woolsack", hardly sat judicially at all. Lord Hailsham, his successor, was anxious that the practice should not disappear altogether and sat judicially very much more often, making time for this and his other work by a liberal use of deputy Speakers in the Lords: there may here be the seeds of a further change in the pattern of the office — though it is no doubt relevant that a Conservative Chancellor is generally more dispensable in the Upper House than a Labour Chancellor, who has fewer colleagues to share the load of debate.

There is no prospect at present of the creation of a separate Ministry of Justice of the type proposed by Haldane. The Home Secretary has retained his responsibility for the criminal law, the magistrates' courts remain in a chaotic limbo where they are the full responsibility of nobody, and suggestions that control of police and prosecutions should come under the same authority as the judicial parts of the legal system have not met much approval. But there have been important developments towards a Ministry of Justice in fact if not in name. The biggest area of growth in the law in the post-war years has been in the proliferation of statutory tribunals, covering an enormous range of quasi-judicial administration or administrative adjudication. The Lord Chancellor has under the Tribunals and Inquiries Act 1956 a supervisory responsibility over these and he is in most cases responsible also for their membership. As the system of criminal legal aid has been extended, so have the duties of the Lord Chancellor's Office with regard to its administration. The reforming chancellorship of Lord Gardiner introduced one of the principal elements of Haldane's proposed Ministry, namely a body, the Law Commission, established by Parliament, in Lord Gardiner's words, "to submit the whole of our law to systematic and continuous review"; the Law Commission, unrestricted in its scope and equipped with a full-time staff, is a radical improvement on Lord Sankey's part-time Law Revision Committee. The most momentous change of all in the recent history of the office also originated under Lord Gardiner, though it only passed into law under Lord Hailsham. This was the Courts Act 1971, which brought under the control of the Lord Chancellor's Office (now the Lord Chancellor's Department) the entire administration of what had been the system of assizes and quarter-sessions. Under the weight of this new burden the Office grew from comprising a small band of officials in the Palace of Westminster to become a government department employing some ten thousand staff throughout the country. Substantially the whole administration of the superior courts is now the Lord Chancellor's responsibility. As a final footnote may be mentioned the Public Records Act 1958, by which the haphazard arrangements for the preservation of records, which had been primarily the business of the Master of the Rolls, were re-organised under the control of his old superior, the Lord Chancellor: in his exercise of these functions a direct line can be traced from the original secretarial work of the medieval chancery.

Such, in outline, are the still expanding duties of the Lord Chancellor. Around this solid functional core the political status of the office has followed an erratic course. The duties of the chancellorship are not such as to carry with them any automatic importance, compared with the power wielded by Treasury, Home Office and Foreign Office. Its influence will largely therefore depend on individual qualities and character of the Chancellor himself. In some respects the Lord Chancellor has been less restricted politically in the twentieth century than were his nineteenth-century predecessors, for the special separate career structure for the barrister in Parliament has disappeared. There are no longer easy seats on the judicial bench available to loyal lawyer-backbenchers, and barristers have not entered Parliament without wishing to be taken seriously as politicians. It has thus become comparatively common for Lord Chancellors to have held other ministerial office at some stage in their careers. Lord Birkenhead, two years after giving up the Great Seal, became Secretary of State for India; the first Lord Chancellor Hailsham (1928-9, 1935-8) was Secretary of State for War between his two spells of office as Chancellor; Lord Simon (1940-5) came to the Woolsack after a period of thirteen years away from the law, in which he had been successively Chairman of the Statutory Commission on Indian Government, Foreign Secretary, Home Secretary and Chancellor of the Exchequer. All three of these had been politicians of the first importance and potential leaders of their parties; after the War the same could be said perhaps of Lord Kilmuir (1954-62) and certainly of Lord Hailsham. And had Lloyd George had his way in 1916, an ex-Prime Minister might have become Lord Chancellor Asquith. The chancellorship in this period has by no means necessarily been a niche for non-entities. These are greater names than most of those from the nineteenth century.

It is noticeable, with all these distinguished and personally influential Chancellors, that they have held the office at the ends of their political careers. The great disadvantage of the Lord Chancellorship to an aspiring politician has been that its holder is lost to the Commons and so denied the chance of winning the highest political prizes. This had not necessarily been so in the nineteenth century, when there was, after all, a Prime Minister in the Lords as late as Lord Salisbury, and perhaps not until the Lord Curzon episode in 1923 was it finally plain that a peer could not head a government. But Birkenhead in 1919 and Hailsham in 1928 both knew that they were giving up a chance of the leadership of their parties; and Simon turned down the chancellorship in 1915 on the grounds that it was "the sack rather than the Woolsack" — he was then aged only forty-two and was the prospective leader of the Liberal party; it was unfortunate that the party slipped away just as Simon's grasp was closing on it. It does not follow from this that the Lord Chancellor's role in the Lords is meaningless. As more and more front-bench spokesmen have moved to the Commons, the burden on the Chancellor of representing the government in the Lords has become greater. This is particularly true of Labour Lord Chancellors. Lord Jowitt (1945-51) played an essential part in passing through a hostile House the controversial legislation of the Attlee government, while Lord Gardiner was one of only two Cabinet ministers in the Lords during his chancellorship. And the slight degree of detachment from the political mainstream which his special position gives him attracts to the Lord Chancellor certain important duties in Cabinet. Recent Prime Ministers have tended to favour their Lord Chancellors as the chairman of Cabinet committees, and also to consult them in particular in sensitive matters of security. The part played by Lord Dilhorne (1962-4) as go-between in the Conservative leadership negotiations in 1963 illustrates this special role in action.

Overall, however, there is no doubt that despite these positive features of the office it cannot attract political figures of the first importance. Nor has it always been thought necessary to give it to politicians at all. Besides Lord Sankey, Lords Maugham (1938-9) and

Simonds (1951-4) were appointed to the Woolsack from the judicial bench and, though of course in sympathy with the government, had when appointed no significant political experience. Lord Gardiner, uniquely, had been neither in Parliament nor on the bench but was already a noted campaigner for law reform and had been chairman of the Bar Council. This trend has probably been inevitable. Whether it matters is not easy to decide. Perhaps for the first time since the sixteenth century the Lord Chancellor has, in the administration of justice, an important permanent role in government. The appointment of the judiciary is now a far more onerous responsibility than it was until recently, and it is one that, above a certain level, cannot be delegated. These are tasks which accrue to him whatever his political standing or lack of it, and he is unlikely to perform them better or worse because of his position in his own party. Indeed a Lord Chancellor known to be a vehement partisan might be less well-placed either to make acceptable judicial appointments or to give convincingly impartial constitutional guidance in Cabinet—though it has never been suggested that either Birkenhead or Hailsham, two of the most active party politicians of this period, were thereby less credible in these respects. But, as has been emphasised, in fact by those very two, what is of unique and essential value about the office of the Lord Chancellor is that he carries both professional and political weight: only thus can he protect the rule of law and the independence of the judiciary from within the Cabinet, and, conversely, keep the courts within their proper sphere. In a country still remarkable for political and constitutional stability the gradual erosion of the political status of the Lord Chancellor's office may not appear to count for very much. It is a matter of opinion whether it will not, in less fortunate times, prove to have been a dangerous development.

Further Reading

The *Lives of the Lord Chancellors and Keepers of the Great Seal* by John, Lord Campbell (7 vols 1845-7, eighth vol. 1869), and its sequels (though they disclaim that description), *The Victorian Chancellors* by J. B. Atlay (2 vols, 1906-8) and the *Lives of the Lord Chancellors 1885-1940* by R. F. V. Heuston (1964), are the only books giving an overall account of the subject, though there is now also an excellent booklet entitled *The Lord Chancellor* by Maurice Bond and David Beamish in the House of Lords Information Office Publications Series (1977). Other generally relevant works are:

The Great Seals of England by A. B. & A. W. Wyon (1887).
Historical Notes on the Use of the Great Seal of England by H. C. Maxwell-Lyte (1926).
A History of English Law by W. S. Holdsworth (17 vols, 1922-72).

Chapters One — Three
The best accounts of the early chancery and chancellors are to be found in editions of writs and charters:

Anglo-Saxon Writs by F. E. Harmer (1952).
Regesta Regum Anglo-Normannorum 1066-1154, ed. H. W. C. Davis, C. Johnson, H. A. Cronne, R. H. C. Davis (4 vols, 1913-69).
Royal Writs in England from the Conquest to Glanvill, ed. R. C. van Caenegem. Selden Society vol. 77 (1959).
Recueil des Actes d'Henri II, ed. H. Delise (Paris, 3 vols. 1909-27).

Other interesting contemporary material available in translation:

Dialogus de Scaccario and *Constitutio Domus Regis*, ed. C. Johnson. Nelson's Medieval Texts (1950).
Glanvill, ed. G. D. G. Hall. Nelson's Medieval Texts (1965).
Fleta, ed. H. G. Richardson and G. O. Sayles. Selden Society vols 72 and 89 (1955 and 1972).

The classic work on the administrative history of this period is T. F. Tout's *Chapters in the Administrative History of Medieval England* (6 vols, 1920-33): vols 1-3 are most relevant to the chancery. The best short introduction is S. B. Chrimes' *Introduction to the Administrative History of Medieval England* (1952). There is a good chapter on the chancery in H. A. Cronne's *The Reign of Stephen 1135-54* (1970). See also *An Introduction to the Use of the Public Records* by V. H. Galbraith (1934).

The chief expert on the medieval chancery and chancellors was the late Prof. Bertie Wilkinson—see *The Chancery under Edward III* (1929), *Studies in the Constitutional History of the Thirteenth and Fourteenth Centuries* (1937) and the chapter on the chancery in vol. 1 of *The English Government at Work 1327-36* ed. J. F. Willard and W. A. Morris (Cambridge, Mass., 1940). Also of importance, if somewhat dated in approach, are his *Constitutional History of England 1216-1399* (3 vols, 1948-58) and *Constitutional History of England in the Fifteenth Century* (1964).

There is little modern work on the judicial work of chancery and chancellors in the Middle Ages, but see these notable exceptions:

The History of the Equitable Jurisdiction of the Court of Chancery before 1460 by M. E. Avery in Bulletin of the Institute of Historical Research vol. 42 (1969).

Select Cases in the Council of Henry VII, ed. C. G. Bayne and W. H. Dunham. Selden Society vol. 75 (1958).

The Cardinal's Court by J. A. Guy (1977). This is on Wolsey, who has been astonishingly neglected by modern historians.

For particular periods and chancellors see:

Roger of Salisbury, Viceroy of England by E. J. Kealey (Berkeley, Cal., 1972).

Thomas Becket by Dom David Knowles (1970).

Henry II by W. L. Warren (1973)—excellent on Becket and on Henry II's government generally.

Hubert Walter by C. R. Cheney (1967).

The Baronial Opposition to Edward II by J. C. Davies (1913).

The Place of the Reign of Edward II in English History by T. F. Tout (revised ed. 1936).

Archbishop Stratford and the Parliamentary Crisis of 1341 by G. T. Lapsley in *Crown, Community and Parliament in the Later Middle Ages* (1951).

The Household of the Chancery and its Disintegration by T. F. Tout in *Collected Papers* (1936).

Thomas Arundel by M. E. Aston (1967) — this covers Arundel's career only up to 1399.

Thomas Langley by R. L. Storey (1961).

At the Deathbed of Cardinal Beaufort by K. B. McFarlane in *Studies in Medieval History Presented to F. M. Powicke,* ed. R. W. Hunt (1948).
Archbishop John Stafford by E. F. Jacob in *Essays in Later Medieval History* (1968).
Wolsey by A. F. Pollard (1929).

Chapter Four

By far the most important work for the history of the office in this period is W. J. Jones' *The Elizabethan Court of Chancery* (1967). Other relevant general works are:

The Tudor Revolution in Government by G. R. Elton (1953).
The Tudor Constitution by G. R. Elton (1960) — N.B. the section on Star Chamber.
The King's Servants by G. E. Aylmer (revised ed. 1974).
The State's Servants by G. E. Aylmer (1973).
The Popular Movement for Law Reform by Donald Veall (1970).

On particular Chancellors there are interesting essays on Wolsey and More in vol. 1 of G. R. Elton's collected *Studies in Tudor and Stuart Politics and Government.* Otherwise:

Thomas More by R. W. Chambers (1935).
'*A Soul as Black as Marble*'? by S. E. Lehmberg (in *Tudor Men and Institutions,* ed. A. J. Slavin (Baton Rouge, 1972)) — on Audley.
Stephen Gardiner and the Tudor Reaction by J. A. Muller (1926).
Nicholas Bacon by Robert Tittler (1976).
Sir Christopher Hatton by E. St. J. Brooks (1946).
Ellesmere and Politics by W. J. Jones (in *Early Stuart Studies,* ed. H. J. Reinmuth (Minneapolis, 1970)).

On Bacon nothing has yet replaced the *Letters and Life of Francis Bacon* by J. Spedding, which forms vols 8-14 of Bacon's *Works* edited by J. Spedding, R. L. Ellis and D. D. Heath (1857-74).

Chapter Five

Clarendon's own *History of the Rebellion and Civil Wars in England* and *Life of Edward, Earl of Clarendon* are the best accounts of his career. There are old biographies by T. H. Lister (1837-8) and Sir Henry Craik (1911).

For Shaftesbury there is a good modern biography by K. H. D. Haley— *The First Earl of Shaftesbury* (1968).

D. E. C. Yale has produced editions of Nottingham's Chancery cases.

Selden Society vols 73 and 79 (1957 and 1961), with a short life of Nottingham in vol. 1 and of his *Manual of Chancery Practice* and *Prolegomena of Chancery and Equity* (1965).

For other Chancellors see:

Lives of the Norths by Roger North (many editions).
Lord Chancellor Jeffreys and the Stuart Cause by G. W. Keeton (1965).
Lord Somers by W. L. Sachse (1975).
Life and Correspondence of Philip Yorke, Earl of Hardwicke by P. C. Yorke (3 vols, 1913).
Lord Camden and his Family by H. S. Eeeles (1934).
Chancellor Thurlow by R. F. Gore-Browne (1953).
Life of Lord Eldon by Horace Twiss (3 vols, 1844).
Erskine by J. A. Lovat-Fraser (1932).

Chapter Six

There are innumerable books on and by Brougham, including his *Historical Sketches of Statesmen in the Time of George III* which cover many of his predecessors as Lord Chancellor. But there is no complete modern biography, that by Chester New (1961) never having been taken beyond 1830. A. Aspinall's *Lord Brougham and the Whig Party* (1927) and G. T. Garratt's *Lord Brougham* (1935) are slight.

For Brougham's successors see:

Life of Lord Lyndhurst by Sir Theodore Martin (1883).
Life of Lord Campbell, being his autobiography, diary and correspondence edited by his daughter, Mrs Hardcastle (2 vols, 1881).
Memoir of Lord Hatherley by W. R. W. Stephens (1883).
Memorials by Lord Selborne (4 vols, 1896-8).
F.E. by Lord Birkenhead (the Lord Chancellor's son) (revised ed. 1960).
Retrospect by Viscount Simon (1952).
A Political Adventure by Viscount Kilmuir (1964).
The Door Wherein I Went by Lord Hailsham (1975).

As well as his own *Autobiography* (1929), there are two full-length biographies of Haldane, by Sir Frederick Maurice (2 vols, 1937-9) and D. Sommer (1960).

Several modern Lord Chancellors have written short accounts of their official duties. The most recent are the Presidential Addresses of Lords Gardiner and Hailsham to the Holdsworth Club at the University of Birmingham, published as pamphlets 1970 and 1972, and an address given by Lord Elwyn-Jones in Gray's Inn, published in *Graya* no. 79 (1975).

Index